John Cordy Jeaffreson

A book or Recollections

John Cordy Jeaffreson

A book or Recollections

ISBN/EAN: 9783743324596

Manufactured in Europe, USA, Canada, Australia, Japa

Cover: Foto ©ninafisch / pixelio.de

Manufactured and distributed by brebook publishing software (www.brebook.com)

John Cordy Jeaffreson

A book or Recollections

CONTENTS OF VOL. I.

CHAPTER I.

CHILDHOOD 1

My Birth and Parentage—George Edwards the Elder—My Grandsire's Gifts—Sunny Memories—Woodbridge Grammar-School—The Rev. Woodthorpe Collett—Hasketon and Bredfield—Boulge and Martlesham—Wilford Hollows and the River Deben—Botesdale Grammar-School—The Rev. Joseph Haddock—A Hunting Clergyman and an Admirable School-master—Redgrave Hall—George St. Vincent Wilson—Steeple-Chases and Cricket-Matches—Botesdale Grammar-School Extinguished by Marlborough College.

CHAPTER II.

MY ACT AND DEED 16

I am Apprenticed to a Country Doctor—Medical Apprentices—The Old School of Family Doctors—The New School of Family Doctors—My Father's Services to Surgery—Professor Erichsen on the most Important of those Services—They are Recognized by the Council of the College of Surgeons—The Birds at the Top of the Tree.

CHAPTER III.

FIFTY YEARS SINCE 33

Framlingham in My Boyish Days—Affluence and Culture of the Town's Principal Families—'The Edwards Family'—Life of the Small Market-Town and its Neighbourhood—My Desire to Turn Soldier—'This Ridiculous Business'—My Eldest Sister and Only Dancing-Mistress—The Greenlaws of Framlingham and Woolwich—My Elder Brother's Death—My Almost Fatal Illness—A Threefold Illusion.

CHAPTER IV.

MY FIRST VIEW OF OXFORD 52

I Turn Religious—And Wish to be a Clergyman—Church-Goers and Chapel-Goers—Pograms and Ranters—The Rev. Joseph Brereton, B.A., of Christ Church, Oxford—He Prepares me for Oxford—My Chief Reason for Wishing to go to Oxford rather than to Cambridge—Matriculation at Oxford—Pembroke College, Oxford—A Middle-Aged Gentleman-Commoner of Magdalen Hall—I Dine with Fellows of Oriel College—Francis Jeune, D.C.L., Master of Pembroke College and (in Later Time) Bishop of Peterborough—Henry William Chandler—The Thirty-Nine Articles.

CHAPTER V.

ALMA MATER 66

Two Grand Blunders—Pembroke College, Oxford—The Admirable Master and Good Tutors—'The World, the Flesh, and the Devil'—The Musical Bursar and Witty Dean—Religious Doubts and Perplexities—An Unhappy Freshman—Holidays in London—Edwin Edwards, Proctor of Doctors' Commons—William Holmes Edwards of the Middle Temple—John Humffreys Parry (in Later Time 'Serjeant Parry')—Meymott 'The Singing Barrister'—Thomas Hay Girtin—Maxwell Miller—Arthur Locker—Edwin Arnold—Henry Kingsley—'The Fez Club'—Its Principles and Purpose—Anecdotes—Notes about Names—George Henry Thornbury *alias* Walter Thornbury—An Unpleasant Dream—My Difficulty with 'The Tutors'—A Way Out of the Difficulty—A Friend in Need—My Last Interview with Dr. Jeune.

CHAPTER VI.

CHARTERHOUSE SQUARE 100

Harry Kingsley—Willie Langworthy—Their Unseasonable Levity—My Design for getting my Livelihood in London—Government Clerks and Classical Tutors—Their Respective Earnings—Boarding-House for Schoolboys—Pupils of both Sexes—Visiting Tutors and Literary Reviewers—Dr. Thunder-cloud, F.R.S.—St. Mary's Hall—Mary Wilderness.

CHAPTER VII.

OLD FRIENDS 108

J. C. M. Bellew on Friendship—Inhabitants of Charterhouse Square—Wedding Bells at Hendon Church—Badge of Disgrace for a Naughty Girl—The Complins of Charterhouse Square—James Hinton, Aurist and Essayist—His quick Passage from Adversity to Prosperity—Scene in the Strand—'The Faculty' in Finsbury Square—Henry Jeaffreson, M.D., Cantab.—His Home in 'The Medical Quarter'—Dr. William Withey Gull, of No. 8, Finsbury Square—His subsequent Celebrity—His good Stories—Bird-like Sisters and their 1820 Port—Sir William Lawrence, Baronet, the famous Surgeon—Fate of the Third Edition of his 'Lectures'—John Jeaffreson, of Upper Street, Islington, Surgeon and Apothecary—His Friendship with the Disraelis—Jews of Islington and Stoke Newington—Anecdotes of Lord Beaconsfield's Birth and Childhood—His first Love-Affair—His early Days at Islington.

CHAPTER VIII.

MY FIRST AND SECOND NOVELS . . . 133

My first Novel, *Crewe Rise*—Messrs. Hurst and Blackett, Publishers—Mr. S. W. Fullom, Author of *The Marvels of Science*—Edward Whitty, Author of *Friends of Bohemia*—Young John Parker, Publisher and Editor of *Fraser's Magazine*—Holidays at

Cheam and Boulogne, in the Channel Islands and the Suffolk Woodland—Changes in the Woodland—The New Agriculture—Steady Impoverishment of Suffolk Farmers—Weeks spent in Devon, at Exeter and Honiton—Months spent in Paris—M. Ricord, the famous Parisian Surgeon—Thomas Chambers Wakley, Coroner for Middlesex, and Proprietor and Editor of the *Lancet*—James Fernandez Clarke, M.R.C.S., Medical Journalist—I act as Hospital-Reporter for the *Lancet*.

CHAPTER IX.

JAMES HANNAY 143

The *Idler* Magazine—My third Novel—Hannay ' at Home '—His charming Wife and lovely Children—His personal Appearance—Gabriel Rossetti's Portrait of Hannay—' Latinless Lubbers '—' Blood and Culture '—Examples of Hannay's Vocabulary—Hannay the Elder—Father and Son—Thackeray's strong Liking for Hannay—Thackeray's ' Thoroughbred little Fighting Cock '—The Tumbler Club—The Tumblers—Quarrel and Reconciliation—Hannay stands for the Dumfries Burghs—Canonbury and Gunnersbury—Doran's Dinner-Party—Misdirected Complaisance—John Bruce, F.S.A.—His Modesty and Embarrassment—A dormant Baronetcy—Bruces of the Suffolk Woodland—A long Walk on a cold Night—Hannay's frequent Visits to Hatton House, Hatton Garden—John George Edgar—The ' Scot of a past Age '—His Opinion of the Queen's Lineage.

CHAPTER X.

FRIENDSHIP, LOVE AND MARRIAGE . . . 163

Novels and Novelists, from Elizabeth to Victoria—My first Letter to Hepworth Dixon—His cordial Answer—His fine Nature—His Manliness—My Place on the *Athenæum* Staff—Applicants for ' a Friendly Lift '—An unscrupulous Enemy—Close Friends—Inns of Court Rifle-Corps—Serio-Comic Incidents—*Miriam Copley, a Novel*—*Sir Everard's Daughter, a Novel*—Life of Robert

Stephenson, C.E., F.R.S.—Six Weeks in Northumbria—Stay at Darlington—George Stephenson and the Steam-Locomotive—Charles Manby's Home at Eastbourne—George Parkes Bidder, C.E., whilom 'the Calculating Boy'—His Talk about Robert Stephenson—Fallaciousness of Memory—Warning to Biographers—My Marriage—My Wife's Father—My admirable Mother-in-Law—Her brave and successful Fight with Adversity—Her noble Traits and beautiful Children—A Brighton School-Girl—Her Love Match—Great Ormond Street, Bloomsbury—From Lodgings to 'our own House' in Mesopotamia.

CHAPTER XI.

No. 5, HEATHCOTE STREET 187

Neighbourhood of Heathcote Street—*Littérateurs* of the District—Welcome Guests at No. 5—The Bensusans of Marylebone Road—Abraham Bensusan and Henri Quatre—Mrs. Bensusan's Last Will and Testament—*Olive Blake's Good Work, a Novel*—The Way in which it was Composed—Thackeray and his Characters—*Live It Down: A Story of the Light Lands*—The Story's Success—Mr. Petter's Praise—*Not Dead Yet, a Novel*—Coincidences of *Not Dead Yet* and the Tichborne Story—Vice-Chancellor Wood's Mention of those Coincidences—Athenæum Gossip—Rider Haggard's too hasty Critics.

CHAPTER XII.

RICHARD COBDEN AND QUEEN ELIZABETH . 202

Life of Robert Stephenson, C.E., F.R.S.—Mr. Smiles's *Lives of Boulton and Watt*—Popular Error touching the Elder Stephenson and the Steam Locomotive—David Roberts, R.A., on 'the Ignoromeousness' of Artists—James Hayllar's Picture, entitled *The Queen's Highway in the Sixteenth Century*—Richard Cobden's Part in the Production of that Picture—The Free Trader at Fault—His Inability to produce his Authority—An Essay in Literary

Misdirection—Maud Ufford's Letter to Margery Pennington—D'Eyncourt's *Memoirs of Maids of Honour*—'Quaint old D'Eyncourt!'—Mr. Smiles's *Life of Thomas Telford, the Civil Engineer*—Explanation of Richard Cobden's Mistake—Light from *Murray's Handbook for Kent and Sussex*—'An ingenious Gentleman' of Queen Anne's Court—Prince George of Denmark—Charles VI. of Spain—Falsification of Personal History—Publication of *A Book About Lawyers*—Letters from learned Lawyers—Edward Foss, F.S.A., author of *The Judges of England*—Letter from the Lord Chief Baron—Sir Fitzroy Kelly's Confirmation of my Exposure of a spurious Anecdote—Sir William Follett's Health in 1844 and 1845—An Idle Tale touching Sir William Follett and George Stephenson—Migration from Mesopotamia to St. John's Wood—Joy and Sorrow—Holiday Trips.

CHAPTER XIII.

'OUR CLUB' 216

Augustus De Morgan on London Club-houses—Tavern Clubs—*The Tumbler* Club—*The Sheridan* Club—*The Rambler* Club—*Our Club*—Notable Members of the last-named Club—Frederick William Hamstede, First Secretary of *Our Club*—Thackeray's Affection for 'little Hamstede'—'I love little Hamstede'—Messrs. Merivale and Marzials on Thackeray—Causes of Thackeray's Tenderness for 'little Hamstede'—Clunn's Hotel, Covent Garden—Dinners at 'Clunn's'—Marrow-Bones and Marrow-Spoons—Drinking in 'the 'Fifties and 'Sixties'—Table-Talk at *Our Club*—George Jessel on Vulgar Prejudices—Songsters of *Our Club*—Robert Chambers on the Waverley Novels—Freedom of Action in Edinburgh—Robert Chambers on the Fictions of Biographers—Insult offered to Frederick Lawrence—Garibaldi's Telegram to Fred Lawrence—A Large Order on Modest Means—Mr. Matthews of Sheffield—Théophile Gautier at *Our Club*—'Who the Devil is *Doré*?'—*Tête-à-tête* of an Englishman who spoke no French and a Frenchman who knew no English—'The Illustrious Goaty'—Théophile at the Salisbury Hotel—Mr. Matthews entertaining 'the brightest Spirits of the Age.'

CHAPTER XIV.

WILLIAM MAKEPEACE THACKERAY . . 246

My Introduction to the Author of *Vanity Fair*—Thackeray's Regard for my Brother George—*Life of W. M. Thackeray* by Herman Merivale and Frank T. Marzials—The Novelist's Ancestors, gentle and simple—Hannay's Perplexity—Thackeray's Dictum touching 'three gentle Descents'—His Pride in his 'no Family in particular'—His Birth at Calcutta—His Preparatory School—Thackeray at Charterhouse School—The Youngs of St. Helen's Place, Bishopsgate—John Young—James Young—Emily Young—Edith Young—Thackeray playing with Children on a sunny Lawn—Thackeray at Cambridge and 'The Temple'—His Patrimony and Poverty—His Marriage at Paris and Married Life in Great Coram Street—His greatest Misfortune—Its sad Consequences—Mr. Edmund Yates's Sketch of Thackeray in *Town Talk*—The Thackeray-Yates Quarrel—Motley's Sketch of Thackeray's Face—Part taken by Charles Dickens in the Thackeray-Yates Quarrel—Thackeray's Avowal touching the Quarrel—Mr. Marzials on the Quarrel—Strife between Thackeray and Dickens—Thackeray's Ambition to surpass Dickens—Abraham Hayward's 'Airs'—His long Neglect of Thackeray—His Quickness in aiding the Successful Novelist—'The Inner Circle'—Thackeray's Admiration of Dickens the Novelist.

CHAPTER XV.

MORE ABOUT THACKERAY 282

My Intercourse with Thackeray—An *Habitué* of Evans's—Paddy Green—The Cyder Cellars—Thackeray the Tavern-Haunter—His solitary Dinners at the Gray's Inn Coffee-House—His Divers Moods—Douglas Jerrold on Thackeray—James Kenney the Dramatist—His Whims and Eccentricities—Charles Lamb Kenney—Portraits of him in *Pendennis*—His Intimacy with Thackeray—His famous Review of *The Kickleburys on the Rhine*—Why did you 'do it,' Charley?—*Essay on Thunder and Small Beer*

—Thackeray's Care for a Friend's Feelings—Thackeray at 'The Derby'—Comrades in Misfortune on Epsom Downs—Thackeray the *Bon Vivant*—His Delight in Good Cheer—The twopenny Tartlet—Consequences of his gastronomic Indiscretions—Curious Anecdotes about George III.—Thackeray and *Live It Down*—Thackeray in the Chair at a Shakespeare Dinner of *Our Club*—Geraldine Jewsbury's Review of *The Story of Elizabeth*—Consequences of that Review—National Shakespeare Tercentenary Committee—Squabbles and Misunderstandings—Thackeray's Withdrawal from *Our Club*—Hamstede's vain Endeavours to recover him to the Club—Thackeray's Death—His few Foibles and his noble Qualities—Andrew Arcedeckne and Mr. Foker.

A BOOK OF RECOLLECTIONS.

CHAPTER I.

CHILDHOOD.

My Birth and Parentage—George Edwards the Elder—My Grandsire's Gifts—Sunny Memories—Woodbridge Grammar-School—The Rev. Woodthorpe Collett—Hasketon and Bredfield—Boulge and Martlesham—Wilford Hollows and the River Deben—Botesdale Grammar-School—The Rev. Joseph Haddock—A Hunting Clergyman and an Admirable Schoolmaster—Redgrave Hall—George St. Vincent Wilson—Steeple-Chases and Cricket-Matches—Botesdale Grammar-School Extinguished by Marlborough College.

ON 14th January, 1831, I was born at Framlingham, in the Woodland of Suffolk, the second son and ninth child of William Jeaffreson, surgeon, (M.R.C.S. 1812, and F.R.C.S. 1844,) of Framlingham aforesaid, and of his wife, Caroline Jeaffreson, *née* Edwards, youngest child of George and Anne Edwards, of the same small, picturesque, and historic market-town.

When I look at the list of the young men whom I knew intimately at Oxford, but have not seen since 1852, the year in which I took my B.A. degree, I fail to recall clearly their features, voices, or aught else of their respective personalities. But I can remember my grandfather, George Edwards the Elder, distinctly, although he died in his eighty-fourth year, when I was only five years old. That I have so perfect a recollection of the old man, who passed from this life in my tender infancy, and remember so little of my academic comrades, may be regarded as evidence that the human mind is more tenacious of its earliest than of its later impressions.

My childish mind was greatly interested by my grandsire's peculiarities. He was the only man of my familiar acquaintance who was bald upon the crown of his head and toothless, whose hair was white as snow, and whose man-servant was black as coal. How the negro—who looked after my grandfather's garden and drove him about the town and neighbourhood in his high-wheeled 'chaise,' (a big, lemon-yellow gig, provided with a hood, and drawn by a tall, brown horse)—found his way into the heart of the Suffolk Woodland, is one of the countless items of social history that have passed from my mind. In my childhood I imagined that my good grandfather had redeemed the black man from cruel bondage with money paid to a slave-dealer 'on Afric's burning sands.' But, on coming to years of discretion, I discovered that the negro did not owe his freedom to my grandsire's beneficence.

Interesting to me by reason of his toothlessness, his baldness, the whiteness of his hair, and the blackness of his man-servant, my grandfather was also interesting to me as the giver of curious gifts. In an autobiographic fragment, Edward George, first Baron Lytton put it upon record that his maternal grandfather never gave him anything more precious than a chastisement, which he did not deserve. Though they were of no commercial value, my maternal grandfather's presents afforded me much pleasure.

As the kindly old man was a chronic invalid in his closing years, it devolved on his medical son-in-law to make him many professional visits; and in fine weather my father often took me with him to the pleasant house to which my grandfather retired, on withdrawing, in his sixty-first year, from his shop upon the Market Hill, with a fortune that would have justified him in spending the evening of his days in a much statelier abode. Placed at a corner of the town, the house stood close against the highway, but was skirted in the rear and towards the north-east by gardens, orchards, farm-buildings, and the big malt-offices which George Edwards the Elder 'worked' on his own account, and to a goodly profit, after ceasing to be a grocer and draper. The professional visits were usually paid in the forenoon, at a time when the veteran was sure to be found in his parlour; and, on closing his medical and other grave chat with his doctor, the cheery, chubby-cheeked invalid never failed to admit his small grandson to a conference, which ended more or less in this manner: 'By-the-way, young Hop-o'-my-thumb, I have something for you. Just wait a minute,' my grandfather would remark, in the tone of a man who had almost forgotten to do the right thing, and was afraid I should run away before he had done it. Thus speaking, he used to rise from his chair, move nimbly (*i.e.*, nimbly for so ancient a man) to an old-fashioned sideboard, and bring from one of its drawers a rectangular piece of paper or thin cardboard, highly-glazed and richly illuminated with colours. To my childish vision, each paper was a thing of beauty. 'There, Hop-o'-my-thumb,' the donor would add, when he had been duly thanked for his latest gift, 'put that along with the others, and take good care of every one of them. If you take good care of them, you'll have, by-and-by, a lot not to be matched in the whole county.'

Years had passed over my grandfather's grave, I had for years lost my collection of beautiful pieces of paper or thin card through the perverse destructiveness of a nurse, who, wilfully and with malice-aforethought, threw the whole collection into the fire, and I had lived to be a Botesdale school-boy, when I saw a facsimile of one of the most beautiful of my grandfather's gifts, at the extreme end of a piece of muslin that had been 'sent in' to my mother from the shop. In an instant it flashed upon me how my grandsire had obtained possession of the ornamental tickets, which he used to give me one at a time. The gifts were alike illustrative of his thrift and kindliness. Knowing that, up to a certain age, children are just as well pleased with a valueless piece of gay paper as with a twopenny or threepenny toy, he had saved his pence whilst getting from 'the shop' the bright tickets that had delighted my eyes.

Though I was a robust urchin, and, in the opinion of my fond parents, a singularly beautiful little fellow, I was not in my early boyhood so strong and healthy as I looked. Excitable and nervous, I was a frequent dreamer of terrifying dreams, that caused me to rouse the house at night with cries of alarm, and throughout my seventh year and the next six months I was a sleep-walker. Of some of the painful dreams I retain clear recollections, and I remember the emotions of affright and shame that possessed me on returning from somnambulism to consciousness under the eyes of the nurse, who on two or three occasions caught hold of me as I was descending a steep staircase in my sleep. One part of the gentle treatment that cured me of this morbid practice was the use of a strong band that, after I had fallen asleep, was put over me and fixed to my bed, so that I could not easily escape from the couch. Apart from my vivid reminiscences of the mental distress that came to me from horrible dreams and my somnambulistic propensity, all my recollections of my tender childhood are pleasurable.

Whenever thought carries me back to the scenes of my childhood, I am in cheery, exhilarating, luxurious sunshine. I remember nothing of the cold winds that swept over the leafless Woodland in winter and early spring, nothing of the rain that rained every day in the humid seasons, nothing of the gloomy clouds that crossed the land for weeks together when I was a boy. I bask in sunshine whilst I am recalling the incidents and familiar haunts of my opening years. My morning calls on my old grandfather were paid in fine weather. The hours I spent in the gardens and orchards about the old man's house were passed under blue skies, and in a warm air, redolent with the scent of flowers and ripening fruit. When my father took me with him for a roundabout drive to picturesque villages, secluded farmsteads, moated halls, and rectories lying in lovely gardens, we felt the sun's full heat on emerging from a leafy lane into a main-road or open common. The sickles of the harvest-men flashed in the sun, when they had returned to their work after 'hallooing the doctor's largess.' It was seldom in these drives that my father had to descend from his gig to open a gate on his way to a farm-house; for the music of his approaching wheels rarely failed to bring to view a child, or group of children, all agog to open gates for 'the doctor,' who paid his gate-openers at the rate of a penny a-gate. Sometimes, as we entered the byway leading to a small land-owner's manorial home, we had view of a covey of little lads and lasses, racing like so many partridges through bracken and gorse, towards the swing-barrier at the end of the lane. Left to myself at the entrance to the grounds about this manorial abode, or any other rural homestead, whilst my father was engaged with his patients, I never grew impatient for his return; so great was the enjoyment that came to me from sitting in the sunshine, and lazily observing the life of the gardens and farm-buildings.

The second stage of my childhood was entered in my ninth year, when I was removed from the control of my sister's governess, and placed under the sterner but far from rigorous discipline of the Reverend Woodthorpe Collett, M.A., at that time Head Master of the Woodbridge Grammar School. One of the famous Dean Colet's proved and certified 'kin,' and the son of a small gentle land-owner who passed his days at Burgh, near Woodbridge, this gentleman is on several grounds entitled to the present writer's eulogistic commemoration. Not that he resembled his famous collateral ancestor in being a great scholar. On the contrary, I learnt in my opening manhood from some of his old college-friends that he resembled William Shakspeare in knowing little Latin and less Greek, and that they had laughed heartily on hearing he had turned schoolmaster. Far from thinking lightly of my preceptor's attainments, I regarded him as the most learned of men, so long as I remained under his government; and I am not aware that I differed in this respect from the oldest and most critical of his pupils. There were occasions in school-hours when he was a slightly terrifying personage to me; but as soon as lessons were over, he was the same amusing, kindly, jocular Mr. Collett, whom I had known at my own home, and who had won all hearts in and about Framlingham, when he was the prosperous rector of Swefling, easy in his circumstances, and unforeseeing the domestic troubles, which constrained him to follow an uncongenial calling.

Naturally a clever man, he was largely endowed with kindliness, and on several occasions was at pains to preserve me from the persecution of a rather rough play-ground. As a small boy's first term at a boys'-school is usually fruitful of vexation to the neophyte, it is not surprising that during my first 'quarter' at Woodbridge Grammar School I made acquaintance with grief. In playing ball-games with my sisters, it had been my use to throw the ball as they threw it, *i.e.*, from a hand raised high above the shoulder. For throwing a ball in this girlish way, I was of course derided by my Woodbridge playmates, one of whom sent the ball back to me together with these stinging words, 'You mayn't throw like a mawther, Miss Polly, when you play with boys,'—words that caused the play-ground to resound with cries of 'Polly.' It was not till several boys had explained to me what was amiss in my way of throwing, that I made my first attempt to throw '*from* the shoulder,' instead of over the shoulder. The effect of this honest essay to throw like a boy was a quick, sharp spasm of some muscle of the arm, that gave me excruciating pain at a point between the elbow and the shoulder. The pain was momentary, but for the moment it was torture. Moreover, the pain was attended by the vexation of knowing that the ball was thrown wildly. Seeing me wince and turn white with pain and annoyance, the witnesses of the exploit of course screamed, 'Polly! Polly!' like a pack of young lunatics.

Here was a painful position. If I threw like a girl, I was derided and called 'Polly.' Every time I tried to throw like a boy, I was rewarded with sharp pain in the ill-conditioned muscle as well as with cries of 'Polly! Polly!' The persecution for some days was hot and fierce; and, so long as it raged, I was an inglorious sufferer from persecution. To my surprise, it ended as suddenly as it began. I was on the point of making yet another effort to throw like a boy, when big Jack Shafto (son of one of the Durham Shaftoes, who had somehow settled at Framlingham, and come to figure as a magistrate for East Suffolk) called to me from the top of the sloping play-ground, 'Put it up, Jeff, any way you like. As there's something wrong in "the go" of your arm, we have agreed not to laugh at you again.' It has often been my fortune throughout life to think of the right thing to say, when it was just a minute-and-a-half too late to say it. On the occasion of which I have just spoken, the happy thought came soon enough for use. As I put up the ball in girlish fashion, I cried out in my jolliest way, 'Thank you, Polly is very much obliged to you!' That this brief speech caught the ear and heart of the play-ground was shown by the play-ground's good-humoured laughter, and its exclamations of 'Well done, little one!'

During the next summer holidays, when Jack Shafto was taking much pains to improve my style of throwing, and to cure what was wrong in 'the go' of my arm, I learnt from him how it came to pass that the persecution ceased so abruptly. Taking the affair into his hands, Mr. Collett had spoken confidentially with Jack Shafto and two other chiefs of the play-ground. He had neither 'lectured' nor 'jawed' nor talked any 'rubbish' about bullying, but had called their attention to my diminutive stature, and expressed an opinion that in consideration of my tender age and general insignificance the boys at large should not be too hard on me, while I was getting my arm into order. In brief, the kindly schoolmaster had flattered and humoured the big boys into taking a sympathetic view of my infirmity, and giving me a 'fair chance.' I do not say he should have been raised to a bishopric or endowed with a deanery; but had kindliness and sterling worth been an effectual title to a good benefice in his time, my excellent Woodthorpe Collett would have become the rector of a wide and fertile parish.

Though I was a poor hand at throwing a ball, I was better than most small boys at walking. Moving with a free step, I delighted in the cheapest of all boyish pastimes, and in this evening of my days I recall with tranquil pleasure how I footed it in the by-ways of Hasketon and Bredfield, and the sandy lanes of Martlesham. Doubtless we boys were often caught by storm and buffetted by blustering winds during our long walks over Wilford Hollows and round about Bromeswell. But the discomforts of existence pass from the memory, whilst the enjoyments of former time remain with us to the end of life's journey. When I fall a-thinking of these wanderings on foot, I walk under a blue sky, and over ground that is steeped in sunshine. It is also a joy for ever to re-visit in imagination the walls and waters of the Deben, which afforded me my earliest opportunity for studying the scenery and humours and various aspects of a tidal river.

Later in my boyhood, when Mr. Collett had retired from the Woodbridge Grammar School, I went to the Botesdale Grammar School, where it was my good fortune to come under the influence of the Reverend Joseph Haddock. A better man than this Mr. Haddock never breathed. A small, spare man, with a fine countenance, strong eyes, and a noble voice, he swayed his pupils by an air that was winningly gentle and at the same time irresistibly authoritative. Brisk in his movements, and no less strenuous than mild in his speech, he overflowed with nervous energy, that in moments of excitement passed in lightning from his eyes, but never in thunder from his lips. He was never known to scold a boy noisily; but if he detected a lad in lying or doing anything mean, this master with a strong face and marvellous eyes punished him terribly with a look that made the culprit contemptible to the whole school. The only instrument of corporal chastisement I ever saw him use was a piece of wood, shaped something like a spoon, and known to the boys as 'the patter.' The thing was the ferula of old-fashioned biographers, and was applied to the palm of the offender's left hand, which doubtless felt uncomfortably hot after receiving half-a-dozen stinging blows from the implement. It was not often that the patter was brought forth from its lurking-place. I forget the culprit's name and his offence; but I remember how Haddock, after administering the chastisement and putting the ferula out of sight, observed on one occasion, with his clear, bell-toned voice, 'The boy who makes me hit him with that piece of wood degrades me and degrades the whole school.' I remember also that for several days the wretched culprit was punished by 'the play-ground,' for having 'degraded the whole school.'

Speaking roughly from mere recollection, I should say that the boys at Botesdale Grammar School in my time—boarders, day-boarders, and day-pupils (including the six free boys or foundationers) who had their meals at home—numbered from forty to fifty lads, all told. Like old-fashioned schools of its sort, Mr. Haddock's school comprised boys of all the different degrees of social quality, from the sons of affluent gentlemen to the sons of mere artisans. The foundationers, who were town-boys of the humblest parentage, were placed in classes with their more fortunate schoolmates; but, unlike the other day-boys, they did not join in the sports of the play-ground. Of the thirty or more boarders, the larger part were sons of county magistrates, clergymen, barristers, half-pay officers, attorneys, doctors, small land-owners of gentle quality, whilst the others were sons of farmers and shopkeepers. Had the sons of the county-justices and rich rectors given themselves any airs of superiority over their less fortunate school-mates, their insolence would have been promptly checked and corrected by the Master, who knew every individual of his promiscuous lot of boys as thoroughly and exactly as a good huntsman knows every hound of his 'pack.'

In some particulars the domestic arrangements of the college were simple and rudely primitive, but in respect to fare, bodily exercise, social diversion, and moral tone, the school was everything that a boys'-school ought to be. The fights were neither frequent nor inordinately savage; and the play-ground never witnessed any conduct on the part of the big boys that could be fairly stigmatized as bullying, though of course youngsters were made to treat their elders with proper respect. That the tone and discipline of the school were maintained with so little corporal punishment and very few penal tasks, was due to Haddock's marvellous power of winning and holding the hearts of his boys, so that they one and all did his pleasure for the pure pleasure of doing it. The man was a veritable boy-charmer; and his power over his boys is the more remarkable, because one does not see how to account for it. Though he was in a grave and grand way companionable with 'his cubs,' he never made the mistake of paying them too much attention, or appearing inordinately desirous of their good-will. Speaking to them courteously and cordially, when he came upon them out of school-hours, he never chattered and gossipped with them, so as to make himself full cheap, and encourage them in the familiarity that breeds contempt. Nor did he ever make the mistake of talking goody-goody to them. Once a week he preached to them and the rest of an approving congregation a plain, short, pithy sermon from the pulpit of the chantry, attached to the 'old school-house.' But he never preached out of the pulpit. No one ever found him guilty of cant, or denied that he was a superb horseman. His extraordinary influence over his boys was in some degree referable to the straightness and judgment with which he went across country. Keeping in his stable two hunters—a clever black hackney (that ran in harness as well as across country), and a wonderful old bay mare, that always went stiff as crutches and lame as a tree for the first half-hour after leaving the stable, and yet on warming to her work never failed to go with the first flight—dear old Haddock (may he have gone to a good hunting country!) seized every opportunity for getting a day or half-day with the hounds.

Botesdale, a fine example of the single-street towns of East Anglia (Kirby calls it 'a long thorough-fare town'), differs greatly from the compact little town of my birth. It is so long, that I am guilty of no Irishism in saying that it lies for the most part in the next parish; for, though the whole thoroughfare goes by the name of Botesdale with the gentry, or 'Buzzle' with the peasants, two-thirds of the way lies in Lower Rickinghall. Moreover, the street (a portion of the old turn-pike road from Norwich to Yarmouth) is not more remarkable for length than for breadth and straightness. In my boyhood this grand way was kept alive, like the narrow main-streets of Woodbridge, with coaches-and-four and the carriages of grandees, 'travelling post.' In this last respect, the thoroughfare changed strangely for the worse, as the railways shut up the posting-houses and drove the coaches from the road: —a sad change for the people who are tied by duty or poverty to the silent and desolate and dolefully dilapidated street!

On coming for the first time to Botesdale, some twenty miles distant from Framlingham, I found myself in novel scenery and a new social atmosphere. Lying in the Woodland, but within a few miles of the Fielding, Botesdale was less remarkable than my native district for redundancy of foliage and boscage. The hedges were less numerous and high, and the fields four or five times as large as the paddocks and pightels about the town of my birth. The humble people of the district differed notably from the subordinate folk of my proper hundred. Comprising a strikingly large per-centage of small men (mere boys in height, though they were grey-haired) with keen countenances and bowed legs, the neighbourhood offered to my boyish consideration fashions of masculine attire that were unfamiliar to me. For head-gear the minute bow-legged men preferred a cloth-cap, showing the size of the skull; and they wore curiously-cut nether garments of corduroy, extremely baggy about the hips and needlessly tight about the lower parts of the bow-legs. At the same time, the number of horses, whose delicacy of breed and constitution required that they should take their daily walks in clothing, was strikingly great. Had I in that opening stage of my career known aught of Newmarket and Dullingham by personal experience, I should have known that the 'peculiar something' of the Botesdale atmosphere came to it for the most part from Newmarket town and heath. True, 'tis a long call from Botesdale to Newmarket, but the influence of a famous school affects the humour of the country for miles round. From Newmarket to Bury St. Edmunds and from Bury to Wortham the moral and æsthetic tone of the heath was strong in every hamlet and homestead. The social life of Botesdale smacked of the famous racing-town. Honoured at Framlingham as a quadruped, serviceable to man in drawing and carrying heavy weights, the 'noble animal' was studied and considered critically at Botesdale as an instrument for making great speeds and flying over railed ditches. Nearly every man in Botesdale who was rich enough to keep a horse, and capable of riding to hounds, kept a more or less virtuous example of the noble animal, and rode it to the best of his ability. In society the noble animal was a frequent topic of conversation with the householders of the long street.

That the long street so greatly surpassed most other long streets in worshipful care for the noble animal was perhaps scarcely more referable to the influence of Newmarket than to the influence of Mr. George St. Vincent Wilson, of Redgrave Hall, the chief squire of the neighbourhood. More interesting to me at the present point of my career as the seat of Lord Keeper Nicholas Bacon, who founded and endowed the Botesdale Grammar School *temp.* Elizabeth, and as the seat in later time of Chief Justice Holt, than as the home of the gentleman who kept house, stables, and a pack of hounds there in my boyhood, Redgrave Park is one of the fairest places of the district of Suffolk, that lies along the Norfolk border. Standing on high ground, the present house (a modern building) is seen to advantage by travellers along the turnpike-road, who, like Kinglake's valet in *Eothen*, are ever on the 'look out for gentlemen's seats.' Between the turnpike-road and the Hall on the upland, a magnificent piece of ornamental water reflects the smiles and frowns of heaven; and, far away to the north, the nobly-timbered deer-park trends towards Redgrave Church (Botesdale's mother-church), where the tourist may find the marble effigies of the two great lawyers. A picturesque and beautiful domain to any observer, Redgrave was a fascinating place to the school-boy who came to it from a district of the Suffolk Woodland, whose stateliest homes were comparatively modest places.

Through the goodness of the reigning squire, who may certainly be commended for neighbourliness, the boys of the Botesdale Grammar School enjoyed several privileges within the park, whose nearest corner was not more than half-a-mile from their school-house. In the hot season they were allowed to bathe in the lake, and all the year through they were permitted to walk through the portion of park lying between the water and the turnpike-road. Yet more, they enjoyed the finest cricket-ground in the county at the concession of the same benignant squire, who allowed them to use Barley Birch for the game as though it were their own property. That amiable enthusiast, the local antiquary, may exercise his ingenuity in discovering how the great meadow, where barley never grew, nor birches flourished in this writer's time, came by its name. Enough for the present historian to record that, year after year in the time of the kindly George St. Vincent Wilson, Barley Birch, lying on the south of the turnpike-road, and well in view of the front windows of Redgrave Hall, was by turns a race-course and a cricket-field,—the course on which jockeys rode hurdle races and flat races after the steeple-chase (the grand event of the Botesdale Races) had been ridden, and the field on which the Botesdale cricketers played many a close match with the clubs of the neighbourhood.

From what I have said of Botesdale's delight in the noble animal and care for affairs of sport, it may not be inferred that hunters and hunting, hurdle-races and steeple-chases, hounds and cricket were the only things in which the superior inhabitants of the long street were strongly interested. Had the town shown an inclination to worship the noble animal with depraving extravagance, the vicious disposition would have been protested against by Mr. Robert Horner Harris, a gentleman of taste and refinement, who was in every respect qualified to be the chief surgeon of a rather aristocratic neighbourhood. The gentle tone—perhaps, I may be allowed to say the academic tone—of the sport-loving town was maintained by several families, whose appetite for news from Cambridge was far keener than their interest in the Newmarket meetings. Though Mr. Mills, a gentle land-owner of the town, was duly honoured for being a capable horseman and clever cultivator of his ancestral acres, he was regarded even by his horsiest neighbours as greatly inferior to his brother, who had distinguished himself at Cambridge, and as a Fellow of Pembroke College might live to be rector of Framlingham, or incumbent of the still richer living of Soham in Cambridgeshire. The two cognate groups of Smiths, leading families of the long town, were more desirous of figuring amongst scholars than of shining amongst sportsmen. Barnard Smith, whose *Arithmetic* and *Algebra* are used by so many teachers and students, had withdrawn from his native town and won his fellowship at Cambridge before I entered the Botesdale Grammar

School; but as a small and insignificant school-boy I enjoyed the privilege of worshipping Barnard's big cousin Hamblin Smith (a gentleman not unknown at Cambridge), very much as David Copperfield honoured the magnificent Steerforth. To this hour the majestic Hamblin lives in my memory as the tallest, handsomest, most gracious, and most benignant boy that was ever offered to the admiration of small urchins as a model of youthful deportment. How exquisitely this superb Hamblin sang ballads of a lightly humorous vein and songs of patriotic feeling! Does he still warble of the 'nice little, tight little island'? More than forty-five years have passed since I last regarded his fine profile and waving locks. Does he still retain those yellow tresses? Were I to meet him face to face this season in a London drawing-room, should I recognize him?

Ben Land, the famous steeple-chase rider, who was believed by the Botesdale boys to have 'never lost a race,' once observed, 'If Parson Haddock had only kept clear of holy orders, he'd have been the best steeple-chase rider in all England.' The clergyman, who won this eulogium from the East Anglian jockey, was ever observant of clerical decorum in the field. He never donned pink coat or green coat. He never wore white breeches or top-boots. Dressed in a close-buttoned black frock-coat, black breeches, and high boots, he was seen at a glance, as he went across country, to be a hunting clergyman. His hat was the familiar chimney-pot, and his cravat as deep and white and perfectly folded as it would have been at a bishop's dinner-table. When Mr. George

St. Vincent Wilson declared that 'the parson rode like the darvil,' he merely meant that the clergyman was a straight, fearless, clever rider. My good master rode boldly, but ever with discretion and humane care for the animal under him. When the day's sport was over, he jogged home. At dinner-tables, where the talk ran on the characteristics and capabilities of the noble animal, he was usually a silent listener, never a noisy talker. Caring nothing for meet-breakfasts and hunt-dinners, he delighted only in the exercise and sport. Neither Bishop Bathurst nor Bishop Stanley saw aught to reprehend in a hunting clergyman of so decorous and inoffensive a type. Still, it points to a great social change, that half-a-century since this good priest and schoolmaster was blamed by no one for seizing every occasion for getting a run with the hounds.

It points to Mr. Haddock's kindliness, that in the holidays he often lent one of his horses to his assistant-master, Mr. Harvey (an excellent horseman), so that he might have a day with the hounds. I remember an occasion during 'quarter' (the Botesdale boys knew nothing of 'terms') when he mounted Harvey and sent him for 'a run.' Between the clergyman and his scholastic assistant there was as wide a difference in air and style as one would expect to find between a regimental captain and a colour-serjeant. But the usher was an honest and capable little fellow, who deserved the almost fraternal regard his employer displayed for him. Marvellously skilful in cutting quills and nibbing pens, Harvey was the inventor and manufacturer of the two inks (a black ink and a red ink) that were used in the school. Some two or three years after I had ceased to be a schoolboy, Mr. Harvey amused and saddened me by telling me that he hoped to provide for his old age by inducing some gentleman with capital to go into the ink-trade, and take him for his commercial partner in consideration of his secret recipes for the two excellent inks. As the poor fellow was seriously out of health, when he spoke to me thus confidentially, it cut me to the heart to think he had no brighter prospect. A few years later, it gladdened me to hear that he had found the needful capitalist, and was doing more than fairly well as an ink-manufacturer.

The school-house doubtless still remains at Botesdale, and I have no doubt that boys of a sort are still being educated in it; but the school which I remember so gratefully perished many years since. It received its death-blow in 1845, in which year Marlborough College was incorporated by royal charter and opened for the higher culture of young gentlemen, to the grievous injury of my dear schoolmaster. Till '45, Haddock was cordially supported by the richer clergy of both divisions of Suffolk. In this work's Postscript, I speak of the rich rectors as momentous personages of my particular district of Suffolk. Some of these fortunate clergymen would have been affluent, had they possessed no estates besides their benefices, but the holders of the best livings round-about Framlingham were for the most part owners of fat farms and money in the consols. The same may be said of some of the incumbents of the inferior livings, with tithes rising from three hundred to four hundred pounds a-year. Besides being clergymen, and (let me observe) most efficient clergymen, these prosperous rectors were active county magistrates, and all that lay-squires of the second degree usually are in our pastoral districts. And, till Marlborough opened its doors, some of the grandest of these grand rectors sent their boys to Botesdale, at least for their preliminary training. Poor Haddock's school died of Marlborough, which deprived the master of his clerical boys in a single year. Having lost his hold on the rich rectors, Haddock lost by degrees the confidence of the small landowners, the half-pay officers, the prosperous solicitors and doctors.

I do not murmur against the success of Marlborough, although it was so hurtful to the old-fashioned schoolmaster, who did me the great service of teaching me in my boyhood to admire sterling goodness. I do not undervalue the good that has come to England's life from the institution of Marlborough and Uppingham and Wellington Colleges, and from the enlargement and re-constitution of such schools as Charterhouse, Dulwich, and St. Paul's. But I regret that the success of our new public schools and the development of several of our old schools should have extinguished so completely and universally the old-fashioned seminaries, in one of which I was well and efficiently trained to the summer of my fifteenth year by a fine example of the old-fashioned hunting clergy.

CHAPTER II.

MY ACT AND DEED.

I am Apprenticed to a Country Doctor—Medical Apprentices—The Old School of Family Doctors—The New School of Family Doctors—My Father's Services to Surgery—Professor Erichsen on the most Important of those Services—They are Recognized by the Council of the College of Surgeons—The Birds at the Top of the Tree.

SOON after my withdrawal from the Botesdale Grammar School in the middle of my fifteenth year, I and my father put our hands and seals to an indented deed, whereby from motives of natural affection he bound himself to instruct me in the arts and mysteries of a surgeon and apothecary, and I promised to be his loyal apprentice and obedient servant during a term of five or seven years (I am uncertain as to the number, but am inclined to think it was *seven* years), and throughout the same term of five or seven years to forbear from gambling, to eschew evil courses and associates, and to refrain from marrying without his consent. To my young mind this indented agreement was a momentous document, and its execution a most solemn, not to say religious business.

When I had signed the indenture, and in obedience to the instructions of the family lawyer in attendance (to wit, my uncle William Edwards) had placed the forefinger of my right hand on a scarlet wafer, and had said, 'I give this as my act and deed,' my father shook me warmly by the same hand, and forthwith put in my hand a small tortoise-shell lancet-case, containing two lancets, sheathed with tortoise-shell. At the time, I regarded my father's act in shaking my hand so cordially as a confirmation of the bargain and compact between us. I also regarded the gift of the lancet-case and lancets as part of the ceremony, that had placed us in a new relation to one another. On these points I may have been mistaken. Anyhow, I went forth from that impressive interview with my father and his lawyer, feeling that I had made a great step towards the attainment of virile importance.

Since I performed this act and deed in the middle of my fifteenth year, the rules and usages touching the education of medical students have been changed in several particulars. To qualify himself to practise as a surgeon and apothecary, it is no longer necessary for the student to serve an apprenticeship to a master. But, speaking from their personal knowledge of the younger members of the medical profession, eminent physicians and surgeons have informed me that the abolition of the necessity to serve an apprenticeship was no genuine reform, but a change for the worse. I have also been assured by clever and resolute medical students, that in walking the hospitals and preparing for their examinations they found themselves at a serious disadvantage from having avoided the preliminary apprenticeship. Moreover, at the present time it is not uncommon for students of the medical schools, who were never apprenticed to practitioners of medicine and surgery, to seek employment as dispensers and assistants to general practitioners and to mere druggists, in order to acquire the particular knowledge and aptitude that are the consequences of the discipline of apprenticeship.

One of the worst consequences of the change that relieved students of the necessity to serve as apprentices is the young general practitioner's disposition to regard the multifarious services of pharmacy as matters beneath his scientific consideration,—as duties to be performed by a mere tradesman, rather than by a professor of medicine and surgery, who is a member of the College of Surgeons and a Licentiate of the College of Physicians. Drugs of the same kind differ in quality almost as much as wines of the same sort; and, instead of deeming it beneath their dignity to trouble themselves about the goodness or inferiority of their different drugs, family doctors of the old school deemed it a chief part of their duty to ascertain that the drugs they administered to their patients were drugs of the best quality, or at least of the best attainable quality. Trained as apprentices to distinguish between good drugs and inferior drugs by sight, smell, savour, or chemical analysis, on becoming practitioners they were at pains to get the best samples of 'materia medica.' Family doctors of the new school too often know nothing of the comparative goodness or inferiority of the medicines which they put into the bodies of their patients, but what druggists tell them. Few persons are aware how much of his pharmaceutical duties and responsibilities the ordinary family doctor of the new school delegates to tradesmen of whom he knows little and his patients know nothing whatever. In these railway-times, many a country doctor with a lucrative practice satisfies the requirements of his numerous patients without the assistance of a dispenser working in his own surgery, and without spending much more than an hour a-day of his own time in pharmaceutical labour. His prescriptions are for the most part dispensed by druggists far away from his home. Instead of making his own pills and tinctures on his own premises, he buys the pills by the gross and his tinctures by the gallon of London tradesmen. The advantages to the doctor of this way of doing business are manifest. Possibly the disadvantages to the sick are not very great. It is conceivable that this new way of dispensing prescriptions is upon the whole no less advantageous to patients than to the family doctors; but, had he lived to consider and deliver judgment upon it, my dear father would have declared with warmth that a professional man should do his duty, instead of paying another person to do it for him.

In August, 1845, the first August of my apprenticeship, my father entered his fifty-sixth year, being in several respects older than his age, though he had lost nothing of his perfect stature of five feet eleven inches, and was still as remarkable as he had ever been for the dignity of his aspect and bearing. On nearing his fiftieth year, he had been so unfortunate as to suffer from an attack of whooping-cough, whose violent paroxysms did him irreparable injury. After that illness he was seldom seen on horseback, and was compelled in the colder seasons to use a close carriage. Fortunately his mental vigour and spirits were not affected by this impairment of his bodily health, and he preserved his enthusiasm for scientific study and all the brighter qualities of his charming personality to his seventy-first year, when his intellectual powers began to decline.

Being human, he was not absolutely faultless. A man of fervid temperament, he suffered throughout his life from a whimsical excitability, that often displayed itself in brief fits of vehement anger at trivial annoyances. But he made no enemies through this infirmity; for his ebullitions of displeasure were not more startling by their suddenness and violence than comical by their brevity, and he was so true a gentleman that even in his fiercest anger he never assailed the object of his disapproval with words, likely to provoke passionate and obstinate resentment. Schoolboys sometimes spoke of him as 'peppery,' but they never feared the capricious storminess of his freakish but always generous irritability.

With the exception of this solitary and venial infirmity, my father had not a failing. Charitable in his judgments of individuals, he was benignant in his dealings with all men. A romantic worshipper of his friends, he was placable to his enemies. Overflowing with sympathy for the poor, he befriended them at every turn, cheering them with kindly words and relieving them with a bountiful hand in the seasons of their urgent distress. It has been my good fortune to know some of the brightest spirits of my period, under circumstances that gave me singularly good opportunities for studying their finest qualities; but I never made the acquaintance of a man in domestic privacy or general society, who was superior in personal dignity and mental refinement to the country doctor who was my sire. And in those respects he was well mated with my mother, who was not more remarkable for the beauty of her noble countenance than for her intellectual refinement.

When he enlivened his remarks on the medical evidence in the Maybrick trial, by remarking that a physician had been defined as a person who spent his time in putting drugs of which he knew little into bodies of which he knew less, Mr. Justice Stephen revived a *mot*, whose antiquity was greater than he probably imagined. Thrown in the first instance at the physicians of George the Third's later period, the piquant definition at the time of its first utterance was neither wholly unjust, nor more unfair than epigrammatic censure is permitted to be. In this closing decade of the nineteenth century, physicians know much of their drugs and very much of the bodies to which the medicines are administered. As my father, by means of the *Lancet* and the scientific literature on which he sometimes spent more money than he could conveniently spare, kept himself well abreast with the leaders of medical science, he steadily improved as a physician from the year in which he withdrew from the Borough hospitals, to the period of his mental decadence. But, were I to say he was a perfect physician, I should declare him to have been miraculously in advance of the physicians of his time. A leader of the physicians he never was. It is, however, an affair of scientific history, that he was conspicuous amongst the surgical leaders of his period. A skilful and successful lithotomist, he was also a no less successful lithotritist at a time when lithotrity was a new and too generally distrusted operation. Indeed, he was an habitual performer of all the more difficult and hazardous operations; and as his generous bearing conciliated his professional neighbours, who would have held aloof from him and even decried him, had he shown any disposition 'to give himself airs of superiority,' he became through his own surgical address and their cordial co-operation the chief of a coterie of Suffolk surgeons, whose proceedings were watched with critical interest by the most brilliant operators of the London hospitals. He had won this honourable position in his secluded district of the Suffolk Woodland, and had enjoyed it for several years, when he was so fortunate as to earn for himself an enduring place amongst the Masters of British Surgery.

On this point it will be best for my father's honour that I should give my readers the testimony of one of the several authoritative writers on British surgery, who have concurred in cordially extolling the most important of his professional achievements. In his *Surgery*, Professor Erichsen says,

'Ovariotomy is probably the greatest triumph of modern operative surgery. In its original conception, as in its ultimate perfection, this operation reflects the greatest lustre on the British School of Surgery. Its history is curious. Its progress was slow, and was marked by those oscillations in the judgment and favour of the profession which frequently precede the final establishment of a great advance in practice. The operation was originally proposed and its practicability discussed in 1762, by John Hunter. It was strongly advocated and its practicability taught by John Bell at a later period. It is said to have been performed in France by L'Aumonier in 1782, in a case of "schirrhus disease with abscess" of the ovary, the patient recovering. A pupil of John Bell (MacDowell of Kentucky, who was the father of ovariotomy) first performed the operation in America in 1802, and in all operated thirteen times. In 1823, Lirzars operated for the first time in this country. But that operation, though several times repeated, fell into discredit, in a great measure owing to the imperfection of the diagnosis of the cases in which it was done, and was not revived until 1836, when Jeaffreson of Framlingham practised it successfully through a small incision one-and-a-half inches long. From this operation we must date the revival of ovariotomy in Great Britain. The operation was followed by others, performed by King of Saxmundham, Crisp of Harleston, and West of Tonbridge. The example of these provincial surgeons was followed by their brethren in London, and the operation was practised by many.'

King of Saxmundham co. Suffolk (a man of fine presence and great ability, who had begun his professional career as a surgeon in the army), and Crisp of Harleston co. Suffolk were leading persons of the group of surgeons who had gathered about my father. How often they performed ovariotomy with the minor incision I am unable to say. My father performed it five times with perfect success in the course of a few years. The five successful cases, without one fatal case to set against them, were enough to dispel all doubt as to the excellence of the operation. All that was needful for the universal acceptance of the operation by surgeons throughout the world was that a young London surgeon of adequate judgment and dexterity should make it his specialty; and such a surgeon eventually appeared in the person of Mr. Spencer Wells, whose splendid performance of what may be called his professional mission was in due course rewarded none too highly with wealth and a baronetcy.

As his singular modesty preserved him from the mistake of attaching excessive importance to his various operations, but on the contrary disposed him to undervalue them, my father deemed himself magnificently rewarded for his services to surgery, when the Council of the College of Surgeons placed him amongst the Fellows of the College. During the thirty-two years that had passed since he gained his membership of the college by examination, my father's visits to London, or to any place outside his native county, had been so few that I believe he could have counted them on his fingers. From the happy season in which he attained to the dignity of F.R.C.S., he went yearly to London for the annual dinner of the Council and Fellows of the College, for the pleasure of regarding the faces and listening to the speeches of the London surgeons. The admiration was not one-sided. The great London surgeons showed their good feeling and good taste in making so much of the fine old fellow from the Suffolk Woodland, that he always returned in the cheeriest of good spirits to his peaceful and secluded neighbourhood, where he was honoured by rich and poor, as no doctor ever had been or will be honoured in that district. These yearly trips to town seldom covered more than one night, but now and then the trip was prolonged for another twenty-four hours, in order that the country surgeon might dine at the private table of some medical celebrity.

On his return from his annual holiday, my good father used to gossip about the incidents of the brief vacation in a way that was vastly entertaining to his wife and children. 'Ah!' he used to say at the close of the story, 'if I had stayed in town when I was a young man, I might be singing with the birds upon the top of the tree!' But the slightly regretful words were never spoken so as to indicate that the speaker envied the songsters in the topmost twigs, or was discontented with his particular perch on one of the lower branches.

CHAPTER III.

FIFTY YEARS SINCE.

Framlingham in My Boyish Days—Affluence and Culture of the Town's Principal Families—'The Edwards Family'—Life of the Small Market-Town and its Neighbourhood—My Desire to Turn Soldier—'This Ridiculous Business'—My Eldest Sister and Only Dancing-Mistress—The Greenlaws of Framlingham and Woolwich—My Elder Brother's Death—My Almost Fatal Illness—A Threefold Illusion.

Though the Cordy-Edwards estate of one hundred thousand pounds had been divided into eighths, and four-eighths of it had been taken out of the little town, Framlingham in the opening year of my apprenticeship enjoyed as large a measure of prosperity as it had enjoyed in the time of George Edwards the Elder. The corn-tax, so soon to be abolished, still favoured the agricultural interest, and enriched all the professional and commercial people of the Suffolk Woodland, who participated in the excessive affluence of the land-owners, the great farmers, and the beneficed clergy. In the particular district of which Framlingham, with two thousand five hundred inhabitants, was the capital town, nothing had occurred to extinguish or even to modify in any great degree the social conditions under which my grandfather Edwards, his brother William Edwards (the tanner of Framlingham), and his brother-in-law John Cordy of Worlingworth had acquired their wealth. As our nearest railway-station was Ipswich, the steam locomotive and the iron road had done nothing to injure the trade of the neighbourhood. On the contrary, by rendering it easier and cheaper for the tradesmen and merchants to journey to and from London, without at the same time causing the ordinary residents of the rural district to buy their stores in the capital, the new locomotion was beneficial to the Framlingham traders. Though the small landowners of the entire Woodland were declining in number, the particular district of the Woodland that surrounded my native market-town still had a goodly number of the superior farmers who farmed their own land.

Though he was the most momentous personage of the parish, the rector, with his Cambridge honours and his grand rectory, and his tithe-rent of some fifteen hundred pounds a-year and his glebe lands, was far away from being the richest man of Framlingham, which numbered amongst its chief laical householders several individuals, who possessed considerable estates apart from their gainful employments.

Like Yoxford, whose inhabitants used to speak of their lovely village as 'the garden of Suffolk,' my native town was in some degree indebted for its prosperity to the peculiar picturesqueness, which lured people from a distance to live for a while in the parish. The parish was seldom without a few residential idlers, who quickened the trade and brightened the society of the place. When my father's old friend Salmon of Pennlyne Court in Glamorganshire—a whilom doctor who had married a Welsh heiress—was educating his boys at public schools and universities, he passed several years with his wife and daughters at Framlingham. Whilst he was waiting for his succession to the living of Dennington, Edward Alston occupied one of the best houses on the Market Place, and lived there at a merry rate for several years, with his charming wife and jolly children.

But Framlingham owed its affluence chiefly to the social conditions that were swept away from our purely agricultural districts by the introduction of railways, the extinction of the small land-owners, and the fiscal change that has resulted in the depression of agriculture and the steady impoverishment of the tenant farmers. If it were written by competent hands, the financial story of the other small market-towns in the purely agricultural districts of East Anglia would closely resemble the financial story of Framlingham. Each of them would be found to have enjoyed during that period a measure of prosperity, which has been greatly reduced or wholly extinguished.

Framlingham 'society' knew nothing of cliques whilst I was my father's apprentice. The society of the little town consisted of eight nearly related households, spoken of by persons to the manor born as 'the Edwards family,' and some seven other households (including the rectory and the other clerical households), who would have been quite able to subdue the arrogance of the Edwardses, had the latter given themselves airs.

Comprising (1) my mother, a chief and charming force of the Edwards connection, (2) her brother George Edwards the Younger, who before 1845 had withdrawn from the shop on the market-hill, and taken to farming and malting on a rather large scale, (3) her brother Charles, yearly growing richer at the old business, whilst he lived at the pleasant house of Broadwater, a mile-and-a-half from the town, (4) her brother William Edwards, the foremost lawyer of the town, and (5) Mrs. John Edwards (daughter of an officer of the army), the richly endowed widow of my mother's first cousin, John Edwards of Framlingham, tanner, 'the Edwards family' comprised also (6) the four Peirsons—to wit, John Peirson, largest of the land-owners living in the parish, his brother Edmund, and their two unmarried sisters—grandchildren of my mother's uncle, William Edwards, the tanner. Coming to them mainly through their father's marriage with the last named tanner's daughter, the prosperity of these Peirsons was greatly enlarged by the last will of their uncle, Edmund Goodwyn, M.D., the celebrated physiologist and experimental philosopher, who bequeathed his real estate to his younger nephew, Edmund Peirson, on condition that he assumed the name and arms of Goodwyn. After complying with the condition, Dr. Goodwyn's younger nephew (known in his time as Edmund Goodwyn Goodwyn of Fairfield House, Framlingham) married a supremely beautiful young gentlewoman—my father's first cousin Eliza Jeaffreson, the heiress of the Fir-Tree House farm at Brandeston.

Their forefathers having acquired wealth as weavers, tradesmen, and farmers, the boys of my generation of the Edwards family were, with only a few exceptions, moved to follow fortune in the learned professions. With the single exception of my uncle William's youngest son, who went to sea in his boyhood and subsequently emigrated to Canada, all the fifteen Framlingham-born grandsons of my grandfather Edwards entered one or another of the learned professions. *Two* became clergymen, *four* were called to the bar, *three* became London solicitors, *one* went to Doctors Commons and flourished there as a proctor up to the time of the Abolition of the Ecclesiastical Courts, *three* went to medical schools and qualified themselves to practise as surgeons and apothecaries, *one* (my brother Horace Jeaffreson, M.D., Lond.) has a place amongst successful London physicians.

So much is said now-a-days by novelists of the dullness and torpor of small country-towns, that I shall probably surprise some readers of this page by speaking of Framlingham, *i.e.*, the Framlingham of my youth and early manhood, as more remarkable for gaiety than sleepiness. Lying twenty miles away from the nearest railway-station and five miles from a turnpike-road, it was an out-of-the-way and secluded place, and very tranquil in comparison with the larger villages on the main highways. The only public conveyance to pass over its market-place was the one coach that made the cross-road journey on alternate days from Ipswich to Norwich and from Norwich to Ipswich. But, though it was secluded and tranquil, Framlingham was far from a sleepy and sluggish place. Life went pleasantly, and sometimes even briskly in and about the picturesque town. As one of a large family, with six elder sisters, and some of them marvellously clever sisters, overflowing with droll gossip, and quick at repartee, I was never in want of bright companions when I had done my work in the surgery. The town had no collection of books to be spoken of seriously as a good library, but every house of the upper ten families had so goodly a lot of books, to which we all had access, that I and my sisters were nearly as well provided with standard literature as we should have been, had my father possessed the finest library of the county. The best of the new literature came to us through one of the old-fashioned club-libraries, far more promptly than books 'in great demand' come to country-towns now-a-days from the monstrous circulating libraries of recent invention. The best novels, the best biographies, the best books of travel, we got them all whilst they were still new literature. Thanks to a spirited little bookseller (Freeman of the Double Street) Dickens's green leaves dropt into our hands wet from the press. Life is never dull to young people who delight in books and are copiously supplied with them.

At some seasons of the year, tranquil little Framlingham had scarce beds enough for the proper entertainment of the visitors who journeyed to her from distant parts of East Anglia,—from Cambridge when 'long' had begun, and, better still, from London as soon as the courts 'were up.' During my apprenticeship and time at Oxford, what with the young men of 'the Edwards family' and the friends who came from Cambridge and the Inns of Court to stay with them, my natal town may be said to have overflowed with young men of academic culture during the long holidays. And we spent those holidays most agreeably in reading, walking, riding, driving, playing quoits and cricket, fishing in the various streams of the neighbourhood, and in other social diversions. On some days we mounted our horses and ponies and rode forth six or eight strong to inspect churches and halls of historic interest and the ruins of suppressed priories. On other days we drove with the young gentlewomen of our acquaintance to Aldborough and Dunwich, and feasted at picnics within view of the dancing waves,—the journeys to the sea-coast being made in early morning, and the homeward drives being taken in the cool of the evening.

Three months later, the young men re-appeared in the small market-town to join in the festivities of Christmas and New Year, to skate and play hockey on the castle moat and the castle mere, to run with a pack of beagles, kept by a gentleman of the Woodland, to waltz from early evening into the small hours of to-morrow with the young gentlewomen whom they had driven to sea-side picnics and flirted with at garden-parties in the previous August and September. What long journeys we young people used to make on cold nights, for the pleasure of dancing round dances, and square dances, and country dances at some hospitable parsonage, or at the manor-house of one of the small gentle land-owners, who still held their own amongst the minor county families. Not once or twice, but often in my dancing days, I have started at five or six p.m. in an open gig in the coldest of cold weather for an eighteen miles' drive to Ipswich, for the delights of a Christmas rout. Sometimes I was accompanied by a youngster of my own age and sex, and sometimes by one of my jolly sisters, thickly veiled, so that the frosty air should not 'catch her complexion.' Boys and girls, who could pursue pleasure under these conditions, thought nothing of six or eight miles for the same sufficient purpose. The rooms in which we danced were not so large as the drawing-rooms of Belgravia; but the dancing and the costumes were perfect. Moreover, the superior families of Framlingham and its neighbourhood gave 'at homes' for music and conversation, if their rooms were not sufficiently spacious for dancing; and my recollection of the mirth and *esprit* of these minor entertainments justifies me in laughing disdainfully at the satire that has been poured by cockney *littérateurs* on country-town tea-parties.

In October, 1846, when I had been his apprentice for some sixteen months, I found courage to tell my father that I had survived all desire to be a doctor, and wished to go into the army—of course, in a way suitable to a collateral descendant of the Colonel John Jeaffreson who had planted St. Kitts and distinguished himself amongst the fighting men of the seventeenth century. My father may well have been startled by this announcement; for I had shown no sign of dissatisfaction with my employment and studies, and so new was my desire to turn soldier, that had my father asked me six weeks earlier whether I liked my vocation, I should have replied emphatically that I delighted in it.

Far from revolting at the drudgery of my calling, I had found much amusement in dispensing medicines and mastering the rudiments of Materia Medica. The three or four hours a-day spent in making pills and powders, putting together the ingredients of mixtures and tinctures and decoctions, compounding lotions and emulsions, spreading plasters and blisters had been to my boyish nature so many hours a day spent in the congenial pastime of a sort of scientific cookery. The light labour of rolling pills and folding powder-papers, corking and capping bottles of physic, adorning the same bottles with neatly written labels of directions had been the reverse of irksome. Moreover, I had earned much sweet praise by my surgical adroitness, which had been pronounced by my father remarkable in so young an apprentice. For months it had been the talk of the town and neighbourhood, how clever a hand I was at bleeding, cupping, vaccinating babes, lancing the gums of infants, applying leeches, drawing teeth, applying bandages, dressing wounds. Before the middle of my sixteenth year, I had performed *propriâ manu* all these minor operations of surgery, and divers other operations not to be set forth in a work of polite literature. I had assisted in reducing dislocations, setting broken bones, and amputating portions of the human body. In confidence, my father had told several of his patients that my extraordinary aptitude and address in surgical matters made him hopeful that I should live to be one of the greatest surgeons of the century.

Whilst I was learning the practice of my profession in this way, I learnt something of its science from books. It was my father's purpose to give me a general view of the various departments of medical and surgical knowledge, before I should apply to the severely exact study of any one of them. He had therefore carried me quickly, but none too quickly for his purpose, through a series of introductory works on pharmacy, nosology, anatomy, surgery, chemistry. Of course, my knowledge of these subjects was superficial; but my father (an excellent teacher, for his mental faculties were still in their perfection, and he was affectionately solicitous for my enlightenment) had given me a general view of all of them, when I startled him and troubled him profoundly by telling him that I had had enough of the medical profession, and wished to 'go into the army.'

At that time I did not know my father as I came to know him in later time. In truth, I knew nothing of the fineness of his sensibilities or of the nobility and sweetness of his generous nature. Had he been a man of ordinary temper, he would have answered my preposterous announcement by snubbing me, telling me I was a simpleton, and bidding me forbear from troubling him again with my egregious folly. I had anticipated one of his transient ebullitions of anger as the first consequence of my astounding communication. But the man, so quick to boil over at trivial annoyances, was ever calm and stoical (as I now began to learn) under grievous vexations. Instead of laughing at me or speaking testily, he encouraged me to speak more fully, and when he had heard my whole case, he observed mildly but with impressive earnestness, 'Ask me to do anything for your happiness which I could do without injustice to your brothers and sisters, and I will do it. But, my dear boy, you are requiring something beyond the power of a father, who has a wife and eleven children, and only a few hundreds a-year, besides the modest income of a country doctor. You forget, my boy, that a subaltern in the quietest foot regiment of Her Majesty's service can't live on his pay.'

'I don't want to go into the Queen's service,' I answered. 'My wish is to go to India—into the Company's service. You could manage that, father.'

These few words caused a look to come over my father's face, that showed I had won a point. I had never seen the look before on his face, and it impressed me by its novelty rather than by its significance, for I could not apprehend its full meaning. Years had to pass before I knew it to be the expression of a brave and generous man, making an effort to resign himself uncomplainingly to a cruel disappointment.

'Yes,' he said calmly, when the look had taken possession of his handsome face, 'I could perhaps manage that.' After a brief pause he added, with a momentary show of his characteristic pride and self-dependence, 'I shall have to go cap in hand, asking favours. But no paltry feeling shall prevent me from doing my duty.—Still, I won't act hastily. Have you spoken to anyone else about this business?' On receiving my assurance that I had spoken to no one else, he remarked in the tone of a man asking a kindness of an equal, 'Then, oblige me by saying nothing about it to your mother or your sisters or anyone else, for the present.'—When I had assured him that I should respect his wish, he observed, gently, 'Now, my boy, go away—I wish to be alone.' At the door, as I was leaving the room, I regarded him for three seconds, and saw the new look still covering his face. Had I known all its meaning, I should not have gone off fairly satisfied with the interview. But I will say nothing to extenuate my puerile selfishness and egotism.

Ten days later, when it was known in the family that I was set on being a soldier, and going to India, my eldest sister, God bless her! spoke a good many words to me that were just, truthful, and altogether creditable to her good sense and good feeling. A woman of great intellect and a charming personality, my eldest sister (ætat. 26) was a sister of whose displeasure I stood in wholesome awe. We loved each other passionately; but whenever I was making a young fool of myself in the domestic circle I feared her censure, and suffered from it all the more, because with all my boyish folly I could appreciate her rare excellences, and knew that she loved me intensely.

I was reading a book on anatomy in the surgery, which was my usual place of study, when my eldest and favourite sister came into the room of bottles and gallipots to give me her opinion of what she was pleased to call 'this ridiculous Indian business.' In a few incisive sentences, she told me that in 'this ridiculous Indian business' I was the mere victim of childish restlessness and puerile vanity. I made an ineffectual protest against this disdainful way of speaking of my design to do my duty to my country, and cover my family with glory. 'Duty to your country, indeed! you to volunteer to cover your family with glory! Fiddlesticks!' my sister retorted, with fervour and high disdain. Then there followed from her dear lips an oration, that made my ears tingle. She laughed at my heroic design, and declared that, instead of burning to glorify my family, I was burning to wear a smart uniform and admire myself in a looking-glass. She told me that my first duty was *not* to serve my country, *but* to serve my father, who was nothing like so strong and active as she could remember him, though he would not be old for some years to come, unless I worried him into premature old age. Duty required me to dispense his prescriptions, and do my appointed work in the surgery. She did not say outright 'Go back to the shop, Mr. John, back to plaster, pills, and ointment-boxes.' But she treated my ambition to be a hero very much as 'Z' of *Blackwood's Magazine* treated John Keats's ambition to take rank with the poets. There was this grand difference between 'Z' and my dear sister: he was unjust, malicious, revoltingly vulgar, whereas her scathing censure was wholly just, righteous, and womanly. My protest having only increased the severity of my punishment, I held my tongue till she had said all she cared to say for that turn.

'Have you done, my dear Carrie?' I inquired, in my politest manner. 'I wish you to tell me your whole mind.'

'I have nothing more to say,' she answered, 'now that I have told you what I think of your folly. I have nothing more to say.'

'Dearest Caroline,' I rejoined, in a fine vein of persiflage,—an art of which I was such a young donkey as to think myself a consummate master,—'I am very sorry that the performance is over. For, whilst you were scolding me, you did look so pretty! Couldn't you give me a little more of it?'

'I don't think the better of you for being a pert little puppy,' retorted my sister, as she whisked out of the room, leaving me to meditate on 'the wigging' she had given me.

Talk of 'an unpleasant half-hour.' I had several most unpleasant hours in the afternoon and evening of that day. Fortunately, when my father returned from his 'round' late in the afternoon, he gave me so many prescriptions to dispense that work diverted my mind from its keen trouble, and did something to soothe the pangs of my wounded vanity.

For several weeks my sister had been giving me dancing-lessons—a lesson for half-an-hour or so just before we went to bed—in order that I should figure effectively in the next batch of Christmas parties. Dancing beautifully herself, she was an admirable mistress of the art in which she excelled: and as the house had no other uncarpeted room on which we could dance at that time without waking the children, she used to give me my lessons in the kitchen, which had 'a capital floor,' that was always swept for our use by the servants before they went to rest. On that floor, by the light of two or three candles and a fading fire, my sister and I used to dance all the round dances then in vogue, marking time with our voices. I had assumed that there could be no dancing for us till we had slept off our mutual displeasure. But, at the usual time, my dear sister opened the door of the room in which I was reading, and cried to me, in her heartiest tone,

'Come away, Johnny; we must dance our feet warm this cold night before we go to bed.'

Jumping from my studious chair, I raced after my sister to our dancing-room.

'It is very good of you, Carrie, to dance with me as though nothing had happened,' I remarked, as I put my arm round her waist.

'Let's dance now,' she answered laughingly; 'let's begin at once, so that we may have warmed our feet before we fall to quarrelling again.'

When we had danced, with unusual spirit, for something more than the usual time, this sweet sister, who was right and just in everything she had said to me in the morning, put her arms about my neck, and, kissing me, said in her sweetest way,

'You are very good, Johnny, for dancing with me, and I am very sorry for having spoken to you so harshly and unfeelingly and passionately. But, dearest, you mayn't go to India without thinking well about it. We sisters are all so proud of you, and you are so dear to all of us; and, if you go to India, you will be as much lost to us as William Greenlaw is lost to the Greenlaws. Don't go from us on a mere impulse.'

A word about these Greenlaws. During the sequestration of the Framlingham living in the time of the Reverend John Norcross, the Reverend William Greenlaw, M.A., (son of the poet Shelley's schoolmaster at Brentford, of whom and whose school Tom Medwin wrote so maliciously and untruthfully,) had for a long term of years been the licensed curate-in-charge of Framlingham, living in the rectory-house, and enjoying a stipend of three hundred pounds a-year. For all purposes touching the spiritual life of the parish, Mr. Greenlaw was the rector of Framlingham: and, as he had some private means, he was more than rich enough for his position. A man of great ability and fine culture, he appreciated my father's qualities at their proper worth; and Mrs. Greenlaw, a woman of rare beauty and a noble nature, conceived a strong affection for my mother and my eldest sister. Though they knew nothing of 'cliques,' the chief families of Framlingham were of course variously affected by friendly feeling. There was warm friendship between the Greenlaws and the Jeaffresons. For several years of her childhood, Fanny Greenlaw (the eldest of the Greenlaw children) used to come daily from the rectory to my sisters' school-room, to be taught by their governess. The intercourse of the two families was so close and affectionate at Framlingham, that it was maintained after Mr. Greenlaw became rector of Woolwich. From time to time Fanny

Greenlaw used to come from Woolwich to the house, in which she had received a part of her early education; and, till William Greenlaw went to India and Robert Greenlaw died prematurely during his career at Cambridge, the Greenlaw boys came several times to Framlingham after their father's retirement from the town.

In my sixteenth year my eldest sister's personal knowledge of the world outside Suffolk had been acquired, for the most part, during her successive visits to Woolwich Rectory, where she was treated less as a visitor than as a daughter of the house.

As I declined to relinquish my wish to go into the Indian army, measures were taken for its gratification. But, ere those measures had proved either futile or successful, I was saved by a domestic calamity and its consequences from entering a profession, in which I was no more likely to distinguish myself than I was likely to win celebrity as a baritone singer or a dancer on the tight-rope.

Affairs were in train for putting me on the highway to discredit and misery, when a letter came to my parents from Bexley Heath, in Kent, where my one elder brother had been in practice as a surgeon for some five years,—a letter saying that he was very ill of typhus fever, and was often talking of his mother in his delirium, though in his lucid moments he had expressed no desire that she should be told of his state. My father and mother went to their sick son with all possible speed; and some few days (perhaps a week) later the intelligence came to Framlingham of his death.

I have only the vaguest recollection of my father's first-born son; but from my sisters' talk about him I know him to have been eccentric, religious, and benevolent. When he was still a student at University College Hospital, he would have entered the Catholic church had not my mother's entreaties restrained him. For a long period after his death, he was remembered at Bexley Heath for his readiness to attend the poorest of poor people; and it was in ministering to some of these extremely indigent folk that he caught the fever which killed him. Some thirty years since I read upon his tombstone at Bexley Heath these words, 'In Memory of William Jeaffreson, M.R.C.S., who died December 30th, 1846, aged 28.—He was the poor man's friend, and sacrificed his life in the arduous performance of his professional duties,'—the brief inscription which my mother caused to be put upon the stone. Dying quite poor, for it was his use to give his destitute patients every shilling of his earnings, which he did not require for his own necessities, the devout and benevolent man left neither child nor widow.

Soon after my mother's return from Bexley Heath to Framlingham, she sickened of the fever which she caught at my brother's bed-side, and communicated to me and several of her other children. The fever dealt so severely with me, that my father and Mr. Mayhew of Stradbroke (the medical friend who aided my father in attending the patients of a home that was for several months a hospital) were amazed at my escape from death. My recovery was tedious, and during my slow convalescence I suffered much pain in my loins and lower limbs, and also from optical illusions, one of which was attended in so remarkable a way with other illusions, that some readers will thank me for recording it.

In an early stage of my convalescence, I had been out for a short walk, leaning on my eldest sister's arm, and I was lying on my back at full length upon a couch, in order to recover from the fatigue occasioned by the exercise, when I saw the nostrils and mouth of a large animal come forth from the middle of the ceiling of my mother's drawing-room. The nostrils and mouth of the animal descended lower, until the whole head was visible. Gradually and noiselessly the whole animal descended to the floor of the room, and stood alongside of the sofa, on which I was reposing,—stood with its head near my face, and one of its fore-quarters within reach of my hand. It was a large, fat, magnificently formed ox. I never for an instant thought it aught else than an apparition; but there the animal stood with all the shape and colour of reality in broad daylight, staring down at me with its dull bovine eyes. To demonstrate to myself (for I was alone) that the show was a mere phantasy, I sat up and struck at the beast's nearest shoulder with my open right hand, being certain that the blow would encounter no resistance. But, strange to say, my hand gave the apparition a spank which my hand seemed to feel, and my ears seemed to hear. Thus I had seemed to see what I did not really behold, I had seemed to feel what I did not really feel, and I had seemed to hear what I certainly did not really hear. It was a threefold illusion. Sight, touch, and hearing had all been at fault.

CHAPTER IV.

MY FIRST VIEW OF OXFORD.

I Turn Religious—And Wish to be a Clergyman—Church-Goers and Chapel-Goers—Pograms and Ranters—The Rev. Joseph Brereton, B.A., of Christ Church, Oxford—He Prepares Me for Oxford—My Chief Reason for Wishing to go to Oxford Rather than to Cambridge—Matriculation at Oxford—Pembroke College, Oxford—A Middle-Aged Gentleman-Commoner of Magdalen Hall—I Dine with Fellows of Oriel College—Francis Jeune, D.C.L., Master of Pembroke College and (in Later Time) Bishop of Peterborough—Henry William Chandler—The Thirty-Nine Articles.

BEFORE I had fully recovered from my severe illness, it was settled that I should 'go to college,' and be a clergyman. From the date of my brother's death, nothing was ever said to me by anyone of what my eldest sister had so properly called 'this ridiculous Indian business.' My wish to be a soldier had probably perished under the shock my brother's death had occasioned me. Anyhow, on recovering from the almost fatal illness which had followed quickly upon that stirring incident, I was too fully occupied by the thoughts natural to a youth, who had just escaped from the jaws of death, with a nervous system seriously weakened and deranged by fever, to have any disposition to enter upon a military career.

Deeply impressed with a sense of the transitoriness of human existence, I desired to be a good man, and to use my talents in making other people as good as myself. The events which had startled me out of one kind of self-conceit had put me under the dominion of another sort of puerile egotism. My mother (a devout woman, though she made no noise about her piety) was well pleased that I should be a clergyman, though she would have been better pleased had I resumed my old purpose to follow my father's profession. Conceiving that I should be sure to distinguish myself 'at college,' and at least become as exemplary a clergyman as her idolized Mr. Greenlaw, my eldest sister expressed her enthusiastic approval of my latest choice of a profession. Though he was far from orthodox in the latent chambers of his intellect and heart, my father cherished an old-fashioned reverence for what he called 'the cloth,' as a grand organization of scholarly gentlemen, who were greatly serviceable in preserving the moral and political health of the country. Honouring the church in this way, he was soon reconciled to the thought of seeing his eldest son amongst the national clergy. He assented to my wish the more readily, because I expressed my readiness to remain his apprentice till the time should come for my departure to one of the universities, and to make myself useful in the surgery during my academic vacations.

During this period of religious energy, if I may

so style the time between my illness and my matriculation at Oxford, I was a more prayerful and conscientious boy than I had been before, and for the first time read the Bible daily and attentively. At the same time, I was preserved from the extravagances of conduct that usually attend the religious agitation of an ignorant youth, by my strong repugnance to the hysterical behaviour of 'the ranters,' and the spiritual peculiarities of the more emotional of those more orderly dissenters, who were ordinarily styled 'chapel-goers' by the church-people of my native town. The ranters, who had not yet acquired a house of meeting and worship, were the forerunners of the Sankey-and-Moody revivalists and General Booth's salvation-soldiers. Having grounds for attributing much of the immorality and some little of the insanity of the humblest folk of the neighbourhood to the disorderly methods of the ranters, my father, who certainly was not deficient in religious liberality, had caused me to regard the 'ranting preachers' as fanatical persons, whose influence was distinctly vicious, and therefore hurtful to society. Of the more orderly dissenters he thought less severely, and would fain have lived in neighbourliness with them. Speaking tenderly of them as 'pograms'—a term that has not passed from Dean Swift's writings to the standard dictionaries of the English language—he used to declare that some of them were most estimable persons.

In some of the Woodland towns, it was the fashion of the principal church-goers to look down upon the chapel-goers as 'low people,' with whom it was impossible for church-going gentry to have familiar intercourse. But the superior church-goers of Framlingham were saved from that sort of insolence, partly by their own good sense and partly by the culture and ancestral worth and gentle bearing of the leading dissenters of the town and neighbourhood. Coming to me from the elders of 'the Edwards family,' and from my father's testimony to the essential worthiness of 'pograms,' my opinion of the leading Nonconformists was that they suffered from some curious intellectual 'cranks,' that caused them to be wanting in spiritual modesty and social sweetness, and to nurse a secret desire to oppress and persecute the church-goers, by stripping them of the churches and tithes and pleasant parsonages which had belonged to them from time long anterior to the first appearance of Nonconformists in the body politic. I had neither a doubt nor the ghost of a doubt that the social severance of the church-goers and chapel-goers was referable to the unsocial temper and sectarian bitterness of the dissenters, and that it would perish in an hour from Framlingham, if the 'pograms' would only get the better of their peculiarities, and become as large-minded and tolerant and reasonable as I and my nearest relations were.

Since my withdrawal from the Botesdale Grammar School, I had gone forward with my classical and mathematical studies. After it was settled that I should go to one of the universities, I went onwards with my Latin and Greek books, and my Euclid and Algebra more zealously than heretofore, under the tuition of the Reverend Joseph Brereton, B.A., of

Christ Church, Oxford. Son of the old Vicar of Framsden and great-nephew of Alethea Brereton, the novelist, this young clergyman had a curacy under the rector of Framlingham-cum-Saxted (who paid him a liberal salary) and the appointment of Reader of Prayers (daily prayers) to the almsfolk and pensioners on Sir Robert Hitcham's charity,—an office that gave him an additional forty pounds a-year and the use of a pleasant little house, called 'the Readery.' Better placed than most curates, he was the husband of a very pretty young gentlewoman, and was endowed with as kindly a nature as a young curate ever possessed. It was arranged that I should read with him on every evening of the week, when no engagement made it inconvenient for him to receive me. For me the whole arrangement was very agreeable and beneficial. Mr. Brereton was no great scholar, albeit he possessed much more scholarship than a mere Oxford passman usually possesses. But he resembled Mr. Collett, and my dear old master, Mr. Haddock, in teaching accurately and soundly all that he undertook to teach me; and I have grateful recollection of the care and efficiency and invariable kindness with which he prepared me for Oxford. Though he was under no obligation to trouble himself about me in aught but my studies, he was good enough to make me his familiar companion, and we remained cordial friends for years.

That I went to Oxford, where no member of my family had ever studied, instead of Cambridge, where several of my cousins had been educated, was probably in some degree due to the influence of Mr.

Brereton, who regarded his own university as greatly superior to the other great seat of learning. But my choice of Oxford (for my too indulgent father left the choice to me) resulted in a greater degree from my desire to see London, of which my cousins of 'the Edwards family' had told me so much. Hitherto I had passed my whole life in Suffolk, with the exception of a few hours spent at Diss when I was confirmed by Bishop Stanley, and the few hours passed in Norfolk when, as a Botesdale school-boy, I walked a mile or so beyond the northern boundary of my native county. I had never seen a greater place than Ipswich. As an Oxford undergraduate, I should pass six times a year through London, and should be introduced to the amusements of the capital by my cousin Edwin Edwards (my particular friend of all my Framlingham cousins), who had promised to 'put me up,' whenever I should be passing through town. Of course, I was a young fool to allow so trivial a consideration to influence me in so important a matter as the choice of my university. But boys *ætat.* 16 are seldom endowed with much discretion; and it is usual for inexperienced lads to attach extravagant importance to trivial pleasures.

I cannot state precisely the exact day, nor can I even state positively the exact month of my matriculation at Oxford. But that important event must have been an affair of Trinity Term, 1848. I remember that I journeyed in summerly weather from Framlingham to Oxford, that my sojourn in London afforded me intense excitement, and that I was inexpressibly delighted with the beauty of Oxford. It lives in my memory that I lodged at the 'Roebuck Hotel' in the Corn-Market, and that at the close of my first evening at the 'Roebuck' I made in the coffee-room the acquaintance of a short, stout, black-whiskered person, whom I regarded as a man of more than forty years, though he was perhaps no more than thirty years old. Instead of putting this gentleman's real surname before the readers of this work, I will call him Mr. William Betts.

I and Mr. Betts were the only occupants of the narrow coffee-room, when he came to my box, and, with a courteous gesture, enquired whether I was familiar with Oxford. On being told that I had never been in Oxford before, and that I had now come to it in order to matriculate, Mr. Betts ejaculated,

'I too am up to matriculate.'

'Surely,' I ventured to remark, 'you are rather old for that?'

'Yes,' replied Mr. Betts, 'I am too old for a college, but I get over that difficulty by going to a hall. I am going to be a gentleman-commoner of Magdalen Hall. You see, I am changing my profession. Hitherto I have been a lawyer; but I love my church —yes, I love my church—and I have resolved to serve her.'

The tone of voice in which Mr. Betts made this announcement caused me to warm towards him, to think him a good fellow, and much less than forty years of age, his stoutness and big whiskers notwithstanding. Ten minutes later I thought less favourably of Mr. Betts. Having told me his name and several matters of his own personal story, he inquired,

'From what part of the country do you come?'

'From Suffolk,' I answered, 'and only last week I could say I had never slept a night outside my native county.'

'Oh, come,' replied Mr. Betts, quickly, with the air of a man who did not mean to be trifled with by a youth of my age, 'you won't get me to believe that. I know all about Suffolk and the Suffolk dialect, and all the rest of it, for I am in the habit of visiting Ipswich, and staying there with my friends, the . . . . I am not the man to be taken in in that way.'

I was amazed and indignant. With freezing dignity, I informed Mr. Betts that it was my practice to tell the truth, and that I never amused myself by 'taking people in.' Moreover, with polite *hauteur*, befitting a grandson of George Edwards the Elder, I remarked,

'I know your Ipswich friends by name and reputation, and know they are most respectable manufacturers and tradespeople. As their guest, you would probably hear the Suffolk dialect spoken with its highest pitch and lowest fall.'

Mr. Betts having apologised most handsomely for his mistake, we talked about the county he had so often visited; and our gossip ran so pleasantly that at its close I assented with some effusion to his proposal that during the next few days we should walk about Oxford and view the colleges in the company of one another.

It lives in my memory that in the course of my first stay at Oxford I dined once at Oriel College, and after dinner took wine with some of the Fellows of that famous society, as the guest of Mr. Charles Peter Chretien, M.A., who had honoured me with an invitation to dine with him shortly before I started from Framlingham for my first visit to my Alma Mater. Mr. Chretien is associated in my mind with my brother's death. If I remember rightly, some of Mr. Chretien's nearest relations lived at Bexley Heath, and had there made my brother's acquaintance; and that, as he happened to be staying with the same relations in the Christmas holidays of 1846, the Fellow of Oriel had been especially attentive to my brother during his illness, and also in the interval between his death and funeral very attentive to my father and mother, whom he of course liked; for no one of culture and fine taste could make their acquaintance without admiring my mother's beauty and womanly judgment, and my father's grand presence and charming manner. I think Mr. Chretien's disposition to take notice of me proceeded entirely from his brief intercourse with my brother and my parents.

On retiring with the Fellows from their high table in the dining-hall of Oriel College to the room (presumably the Fellows' Common Room) in which we took wine, I suffered from a fit of boyish shyness that must have been manifest to my companions; but they soon took the best course for putting me at my ease by talking amongst themselves, and leaving me to play the modest part of listener,—a part that was always congenial to me in the society of my elders, even when I was not overborne, as I was just then, by a sense of the intellectual and social superiority of my companions. Whatever else could be alleged to my discredit, my severest censor would never at any time of my boyhood have charged me with a want of reverence for my superiors by age and knowledge. At the Framlingham dinner-parties, when the ladies had left the table, I enjoyed listening to the veterans of the social gathering, whilst they argued with and bantered one another. In the company of the Fellows of Oriel the listener's part was appropriate to a youth of my inexperience and obscurity, and I enjoyed it greatly.

Turning on matters that were light and trivial, though in no degree unbecoming so grave a society, the conversation was enlivened and controlled by a gentleman who told some extremely humorous anecdotes, that did not seem to be appreciated at their full worth by the company. Instead of laughing outright, the clerical auditors only smiled at the pleasantries of this principal talker, and smiled in a way which caused me to feel that, though they valued him in a degree for being a droll and funny fellow, they regarded him as something of 'a jack-pudding.' But their coldness did not lessen my sense of the merit of the performer, who, seeing from my countenance that I was agreeably excited by his stories, gave me every now and then a glance of approval. The *raconteur's* concluding story tickled me to such a degree that I first laughed gleefully, and then, reclining on the back of my chair, screamed with delight—an outbreak of feeling that caused the rest of the company to regard me with condescending sympathy and amusement.

'Ah,' remarked the *raconteur* to the other dons,

'that is how you should acknowledge the excellence of my stories! Our young friend from Suffolk can recognize merit and reward it.'

'Our young friend from Suffolk is new to the world, and your stories are new to *him*,' replied one of the dons, laying on the last word a slight accent, which raised a light titter at the table,—a titter in which I forbore to join.

Instead of showing any disapproval of my uproarious laughter, the grave and reverend dons seemed to like me for the riotous mirth that may have reminded some of them how merrily and madly they used to laugh when they were striplings. Anyhow, they chatted very jollily with me on subjects about which I could speak freely, towards the close of the brief symposium; and, when the party broke up, I went back to my Inn with a high opinion of the sociability of the Fellows of Oriel, and a pleasant sense of having won their momentary good-will. The pleasure of dining with them, however, was slight in comparison with the pleasure of saying I had dined with them.

On returning to the 'Roebuck,' I found Mr. William Betts (late a proctor of Doctors Commons) arrayed in the silk gown and velvet cap of a gentleman-commoner of Magdalen Hall, who had been waiting for an hour or so for me, in order to show me how he looked in his new costume. After complimenting him on his appearance, I told him that I had been dining at Oriel College,—an announcement that caused him to inquire quickly, whether I sat near enough to the high table to be able to examine and study the faces of 'the dons.' On hearing that I had myself sat at the high table, and had wined with 'the dons,' Mr. Betts opened his eyes with astonishment, and became wildly eager for particulars. Was .... of the party? Was .... at table? I told him I could not say, as Mr. Chretien had not introduced me particularly to anyone of 'the dons,' and they were not ticketed like reserved seats or labelled like decanters of wine. Mr. Betts begged me to describe minutely the appearance, voice, and manner of Mr. Chretien. After I had done my best to gratify my questioner on half-a-hundred points, he ejaculated,

'What an honour has been paid you, and you take it just as coolly as if you had been dining with half-a-dozen undistinguished country clergymen. But you'll talk about it, when you get back to Suffolk.'

Whereupon, as my pride was touched by his talking in so extravagant a way about the honour that had been conferred upon me, I informed Mr. Betts that I had dined with Fellows of colleges too often to be so greatly excited even by Mr. Chretien's civility. The rector of Framlingham had been senior Fellow of Pembroke College, Cambridge; every year one of the Fellows of that college presided at the audit-dinner of the Hitcham Trust Estates at Framlingham. Of course, I held Fellows of colleges in the highest reverence, as intellectual personages; but I had been on friendly terms with too many Fellows (including my own father, who was a Fellow of *his* college), to be so greatly agitated by the honour of which he made rather too much. What a droll couple we were!—the simple, middle-aged, newly-gowned gentleman-commoner, who 'loved his church' and was yearning to serve her, and the ludicrous young simpleton, crude and green as a cucumber from a little market-town in the Suffolk Woodland, who forbade his casual acquaintance to under-rate him!

The impression made upon me by the personality of the Reverend Francis Jeune, D.C.L., at that time Master of the College (Pembroke) which I was about to enter, is what I most clearly remember of my first visit to Oxford. To readers who know Mr. Justice Jeune by sight, it is not difficult to give a life-like description of his father. Let them by efforts of the imagination deprive Mr. Justice Jeune of some four (perhaps six) inches of his height, make him proportionately broader in the face, the shoulders, the breast, the body, lower his complexion almost to paleness, and make him into a massive man, and they will have before their mental vision the Dr. Jeune, Master of Pembroke College, and subsequently Bishop of Peterborough, whose handsome face, strong eyes, and commanding air made me, in the middle of my eighteenth year, feel myself in the presence of a remarkable personage. Twenty years since, not long after his death, I ventured (vide, *Annals of Oxford*, vii, pp. 304—6) to put on record my admiration of Dr. Jeune's academic services, mental force, and rare goodness. I would not by a single word alter that attempt to exhibit some of the doctor's claims to grateful commemoration. It is indisputable that he was an able ruler of his college, and at the present date, when time has silenced the voices that used to disparage him, no one is likely to deny that he was an energetic and beneficent bishop and a supremely good man. Speaking to me and Henry William Chandler at the time of our matriculation, Dr. Jeune said,

'I don't ask you whether you positively and reasonably agree with everything contained in the Thirty-nine Articles, for they doubtless contain several things which you have not fully considered, and they certainly contain some things which boys of your age are incapable of understanding. I have asked you solemnly whether you are aware that they contain any doctrine with which you do not agree: and you assure me that you are not aware of anything in the Articles, from which you dissent. That is enough. But mind, if you are aware there is anything in respect to which you differ in opinion from the Articles, you will do a terribly wrong thing to declare that you agree with them.'

Uttered as they were in Dr. Jeune's strong voice, these words would have restrained me from doing the terribly wrong thing, had I been about to subscribe the Articles with any dishonest reserve or untruthful qualification. But as I had studied the Articles, sentence by sentence, and clause by clause, with my tutor at Framlingham, and as he had crammed my trustful mind with the usual proofs of every doctrinal sentence and every doctrinal clause of the Articles, I was not disturbed by the master's warning. At the time of my matriculation, I believed the things which my spiritual pastors and masters had taught me to believe. Some months later, I believed certain other things, which books had compelled me to believe. And between the two sets of things there was a momentous difference.

CHAPTER V.

ALMA MATER.

Two Grand Blunders—Pembroke College, Oxford—The Admirable Master and Good Tutors—'The World, the Flesh, and the Devil'—The Musical Bursar and Witty Dean—Religious Doubts and Perplexities—An Unhappy Freshman—Holidays in London—Edwin Edwards, Proctor of Doctors' Commons—William Holmes Edwards of the Middle Temple—John Humffreys Parry (in Later Time 'Serjeant Parry')—Meymott 'The Singing Barrister'—Thomas Hay Girtin—Maxwell Miller—Arthur Locker—Edwin Arnold—Henry Kingsley—'The Fez Club'—Its Principles and Purpose—Anecdotes—Notes about Names—George Henry Thornbury *alias* Walter Thornbury—An Unpleasant Dream—My Difficulty with 'The Tutors'—A Way Out of the Difficulty—A Friend in Need—My Last Interview with Dr. Jeune.

It is an old saying, that youth is a blunder, manhood a struggle, and old age a regret: and it is a true saying, in respect to a large minority of the men who live to enter their seventh decade. In my youth, I was guilty of several grave mistakes, and two grand blunders,—(1) the blunder of declining to enter the profession for which my father designed me, and (2) the blunder of going to Oxford, in order to qualify myself for the clerical profession. Though it has afforded me some satisfaction, a few passages of transient triumph, and a far larger measure of domestic happiness than is allowed to most men, my manhood has been a struggle. In my sixty-third year I regret those blunders.

Had I been qualified by nature for the career which I selected for myself in my seventeenth year, a better college than Pembroke College could not have been chosen for me. Though it numbered a few 'fast men,' it was upon the whole a quiet and economical college. Though it comprised a good many academic loungers, it was a reading college. Governed by an admirably able Master, it was a house with three excellent tutors,—gentlemen whom I regarded with sincere respect, whilst they regarded me with reasonable disapprobation. Dr. Jeune and two of these exemplary tutors (the Rev. Thomas Frederick Henney, M.A., and the Rev. Evan Evans, M.A.,) were spoken of by flippant undergraduates as 'the World, the Flesh and the Devil.' Dr. Jeune was called the Devil, merely because his 'boys,' as he used to call the undergraduates, discovered something satanic in his handsome face which would have well become an impersonator of Mephistopheles in *Faust and Marguerite*. Heaven knows there was nothing satanic in the good Master's nature or way of living! Mr. Henney (the Flesh) was a stout man, with better reason than Hamlet had for exclaiming,

'O that this too, too solid flesh would melt,
Thaw, and resolve itself into dew!'

But the burden of his bodily grandeur never made the sound scholar indolent in the discharge of his duties.

I am not aware there was any sounder reason for crediting Mr. Evans with worldliness than that he dressed well, and was believed to move in 'the world' when he was away from Oxford. All three tutors were popular with the undergraduates; but Mr. Evans (the Dean) was the most popular of the three. The admiration with which the young men used to speak of him was enthusiastic and universal. If nothing more than truth was said of his cricket, he must have been in his earlier time as superb a cricketer as ever handled a bat or sent a ball flying to the middle stump. I honoured him for his wit and humour, albeit he sometimes displayed them to my discomfort. The pleasantries with which he occasionally enlivened his lectures were the more effective, because they were made with the fewest possible words. The rooms of the college-bursar, the Reverend Haviland De Sausmarez (a member of the Guernsey family) were on the same floor of the same staircase as the Dean's rooms; and one sweltering hot day, when the door of the tutor's lecture-room had been left open for the passage of fresh air, his Herodotus lecture was slightly disturbed by the bursar, singing a jubilant operatic air as he went downstairs. In reference to this disturbance, the lecturer observed lightly, as though he were speaking to himself rather than to his class, 'The finances of the college must be in a flourishing state!' The twenty or thirty youthful hearers of these few words were of course thrown into riotous laughter by the droll suggestion that tuneful gladness in a bursar necessarily pointed to a cheering balance-sheet. One line of commemoration to the third of Pembroke's three excellent tutors. Greater mathematicians than the Reverend Bartholomew Price, M.A., (or 'Bat Price,' as his pupils used to style him admiringly) may have arisen in Oxford in recent time; but forty years since he was regarded as the best mathematician of his day at Oxford, and I have been assured by competent judges that he was even greater and brighter than his reputation. Dr. Jeune, Mr. Henney, Mr. (in his closing years Dr.) Evan Evans have passed from this life. The mathematical professor survives them, and has recently become the Master of Pembroke.

In the absence of contemporary memoranda touching my passage from religious orthodoxy to the state of opinion that disqualified me for the clerical profession, I am unable to state precisely the exact time at which, or the exact circumstances under which, the journey was made. As I was a sincere, earnest, and highly nervous youth, I must have begun the journey with emotions of alarm, but I do not remember having experienced any feeling of terror at the outset of my gradual passage from the spiritual condition of a trustful believer in the doctrines of the Church of England to the spiritual and intellectual condition of a disciple of Theodore Parker, the Unitarian minister of the second church in Roxbury, Massachusetts, U.S., in which last-named state of feeling and opinion I remained for many years. Whether the first steps of this journey were made before I came into residence at Oxford, I cannot positively say at this date, but I think that they were taken immediately after that event. They certainly were not taken in boyish levity; for, though I cannot recall any violent paroxysms of terror at the first disturbance of my faith, I can aver that my change of religious sentiment caused me deep distress, and that, whilst pursuing the theological and critical studies, which eventually put a wide gulf between myself and the church in which I had been reared, I should have experienced great relief in discovering reasons why I should return to the state of mind from which Free Thought had withdrawn me.

One consequence of these theological and critical studies was that they withdrew my mind from those academic studies which I should have been pursuing strenuously, had I surrendered myself dutifully to the discipline of my college. I went to as few lectures as possible, and I seldom prepared myself for them, because my mind was wholly engrossed by the inquiries which I was making without the aid or cognizance of my official teachers, who naturally regarded me as a commonplace idler, when I was, in fact, an anxious and strenuous student of the literature that was most likely to enlarge my new religious views, and also of the literature that was the most likely to show me the erroneousness of those views.

I have never possessed the mental self-control that enables some students to go forward with three different and strongly interesting kinds of study at the same time, or the faculty that enables some writers to work simultaneously at three different literary enterprises—say at an epic poem in the morning, a work of history in the afternoon, and a novel in the evening. Commenting on my inability to distribute my mental energy on three different undertakings upon the same day, as Southey could do, a friend some thirty years since was so civil as to call me 'a one-horse man.' By reminding him that I had several mental nags in the stable, I only caused my censor to remark, 'Yes, but you don't work them evenly. You ride the same nag day after day, and *all day*, whilst you let the others fall out of condition for want of exercise.' In my later years I have been less faulty in this respect, and can ride three hobbies on the same day, provided no one of them interests me strongly. But in my earlier time I used to mount the same horse day after day, till it could carry me no longer.

During the first four of my residence-terms at Oxford, literature relating to the questions of belief and disbelief, that were vexing my brain and conscience, was the only literature to which I paid any serious attention. The work to which as an undergraduate I should have given my best powers was work from which I revolted. Having every reason to think me an idle boy, who would probably disappear from the university before the end of his second academic year, the tutors were right in making me feel I had no place in their esteem; and, though the annoyance had no effect on my conduct, I felt their disapproval acutely. From other causes, I was miserable during those four terms. One consequence of my religious disquiet was that I became for the first time in my life an unsocial creature, and avoided the society of the undergraduates who showed a disposition to be intimate with me. Sporting my oak whenever I was in my rooms, I seldom opened it to a caller, however noisily he knocked. Declining invitations to go upon the river or join in other amusements, I took my daily exercise in long and solitary walks about the country. In the hall I spoke as little as possible to the men of my table, without being deficient in courtesy. In short, I took pains to make the college see that I wished to lead the life of a collegiate recluse, and to be left alone. My absurd behaviour in this respect resulted from ungenerous suspicion and groundless fear. I feared to speak freely with the undergraduates of my year, lest they should discover my heterodoxy, and talk about it to my disadvantage. I was so ignorant of the genius and temper of the university, as to imagine that, if my heterodoxy came to the knowledge of the authorities of my college, I should either be dismissed from Oxford for ever, or at least be sent to the country, there to remain till I should have recovered from my spiritual disease.

The comparative isolation and the mental distress, which I endured in those opening terms of my residence at Oxford, would have been more afflicting to me, had it not been for my cousin Edwin Edwards, for whom I cared in those days far more than for any of my other friends, with the exception of my parents and my eldest sister. My senior by something more than eight years, he was in his heyday a man of lively humour, high spirits and brilliant parts. To the many artists and connoisseurs, who made his acquaintance in his later time, after he turned from his original profession to Art, at a period of life when he had lost much of his alertness and gaiety, he was nothing more than a droll and eccentric 'good fellow,' who would have been a great painter, had he pursued Art as enthusiastically and seriously in his youth and early manhood as he pursued her after his fortieth year. They knew nothing of the personal comeliness, the intellectual graces, the mirthful temperament, that made him an inexpressibly delightful companion at every season from his twenty-first to his thirty-sixth year. His education had made him different from the other young men of my acquaintance. When he had acquired the rudiments of classical culture at the Dedham (Essex) Grammar School, an excellent school in the time of Dr. Taylor, he was sent for several years to a large school in Paris—a school where the boys, with few exceptions, were French boys. From this seminary he returned to England a perfect master of the French language and a critical student of French literature. Before I went into residence at Oxford, he had acquired during successive trips to Germany a similar acquaintance with the German tongue and literature.

A critical reader of the *belles lettres* of Germany and France, he was a serious student of English history, and for several years nursed a design of writing a complete history of the Ecclesiastical Courts; but all that resulted from his reading for the accomplishment of this ambitious project was his *Ecclesiastical Jurisdiction: A Sketch of Its Origin and Early Progress*, which he published in 1853, just twelve months after my withdrawal from Oxford. Whilst spending the greater part of his leisure in these studious pursuits, he found time for the pursuit of elegant accomplishments. Amusing himself with pencil and brush, he was already an art-amateur of considerable ability. Delighting in music, he performed so well on one instrument that an eminent master of the flute used to speak of him as the best amateur-flutist in London.

On being admitted a Proctor and an Examiner in the Courts of Civil Law in Doctors' Commons, he stept almost in his boyhood into good practice, the greater part of his income being made in the way of 'an examiner,' *i.e.*, a functionary appointed to take in writing the answers made on oath by witnesses in reply to interrogatories prepared by counsel.

Enjoying so good an income, that he could well afford to entertain me, my cousin Ned was only too happy to fulfil his promise to 'put me up,' whenever I should be passing through London. Occupying the whole of a house in Knightrider Street, Doctors' Commons, (with the exception of the rooms on the ground floor, that were let to another proctor,) he had his own offices on the first floor, and some seven or eight rooms (one of them a well-furnished library) on the higher floors. He could therefore give me a bed-room at a moment's notice. My hospitable cousin did more. The bed-room, which I occupied on the occasion of my first visit to Doctors' Commons, was assigned to me, so that I could take possession of it, if he were out of town at the close of an Oxford term, or an Oxford vacation. In short, I was taught to regard the roomy house in the quietest street of about the quaintest and most interesting nook of Old London as my 'home in town.' I have no memoranda that would enable me to state precisely for how many months during the four years of my Oxford course I occupied this 'home in town:' but speaking from recollection I should say that I was my cousin Ned's guest in Doctors' Commons during eight or ten weeks of each year.

Industrious in his profession and persevering in his studies, my amusing and blithe cousin had a keen appetite for pleasure. For some of the diversions of life, on which young men of ample means often squander a good deal of money, he had no liking. He neither played cards nor cared for any game in which dice are used. I never knew him make a bet, and he disliked dancing. Honourable in all things, he was never concerned in any *liaison* that he would have blushed to acknowledge. But he delighted in most of the worldly enjoyments. Something of an epicure, he was a prodigal at the dinner-hour. A connoisseur of wine, he drank freely but without crossing the extreme limit of temperance. A good horseman, he was as well-mounted as any of the dandies who 'sneered from Rotten Row' at the unfinished Crystal Palace. Passionately fond of music, he was a frequenter of the Opera. Rather too foppish in his attire, he was probably often mistaken by critical street-loungers for a smart, handsome, rather small would-be-Brummell, who valued himself chiefly on the virtues of his tailor, and

> 'The merits of a spotless shirt,
> A dapper boot—a little hand,'

and had no right to value himself on anything more

important. This was the cousin with whom I made holiday in my later boyhood,—the Edwin Edwards who sloughed his superficial smartness as he entered middle-age, and in his closing term was the bluffest, burliest, hairiest 'good fellow' of the studios.

In the years when I used to stay with my clever cousin Ned in Doctors' Commons, I was on familiar terms with a still cleverer cousin,—William Holmes Edwards, a Bohemian barrister, who for some years gathered about him in his chambers in the Middle Temple as droll a lot of gentlemen, as could have been found in all London. One of the lot was Meymott, 'the singing barrister,' who after surviving the favour that was shown him in the drawing-rooms of 'the great,' as the best amateur songster of the town, carried his broken voice and fair knowledge of the law to Australia, where he became a judge, and some few years since died a judge. Another of the amusing set was John Humffreys Parry, the manliest and most cultivated of the 'self-made' barristers of his period. Known in his earlier time as 'the Chartist barrister,' he was known as Serjeant Parry in his later days, when he enjoyed a fine practice in Westminster Hall and on the Home Circuit, and, though he remained a staunch liberal to the last, had survived the ultra-radical fervour which animated his hustings speeches at Norwich in 1847, on the occasion of his contest with the Marquis of Douro (in his later time the second Duke of Wellington.)

Parry and William Holmes Edwards came together in the Middle Temple Hall, when the former was still 'eating his dinners' as a student, and sustained himself by working as a transcriber on the British Museum Catalogue of the Printed Books. Companions on the same circuit, they remained friends for years, whilst the man of stronger purpose was fighting his way to the fore at the Old Bailey, and the man of keener and brighter wit was falling into the moral, social, and bodily disorder, of which he eventually perished. Long after my cousin's death, Parry spoke to me with much feeling of his friendship for the brilliant ne'er-do-well, who might have risen to dignity had he possessed ordinary prudence and self-control. 'In my first wife's time,' Parry continued, 'he was the life of the little gatherings in her tiny house in Frederick Street, Gray's Inn Lane,—the house in which I spent the happiest years of my life. Before his health began to fail, he was one of the cleverest men I ever knew. Without any exception he was the wittiest. There, there, I'll say no more of him. It saddens me to think about him, even now that so many years have passed over his grave.'

Parry rated his old friend's powers none too highly. William Holmes Edwards (the only offspring of George Edwards the Younger, of Framlingham, farmer and maltster) was a singularly clever man and charming companion. Together with most of the usual infirmities of his sub-species of Bohemian humankind, he displayed several fine qualities that were not always visible in the sort of gentlemen, who in the opening decades of the present century were called 'fast men,' because they lived so as to come to the end of their vitality some five-and-thirty years sooner than they would have come to it, had they lived temperately. An exactly honourable man, he injured no one but himself by his irregularities. Whilst paying the penalty of those irregularities, he endured the long and severe punishment with uncomplaining fortitude. To the last, each tone of his noble voice was clear and musical; and even in the final stage of his downward course his worn and wasted countenance drew children to his knees and softened his sternest censors. Holding firmly to his early faith, he preserved also his early reverence for good women throughout a long course of dissipation, that would have utterly depraved him, had he not been sound and chivalrous at his heart's core.

The cloud that covered me during my earlier terms at Oxford dispersed, when time and use had reconciled me to a painful position; and at the opening of my second year of residence I surprised my few acquaintances by becoming as light-hearted and social as I heretofore had been gloomy and uncommunicative. At the same time, new men appeared in the college to take the place of youngsters who had retired from the university, with or without a degree. And amongst the freshmen I found several congenial companions. Of these new arrivals at Alma Mater's knees none was more acceptable to me than Thomas Hay Girtin, grandson of the great artist who is sometimes styled the Father of Water-Colour painting. An equally clever and unconventional youth, Tom Girtin was the son of an eccentric surgeon, who preserved a fine collection of his father's sketches, which I had many opportunities of examining. In Germany my friend would have developed into a great Professor, for he was a serious student and a man of great ability; but, though he took honours at Oxford, he was ill at ease in the university, and throughout his undergraduate career longed to escape from what he used to call 'clerical domination.' In later time I saw a good deal of him in London, when he figured as 'a city man' in a curious corner of Old London, in the neighbourhood of Mincing Lane; and after he left England, to establish himself in southern Europe, we corresponded with one another, even to the year when he was drowned whilst bathing in one of the Italian rivers.

A whilom Pauline, who had been very popular with his school-mates at St. Paul's, Tom Girtin knew the old Paulines of the Oxford colleges, and introduced me to them. It was through him that I made the acquaintance of that bright, enthusiastic, loveable Anglo-Irish youngster, Maxwell Miller, of Queen's College (one of the sons of the late Serjeant Miller), whose academic splendour died all too soon of its own excess. Maxwell Miller was said to have spent in a single Trinity Term more money on cut flowers than any previous Oxford man had ever squandered on things of beauty and sweetness during an entire year; and it was at one of his too frequent and chargeable feasts of wine and roses that I first saw Harry Kingsley of Worcester College, whom I knew intimately in the closing years of my academic course.

It was also in Maxwell Miller's rooms (unless my memory is at fault) that I made the acquaintance of another man, who in later time won a place amongst the celebrities of literature, Edwin Arnold of University College. Forty years have of course made him other than he was; but in some respects the Sir Edwin Arnold, whose Star of India shines with mild effulgence in the salons of the London season, differs little from the undergraduate of University College, who was greatly popular with the Oxonians of his academic period. Time has thinned his tresses and ploughed deep lines in his vigorous face; but fortunate in escaping the great disfigurer, who so mercilessly transforms graceful youths into corpulent veterans, he is also fortunate in preserving the facial lineaments of his boyish age. He preserves also the enthusiasm and winning cordiality of his youthful manner, and the same musical, nervous, and persuasive voice that, in 1852, was heard to such advantage during his delivery of his prize poem, *The Feast of Belshazzar*.

Harry Kingsley had not been many days in Oxford when I took my first view of his weedy frame and curious visage. Resembling Charles Kingsley (who was far from well-looking) in the straight mouth, and the deep line, descending on either side of the face from the unshapely nose to the corner of the graceless lips, which distinguished the clergyman's visage, Harry Kingsley was far plainer than his brother. That he was painfully sensitive of his extreme plainness appeared from the frequency with which he called attention to it. When he asked me at the outset of our acquaintance whether I did not think him the ugliest man in Oxford, I could not reply in the negative, although in my desire to soothe his troubled vanity I encouraged him to hope that next term a plainer undergraduate would come into residence. Later in his academic career, truth was in no degree outraged by the young lady, who with droll *naïveté* replied, 'There was no need for you to say so,' when at the moment of his introduction to her he proclaimed himself the ugliest man of all Oxford. But, notwithstanding its obtrusive ugliness, his countenance was not repulsive. On the contrary, the comical unsightliness of his grotesque visage disposed people to like him. The proverbial five minutes were all the time he needed for putting himself on equality with any personable youngster in a woman's regard.

I have already spoken of Harry Kingsley's weedy frame. In his freshman's term he was so slight and seemed so deficient in physical vigour, that his friends smiled compassionately at his ambition to distinguish himself amongst the oarsmen of the river. But they ceased to smile a few terms later, when by strenuous exercise and training he had not only rendered himself one of the best scullers on the river, but so changed the habit of his body that he had the appearance as well as physical capability of an athlete. The body, that was so greatly strengthened and altered in a single year by physical education at Oxford, acquired a larger measure of muscular development in Australia, and eventually became as remarkable for robustness as it had been remarkable for slightness and tenuity.

Harry Kingsley and Edwin Arnold were both concerned in a droll and innocent affair, that amused the younger and lighter sort of Oxonians, towards the close of my academic career. Indeed, unless my memory is at fault, they were the originators of the short-lived Fez Club,—a society of some fifty or more members of the university, who declared themselves haters of womankind, and vowed to pass their days in celibatic freedom, to do their utmost to diffuse the sentiment and principles of misogyny in every grade of English society, and after reducing women to their proper position to keep them in it. It was the opinion of the Misogynists that the influence of the gentler sex had increased, was increasing, and ought to be diminished. I was a member of the Society, and held (if I remember rightly) the office of Door-keeper, duly sworn to prevent persons, not being members of the Society, from coming into the Society's rooms during any meetings of the brotherhood. Besides a book of principles, a code of laws, divers volumes of record, and a staff of officers, the Society had secret signs whereby members meeting one another for the first time should become cognizant of their mystic fellowship, and also had articles of costume, to be worn by members at meetings of the Society. Every member of the Society was bound to wear at those meetings a fez cap, duly embroidered with symbols general or particular, my particular office of Door-Keeper, if I remember rightly, being indicated on my fez cap by the semblance of *A Key*, embroidered on the crimson cloth with yellow silk. It was provided by a rule of the Society, that should any member turn recreant and apostate, and commit matrimony, a mark of perpetual infamy should be put against his name on the roll of members. Besides meetings for the transaction of business, the Society met in full force once a week for enjoyment and fraternal edification.

The meetings for social enjoyment and fraternal edification were held in broad daylight at a table fitly provided with materials for a rather luxurious breakfast at Dickenson's Hotel and Coffee-House in Turle Street. No serious business was done at the meetings for social enjoyment (at which assembly every M.F.C., to wit, Member of the Fez Club, wore his fez cap, together with other ornaments appropriate to his position in the Society): but after breakfast, whilst the be-capped brethren were smoking oriental tobaccos from eastern pipes, it was competent for any member to rise in his place, and make *ore rotundo* to the President any communication, calculated to confirm members in their reasonable and wholesome opinion that womankind should be reduced to subjection, and held steadily in the subjection, befitting light, weak-minded and incorrigibly frivolous creatures.

The excitement, into which they were thrown by the Fez Club, caused the lighter sort of gownsmen, not being members of the Society, to talk with more fervour than justice of the misogynists. It was averred that the Fez Club was a disloyal and revolutionary association, that it was set on abolishing marriage and replacing it with free-love. There was also a stir amongst the free-masons of the university and city, who detected in the proceedings of 'the Fez' a malicious purpose to cover free-masonry with ridicule and contempt. To believe all that was declared from the house-tops or whispered secretly against the misogynists, was to think them conspirators against the throne, enemies of the church, free-thinkers, infidels, atheists, libertines,—whereas they were merely some fifty young gownsmen who thought it pleasant to play the fool for a season, and who in later time showed themselves healthily eager to associate in lawful wedlock with young gentlewomen of fit quality. The misogynists one and all married early, —some of them married early and often.

Soon after I donned my B.A. gown and hood, I backed the only bill I ever backed in my life, the person in whose interest I did the rash act being Harry Kingsley. The bill was for no large sum (I think it was for eighty pounds), and Harry showed such good reason for raising money by an objectionable process, that I could not refuse to 'give him my name.' The poor boy (yes, boy—though he was something older than myself) had for weeks and months been worried by a few contemptibly small creditors, whose importunities caused him so much mental distress, that he was incapable of preparing himself for 'smalls.' My 'name' would enable him to satisfy the pestiferous duns for ridiculously trivial sums, and would give him the peace of mind, without which he could not prosecute his studies. Of course, 'the accommodation' that came to him from the transaction in paper was of no real service to him; and of course, during the next few months, some disquiet came to me from thoughts about the wretched piece of paper, with my autograph upon it. But no harm came to me from the little kite. People occasionally die at the right moment, leaving legacies to the right people. Some one died at a happy moment for Harry Kingsley, and left him the few hundred pounds with which he wiped off his Oxford debts and paid for his outward passage to Australia, where he acquired the intellectual vigour, the humour, the worldly experience, and the knowledge of human nature, that enabled him to write *Geoffrey Hamlyn* and *Ravenshoe*—two novels, that are equal to any two novels that proceeded from the pen of his more fortunate and famous brother.

The poor fellow missed the death (the 'cheesy death,' as he called it) with which he desired in his merry boyhood to close a brief and brilliant career. In that sunny time he used to declare that he would fain fall back in his outrigger and expire suddenly at the close of a triumphant match with the champion sculler of the whole universe. To perish of violent delight, as his boat shot past the goal, three clear lengths ahead of the universal champion's outrigger, and the acclamations for the conqueror rent the air and rose to the blue sky, would be a blissful exit from a troublesome life. Good fellow! It was not appointed that he should die thus quickly and sweetly in the arms of Victory, either on water or land. Though it opened with bright achievement and brighter promise, his literary career was in its later stages less fortunate than the admirers of his earlier books hoped it would be; and he did not escape from the cares of this world until he had endured bravely a painful illness that was aggravated, if it was not caused, by disappointment. His least powerful works have already passed from the regard of readers, but it may be confidently predicted that the excellencies of his best works will preserve him from the limbo of forgotten authors.

At Oxford I had in Arthur Locker another friend, who was destined to make his mark in literature and win a place of high consideration amongst journalists. A member of my own college, Frederick Locker's younger brother confirmed me in my disposition to become a man of letters. To him also I was indebted for my agreeable intercourse with Thornbury—the first author to admit me to his intimacy. Introducing me to nearer and dearer members of his domestic circle, while I was still an undergraduate, Arthur Locker also made me known to his cousin-by-affinity, George Henry Thornbury, as he was called when he came to Oxford for ten days shortly before Locker took his B.A. degree (1851). As I knew the whilom literary critic of the *Times*, and late editor of the *Graphic*, thus intimately more than forty years since, and as no single gust of discord ever vexed the current of our long friendship, I feel some difficulty at the present moment in adhering to my determination to say little or nothing of the virtues of my living friends in this book. Would that the same rule forbade me to become garrulous about the winning qualities and generous endowments of Walter Thornbury, as he preferred to style himself in his later years. But alas! full fifteen years have passed over the grave to which he was consigned in his forty-fifth year.

Soon after George Henry Thornbury dropt his

baptismal names and took to signing himself Walter, I asked him why he had so changed his name. 'As my ballads have made so distinct a hit,' was the reply, 'I have decided to call myself Walter.' Possibly I showed by a smile that the explanation had not made the matter any clearer to me; for he added, snappishly, 'Surely, you must see that Hen-e-ry, Hen-e-ry is not a fit name for a writer of ballads, and that George, George, George is almost as bad, though no doubt Byron was a George. Walter is a much better name for a poet. So henceforth, be good enough to speak of me and think of me as Walter.'

Authors are apt to be fanciful about their names. My good old friend William Stigand (long may he flourish as Her Britannic Majesty's consul at Manilla or elsewhere!) was uneasy about his surname till he had changed the spelling of it. On the title-page of *A Vision of Barbarossa* (1860) the author stands forth in clear type as William Stigant; and on the title-page of *Athenais: or, The First Crusade* (1866) the same author stands forth as William Stigand. William Hepworth Dixon, my ever dear friend, did not receive the name of Hepworth from his god-parents, but assumed it at his own discretion. Charles Shirley Brooks, whilom editor of *Punch*, called himself Shirley not because it was his name by baptismal rite, but because he wished to hear himself called Shirley. Had he foreseen that the satiric humour of the literary coteries would convert 'Shirley' into 'Shallow' as a more appropriate name for a gentleman who was the reverse of profound, he would perhaps have remained plain Charles Brooks. And why should a man hesitate to make his name agreeable to his ear and sight? It is surely more sensible for a gentleman to change his name, than to squirm with fury at seeing or hearing himself described by a name that is distasteful to him. When I wrote a rather angry letter to the *Athenæum* in the summer of 1883 about the late Mr. Abraham Hayward, Q.C., and spoke of him repeatedly as 'Mr. Abraham Hayward,' I was ignorant that he detested his own Christian name as passionately as he detested Lord Beaconsfield, and winced with anguish whenever anyone called him 'Abraham.' Soon after the appearance of that letter, I learnt from my dear old friend Dr. John Percy, who knew him well, that Mr. Hayward's abhorrence of his Christian name was one of his several foibles. In the February of the ensuing year, when the literary veteran had just died of a malady from which he had long suffered, Percy worried me by declaring with malicious jocosity that I had killed the essayist by my cruel use of his Christian name. What a strange aversion to a name that is associated in the minds of most men with patriarchal dignity and with the natural grandeur of those Heights of Abraham, where Wolfe and Montcalm met and fell. As he hated the name so vehemently, Mr. Hayward should have dropt it. He might with propriety have re-named himself after the Philippus of Xenophon's Symposium. Philip Hayward would have sounded well.

A tall, fair young man, with straight hair and a very pleasing though plain face, Walter Thornbury at the outset of our acquaintance was a very interesting and winning person. The son of a London solicitor, who had passed several years in an asylum for mental invalids, my friend inherited from his father the highly nervous temperament, that in more than one passage of his career caused his familiar well-wishers to regard him with anxiety. Reared in his tender years by his father's only sister, and educated in his boyhood by her husband, the Reverend Barton Bouchier, M.A., Oxon. (a gentleman of some literary achievement) Thornbury was for a few years an apprentice in the office of a Bristol newspaper. On approaching manhood he went to London, and became a student in 'Dagger' Leigh's art-school in Newman Street: and for some time it seemed more probable that he would be a painter than become an author. That he relinquished his design of following art as a profession, because he soon discovered his natural incapacity for the calling, has often been alleged; but the statement is erroneous. The story that during his brief term of pupillage in Mr. Leigh's studio he produced a sketch of the Apollo Belvidere with six toes on the right foot was the fiction of an angry artist, who resented certain criticisms from Thornbury's pen, that had appeared in the *Athenæum*. Thornbury withdrew from the Newman Street school, because he saw his way to earning in literature an income, that would enable him to assist his uncle and aunt Bouchier and also his father, who were living at Cheam on a painfully narrow income. Whether he did wisely for himself in throwing himself resolutely into literature is questionable; but it is certain that his nearest and dearest relations had reason to congratulate themselves on the step he took for their sake.

Although he endured several sharp annoyances, in his literary career, Thornbury had a fair share of happiness during the twenty years, next following his appointment to the post of art-critic on the *Athenæum*,—a post, by the way, which he occupied for only a few years. Literature was his proper vocation. A lover of books, he delighted in the labour of the British Museum reading-room. Enjoying the labour of producing 'copy,' though he loathed the drudgery of correcting it, he made for many years a considerable income,—at least, so good an income, that he had the satisfaction of seeing his uncle and aunt and father in comfort, and could indulge in 'touring.' At the same time he had the delight of helping other persons besides the trio who were entitled to his assistance. As the warm-hearted fellow delighted in aiding people, he, of course, had several candidates for relief from his helpful hand. I question whether any professional author, wholly dependent on his pen, ever gave away in charity a larger percentage of his income than Thornbury gave from his precarious income to necessitous comrades. Giving them money, he was also at great pains to find employment for them. One of them he employed for several years as a reading-room hack and copyist. In one department of his duties this particular drudge rendered his patron good service, as he was the only person in London who could read at sight the worst examples of Thornbury's execrably bad hand-writing. When the compositors in a printing-office 'struck work,' as they sometimes did, over Thornbury's 'copy,' on account of the difficulty they experienced in deciphering it, the author's peculiar *protégé* used to make a fair copy of the puzzling manuscript for the indignant workmen. Moreover, so many of Thornbury's articles were returned to him by editors of magazines because they could not read his writing, that he found it to his advantage to make his hack produce fair copies of his articles, for the convenience of the editors. For some years the one clever expert in Thornbury's penmanship lived for the most part on money paid him by Thornbury for clear copies of articles in manuscript, whose most puzzling passages the author himself was sometimes unable to read.

Thornbury's practice of employing his especial hack in this way, and his perfect confidence in the accuracy of that gentleman's transcripts, had ill consequences. It is not wonderful that the transcripts of copy, which was in places illegible to Thornbury himself, occasionally misrepresented the author. Nor is it matter for surprise, as Thornbury in his reliance on their accuracy did not hesitate to correct his proofs by them, that strange errors often appeared in the author's published work. Thornbury's reputation for inaccuracy resulted in a far greater degree from the slips of his transcriber, than from his own want of knowledge. The author's way of feeding the press also resulted in absolutely false rumours that his articles were sometimes the productions of the gentleman who was merely his copyist. Honourable in all things, Thornbury was quite incapable of publishing as his own work the product of another man's brain. He was 'true as steel,'—the motto that he used as a title for his best novel. The nervous and too sensitive man had the failings of his temperament; but he was exempt from all the more serious infirmities and guiltless of all the darker irregularities of poor humanity. Lord Beaconsfield once remarked with delightful drollery of Mr. Gladstone, that he had not 'a single redeeming vice.' The words may be spoken in all seriousness of dear Walter Thornbury, whose many virtues were unattended with a single evil propensity.

Having said more than I intended to say of my first literary associate, I will return for a moment to my last days at the university, within whose bounds it was my good fortune to make his acquaintance. After passing a wretched 'first year at Oxford,' I enjoyed the remainder of my academic time. I should have enjoyed it thoroughly, had I been indifferent to the disfavour with which the tutors of my college reasonably regarded me for being a mere idler, and had I been free from thought for the disappointment which my neglect of academic work would occasion my people at home. How greatly I enjoyed the colleges, the gardens, the river, the gaiety of my comrades, I know from the pleasure that has come to me during forty years from dreaming of them.

During the last twelve or fourteen of those forty years I have also been repeatedly visited by a dream about Oxford that is the reverse of agreeable. As I cannot remember that as an undergraduate I was distrustful of my ability to pass either of my two examinations in 'the schools,' and fearful of being compelled to leave Oxford without a degree, I am at a loss how to account for the dream that caused me acute distress for the first time some twelve or fourteen years agone, and ever since its first assault on my peace of mind has disquieted me in the same degree twice or thrice in every year. The dream is this: I am journeying to Oxford, in order to wipe out a blot on my honour by taking the degree which I failed to take in my boyhood; crowned with grey hair I am again at Pembroke College for this purpose, taking my place in a class of students who regard me derisively; a few minutes later an officer of the college approaches me, and informs me that I must leave the lecture-room and quit the college, from whose books I removed my name in my twenty-second year; in my anguish at the announcement I give utterance to a cry, that dispels the illusion.

Had I been ploughed either for my 'smalls' or my 'greats,' or could I remember myself to have been painfully apprehensive of misadventure in the schools, it would be easy to account for this dream, which has disturbed my rest so often during the last twelve or fourteen years. But I endured no humiliating misadventure in the schools, I passed both examinations easily, and I took my degree in the ordinary way on 19th May, 1852. I can remember that shortly before each examination I was at pains to prepare myself thoroughly for the not severe ordeal; but I have no recollection that I took these pains at the instigation of fear. Why, then, the curious dream? Why did it not trouble me sooner?

Having taken my degree, I remained at Oxford till the close of Trinity Term; and shortly before leaving the university, that had become inexpressibly dear to me, I called on Mr. Henney, vice-gerent and senior tutor of my college, and asked him to give me a testimonial, that would be serviceable to me in London, where I meant to find employment as a visiting-tutor. To my surprise, he declined to give me a testimonial, and told me I might spare myself the trouble of applying to either of the other two tutors for a credential letter; as he and they had all three agreed to decline to give me a testimonial, should I ask them for one. He was frank respecting the grounds for their determination.

'Apart from what your degree declares, we know nothing whatever about you,' he said, 'save that you possess some natural ability which you have forborne to turn to good account in the studies to which you ought to have devoted all your powers. We know that you have lived in the college, or in lodgings near it, that you have passed your examinations, that you have taken your degree, that instead of taking honours you are a mere passman. We know nothing more of you, and you have taken care that we should know nothing more of you. Does this statement do you any injustice?'

'None whatever,' I answered. 'On the contrary, you might put the case more strongly against me. You might say that in a quiet way I have been a disorderly undergraduate, that I attended the fewest possible lectures and never prepared myself for them, and that I was so infrequent an attendant at chapel that I was always "gated" at the end of term by the dean. I am quite sensible that I have not done my duty to the college.'

'Well, well,' he replied, in a kindly way, 'I am glad you speak so reasonably.'

I have no doubt that, had my pride permitted me to make the attempt, I could have persuaded Mr. Henney to give me a sufficient testimonial, his compact with the other tutors notwithstanding; for he was a kindly man, as well as a conscientious and able tutor. Making no effort to shake his resolution, I took my leave of him, without any sort of ill-will to him. As I had always respected and in a certain way liked him, it was not in my nature, faulty nature though it was, to be angry with him for acting in accordance with his view of duty.

After my staggering interview with Mr. Henney, possibly on the day of the interview, but more probably a day or two later, I called on Dr. Jeune, and was so fortunate as to find him at home. I do not think I had written to him asking for an audience, but I may have done so.

'Well, Mr. Jeaffreson,—come to say good-bye?' the Master remarked, in a tone which implied that, if that was my object in calling upon him, our interview need not be long.

Going at once to the heart of the matter on which I wished to speak with him, I observed that the tutors had refused to give me a testimonial.

'You have not come to me to complain of that?' observed the Master.

'I don't complain of them,' I answered. 'On the contrary, I am disposed to think that from their point of view they are quite right.'

'Then why mention the matter to me?'

'Because I have come to ask you to give me a testimonial, and it would not be right for me to make that request without first telling you of the tutors' refusal.'

When it pleased him to do so, Dr. Jeune could set his fine face so firmly and render it so motionless, as to give it the appearance of a mask; and, whilst his countenance remained thus still and rigid, no observer could divine what was passing in the strong man's mind.

'You can say what you like,' he remarked; and, as he gave me permission to talk, the Master made his features as still as stone. For some minutes I talked to the mask, telling the motionless listener how it came to pass that I could not give my mind to my proper studies during my first year at Oxford, and on coming to a healthier frame had not the heart to read for honours, after losing so much time, and that I had shirked chapel throughout my whole time in the university, because I did not concur in the fundamental doctrines of the Church, and therefore never appeared in chapel with an easy conscience. Moreover, I ventured to tell the mask that, if I went in search of tutorial work without any certificate from him or the tutors, the want of the testimonial would expose me to suspicion of having been a collegiate black-sheep, instead of having been a mere idler against whom the tutors alleged nothing worse than academic idleness.

'How much money have you spent since you came into residence?' the Master inquired, when I had stated my case. Fortunately I was in a position to answer the question precisely, for I had just been taking a view of my financial doings since the opening of my academic career. 'You have debts, of course?' observed the Master, dropping his mask as he put the question, quickly.

'None,' I answered, 'over and above the sum I have just named. The cheques I have received from my father amount to . . . , my debts amount to . . . ; I don't owe a shilling to anyone outside Oxford.'

The Master's comment was re-assuring.

'Then, you have not been extravagant; you have spent in all more than you need have spent, but the excess doesn't amount to extravagance.'

'In some things,' I replied, 'I have been severely economical.'

Then came from the Master's lips a stream of short questions, touching my designs for getting employment, and my knowledge of London, to which questions I answered in a way that caused my interrogator to remark at the end of the examination,

'You know what you mean to do. That's in your favour. But you'll have a harder struggle than you seem to think.'

A few seconds later, he remarked, 'Wait a minute, while I write a few lines,'—the words being uttered in a tone that made me think he was going to write a note on some of his private affairs.

'There,' he said, two or three minutes later, when he had written a few lines on a sheet of note-paper, and signed them, 'that, I think, will be sufficient for your purpose. Just look at it, and say if it will do.'

On looking at the brief note, I found the writing to be precisely the testimonial I wanted from the writer.

'Dr. Jeune,' I said warmly, 'you are very good to me! It is the very thing I wanted!'

'Then give it to me for a moment, for the ink is wet. I'll dry it, so that you can carry it away with you.'

On returning the paper to me, when he had folded it and put it in an envelope, Dr. Jeune observed,

'Of course, I shall tell Mr. Henney what I have done, but you may as well be silent about the matter till you have left Oxford. Keep that paper in your pocket and show it to no one, till you have occasion for using it.'

In the following Christmas holidays, when I dined with him at Islington, Tom Girtin told me that on an early day of Michaelmas Term, next following my withdrawal from Oxford, Mr. Henney amused a class of young men by speaking of me, as though the college were well rid of me, and at the same time as though he rather liked me.

'We knew nothing about him,' said the tutor, in the semi-jocose way of speaking in which he indulged when his sense of humour was agreeably tickled, 'we tutors knew nothing whatever about him, literally nothing whatever about him, and therefore we refused to give him a testimonial. What could we have said about a gentleman of whom we knew nothing? But he managed to get a testimonial. He went to the Master, and talked the Master over. Yes, he actually talked the Master into giving him a testimonial.'

According to my informant, the vice-gerent's kindly face beamed with amusement, as he told how I had 'talked the Master over!'

I have the kindliest recollection of Mr. Henney, who was as good a man of his sort as ever breathed. But he ought not to have said that I 'talked the Master over.' As though a boy of twenty-one years—a mere idle stripling—could have 'talked over' Dr. Jeune, who had as clear and strong a head as any Englishman of his period! The notion is preposterous! There was no 'talking over' in the affair. I made no cunning speech, but a simple statement of my case to an extremely able and fair-minded man, who saw that, though my conduct had been faulty, it had not been heinous or unattended by extenuating circumstances. A pre-eminently just man, Dr. Jeune was also a sympathetic and charitable man. Compassionating me for the mistakes and perplexity of my youth, he took a lenient view of my collegiate misdemeanours. The brief letter, which he wrote in my behalf at the moment of my departure from Oxford, may be spoken of as one of 'those actions of the just' that 'smell sweet and blossom in the dust.'

It is needless to say, that for my purpose Dr. Jeune's testimonial was more serviceable than any letter signed by the tutors of my college would have been; for, though they were able and excellent gentlemen, no one of the tutors was a man of great influence or reputation outside Oxford, whereas the Master of Pembroke was an intellectual celebrity and a moral force in London.

CHAPTER VI.

CHARTERHOUSE SQUARE.

Harry Kingsley—Willie Langworthy—Their Unseasonable Levity—My Design for getting my Livelihood in London—Government Clerks and Classical Tutors—Their Respective Earnings—Boarding-House for Schoolboys—Pupils of both Sexes—Visiting Tutors and Literary Reviewers—Dr. Thundercloud, F.R.S.—St. Mary's Hall—Mary Wilderness.

My university career was in its last week, when Harry Kingsley and his particular friend Willie Langworthy (both of Worcester College) pressed me to tell them by what means I hoped to maintain myself in London.

'I know just nothing,' I replied lightly, 'and my design is to make a sufficient income by teaching it to other people.'

On coming out of the long fit of screaming laughter into which they were thrown by this airy speech, my friends begged for a full statement of my plans for getting pupils, who would be willing to pay me for teaching them 'just nothing;' but I declined to gratify their curiosity, observing, with some stateliness, that the boisterous merriment which my few wordshad occasioned them showed their incompetence to deal with grave questions. Had I cared to enlighten them, I could have easily convinced them that I was a practical young man, who knew what he meant to do in great London. For I had formed a plan for achieving my purpose, and had begun to act upon it. Indeed, I was already in negociation with an advertiser in the *Times* newspaper, who was looking out for a young tutor.

It is usual for young men of slender resources, who have left Oxford or Cambridge with a degree in Arts, a desire to establish themselves in London, and a firm resolve against taking holy orders, to seek employment in one of the great government offices. Forty years since it was easier than it is at the present time for a young man to get a goverment clerkship, and I had friends who could have put me into such a berth. But, after thinking the matter over, I decided not to be a government clerk. My reasons for this decision were sound. I had resolved that, whatever else I might be in the future, I would be a man of letters. I had already seen two papers by my pen printed in clear type in London magazines, and had produced some sketches for a provincial journal. The rate at which I was paid for these crude and slender trifles was low; but I was paid for them, and had looked with delight on pieces of gold and silver earned by myself. Having tasted blood, I thirsted for more of the same drink. Moreover, I was so simple a lad as to yearn for literary fame, and to imagine I could win it, if I took the right course and sufficient pains. But the labour of producing those printed trifles had taught me I could not earn a bare subsistence by my pen, till I should have acquired greater facility in handling the tool, larger knowledge of the world, and a far wider acquaintance with books. To educate myself to be a writer, I must so arrange my life, as to live in London, have access to a great library, and reserve a sufficient time for study.

The daily labour of a government clerk would preclude me from reading effectively at the British Museum, and would consume a larger proportion of my time than I could afford to spend on labour for bare sustenance. I calculated that a government clerk in the receipt of one hundred pounds a year was paid at the rate of about one shilling and twopence halfpenny per hour, whereas a classical tutor with an Oxford degree was paid at the least two shillings and sixpence per hour, was ordinarily paid five shillings per hour, was sometimes paid seven shillings and sixpence, and even half-a-guinea per hour. I put the case in another way, and considered that a visiting classical tutor of my own academic quality, who worked six hours a day for a payment of five shillings an hour during forty-six weeks, would earn more than four times as much as a government clerk, with a salary of one hundred pounds a year,— to wit, one hundred pounds for fifty-two weeks less six weeks of holidays, i.e. for forty-six weeks. From the calculations, it was obvious that until he earned a salary of four hundred and fourteen pounds a year a government clerk, working six hours a day at his office during forty-six weeks of each year, was not so well paid as a visiting classical tutor, who worked the same time. I was prepared to live on one hundred pounds a-year for a few years; but, as I wished to earn the money requisite for my sustenance in as short time as possible, I thought it would be better for me to earn the first one hundred pounds, in four hundred hours, as a classical tutor, paid at the rate of five shillings an hour, than to earn it in sixteen-hundred-and-fifty-six hours, as a government clerk, with a salary of one hundred pounds a year.

The considerations of time and remuneration would have determined me to be a visiting tutor in London rather than a government clerk. But I regarded the question from other points of view before I came to a final resolution. I knew that, on leaving youth behind them, visiting tutors were at a disadvantage; but this consideration did not affect me, as I had no intention of being a tutor for many years. As I meant to have only a few pupils at a time, I was not troubled by considering that visiting tutors with many pupils on their hands have to hurry-and-skurry about London in order to keep their engagements. I thought of the difficulty of finding pupils, and formed a strong opinion that the difficulty could not be great for a young tutor.

I had a numerous acquaintance in London, an acquaintance of different sets and connections into which I had been brought by different introducers, and I knew much more of the town than most young men from the country know of it. I was, therefore, competent to think rightly about the supply of and demand for visiting classical tutors, and after due deliberation I came to the conclusion that the demand exceeded the supply. Moreover, I asked myself whether the employment would be distasteful to me. I never thought for a moment that I should be enamoured of it. Of course, if I had possessed two hundred pounds a year from consols, I should not for a moment have thought of teaching Latin and Greek, Logic and Euclid to strangers for money. The question was whether the employment would be more or less disagreeable to me than the vocation of a government clerk? This question I also answered in favour of the teaching trade.

So I decided to turn tutor, and though I have done many things that I regret and several things that I deplore (as Lord Beaconsfield said of himself towards the close of his career), I have never regretted the decision. Experience justified the several opinions that determined me to teach 'just nothing' to pupils who needed to learn it. I had not been six days in London, before I was engaged to act as tutor to a party of bright, cheery, gentlemanly lads, who had their home in a boarding-house for boys, attending the Charterhouse School or St. Paul's School. My function in this post was to see that the boys prepared and to aid them in preparing their school-lessons,—work that occupied me for some two or three hours of each secular evening of the week. A few weeks later, I was also preparing for his matriculation examination at Oxford a young man (some few years my senior), who had decided at the eleventh hour to relinquish a worldly vocation and qualify himself for taking holy orders. Knowing little Latin and less Greek, this amiable, well-mannered and intelligent gentleman found in me a tutor, quite as competent to guide him in his rudimentary studies as any first-classman would have been. At the same time I was retained to coach a younger student (the only son of a wealthy father) for the matriculation examination of the London University. Whilst my obligations to these students left me sufficient time for my own studies, the payments which I received for ministering to their educational necessities were more than sufficient for my wants.

Finding pupils thus easily at the outset of my tutorial career, I experienced no difficulty in finding other pupils when I wanted them. In the course of the six or seven years, during which I sustained myself chiefly by tutorial work, my pupils differed in character, style, aim, social quality, sex; but they invariably interested me. For the most part they were of the sterner sex,—the boys of the boarding-house, youths who wanted to be prepared for some particular examination, young men who, after labouring for several years in some unscholarly vocation, were set upon taking a degree in Arts at one of the universities. But some of my pupils in that far-away time were of the gentler sex. I remember with pleasure how I was permitted to give instruction to a gentlewoman, who wished to recover her former familiarity with the classic languages, so that she might aid her little sons in preparing their school-exercises, and also how I acted for a while as teacher of a highly intellectual young lady who wished to read Greek plays. In the longer and closing stage of my tutorial career, *all* my pupils were of the gentler sex; for I continued to act as a teacher of Latin and Mathematics and lecturer on English literature in a College for Gentlewomen, long after I ceased to 'coach' boys and young men.

Enough has been said to indicate the rates of of remuneration for the services of visiting tutors; but to give greater effect to my previous remarks on the pecuniary question, I may observe that besides being very much better paid per hour than clerks in the lower grades of the Civil Service, visiting tutors are also much better paid than reviewers of books on the best literary journals, who, after the practice of most reviewers, read with due deliberation the books on which they pass judgment. The reviewer has a distinct advantage over the visiting tutor in that he works at home by his own fire-side. On the other hand, the visiting tutor has a great advantage over the reviewer in the good-will of his former pupils. The gratitude of authors to their friendliest reviewers seldom endures for a month. When I met Dr. Thundercloud, F.R.S., a night or two since at a scientific assembly, he gave me the coldest of nods, though he knows it was I who years syne sent his book on *The Forces of Nature* into a third thousand, and thereby opened to him the doors of the Royal Society. But my old pupils overflow with kindness to me, when they come upon me. 'Tis no long while since that a far greater scientist than Dr. Thundercloud, F.R.S., said to me, 'You have forgotten me, but I remember and often tell my friends in Dublin how you taught me to delight in Euclid, as though it were a mere book of puzzles.' And 'twas only last season that a lady came up to me with a radiant face and an outstretched hand, and said to me, ' You'll remember me, when I tell you that I used to be Mary Wilderness, and one of *your girls* at dear old St. Mary's Hall.' When the lady, who used to be one of my girls, went off to another assembly, I went to my pillow in high good-humour with myself and the whole world, and next morning I woke in the middle of a dream about Mary Wilderness.

CHAPTER VII.

OLD FRIENDS.

J. C. M. Bellew on Friendship—Inhabitants of Charterhouse Square—Wedding Bells at Hendon Church—Badge of Disgrace for a Naughty Girl—The Complins of Charterhouse Square—James Hinton, Aurist and Essayist—His quick Passage from Adversity to Prosperity—Scene in the Strand —'The Faculty' in Finsbury Square—Henry Jeaffreson, M.D., Cantab.—His Home in 'The Medical Quarter'—Dr. William Withey Gull, of No. 8, Finsbury Square—His subsequent Celebrity— His good Stories—Bird-like Sisters and their 1820 Port—Sir William Lawrence, Baronet, the famous Surgeon—Fate of the Third Edition of his 'Lectures'—John Jeaffreson, of Upper Street, Islington, Surgeon and Apothecary—His Friendship with the Disraelis—Jews of Islington and Stoke Newington—Anecdotes of Lord Beaconsfield's Birth and Childhood—His first Love-Affair—His early Days at Islington.

THE Reverend J. C. Montesquieu Bellew, who was a much better fellow than his indiscreet tongue caused many people to think him, once staggered a party of matter-of-fact people by observing at a dinner-table, 'What, have you lived with the same people for so long as thirty years? In my opinion, three yea s is quite long enough for a friendship. By the end of the third year of our friendship, the most amusing persons cease to amuse me.' The present writer is one of those common-place and simple folk who prefer old friends to new acquaintances; and he thankful to say that he enjoys the kindly regard of several people whose acquaintance he made some forty years since amongst his neighbours in Charterhouse Square.

It was a quiet, secluded, picturesque, rather ungeometrical old Square, peopled for the most part by clergymen, solicitors, doctors, but harbouring a few householders of illiberal vocations. The quaint and irregularly built old Square had one or two lodging-houses, one or two big boarding-houses, and two houses in which young women earned their living by making artificial flowers. Though it lay in a noisy neighbourhood, it was a tranquil Square, for its high iron-gates were in the keeping of beadles, who were forbidden to open them to any carriage that was not *en route* for a door-way within the enclosure.

By many of my friends the Square was decried for being out of the way, but for me it was conveniently placed, for I was within an easy walk of the British Museum, a mile of my cousin Henry Jeaffreson's house in Finsbury Square, and a ten minutes' walk of Doctors Commons, where my cousin Ned Edwards continued to follow his calling by day, long after he had married a very charming young woman, the daughter of a gentleman who was in his day a personage of eminence in the Indian Civil Service. When the young people were married at Hendon Church in the autumn of 1852, I figured at the ceremony as 'best man.' It lives in my memory also that, whilst the witnesses were spending a needless amount of time in signing the register, I espied in the vestry a number of wooden labels (or should I call them panels?) in size about six inches by four inches; each of these labels was fitted with black ribbon, so that it could be hung upon a child's neck, and was painted in black and white,—white letters on a black ground, the lettering being to this effect: 'For A Girl Who Behaves Badly In Church.' One of these penal labels found a way into one of my pockets; and I took an early occasion to give it to the bride, as a memorial of her recent misbehaviour in Hendon church; and I rather think that Mrs. Edwards, of Golden Square, has preserved this badge of disgrace even to the present date. If the critic of this page is on the point of charging me with having committed sacrilege in respect to this article of church goods, he will do well to observe that I have said nothing tantamount to an admission that I stole the label.

Of my neighbours in Charterhouse Square none were dearer to me forty years ago, none are dearer to me and my wife at the present date, than the Complins, whilom of No. 24. More than fifty years old when I first crossed his threshold, and made the acquaintance of his group of clever and charming daughters, Edward Thomas Complin, surgeon, scientist, and raciest of *raconteurs*, preserved even to his ninety-third year, at his pleasant home at Eastbourne, something of the personal grandeur and comeliness that distinguished him in his middle age, and much of the mental vigour and colloquial energy that made him for many years a man of light and leading in the Merchant Taylors' Company, of whose Court he had long been the oldest member.

It was in Charterhouse Square that I made the acquaintance of my old friend James Hinton, aurist and essayist, chiefly remembered for *Man and his Dwelling-Place*, a series of philosophical essays that attracted much attention, as they ran through certain early numbers of the *Cornhill Magazine*, and may be found in many libraries as a separate volume. A kindlier, brighter, sweeter being than James Hinton never breathed. Comical in his personality from the weird and wild expression of his slight and colourless visage, the thinness and angularity of his short and fragile form, the extravagance of his gestures, and the acuteness of his penetrating treble voice, he was loveable for his enthusiasm, benevolence, and sincerity. My brother Horace (Horace Jeaffreson, M.D. Lond.), who during a considerable period of his student days lived in Hinton's house, regarded him with affection, and, though he had the best opportunities for discovering his infirmities, honoured him for his goodness. It never occurred to any of his neighbours in Charterhouse Square, where he suffered severely from adverse circumstances, to think that James Hinton might become famous and prosperous. Whilst they talked of him as an amiable failure, the curiously modest fellow took the same view of his case. On that matter he and they were alike wrong. Producing a book that set the world talking, he sprang with a single leap into fine practice in the West End, on the death of a celebrated ear-doctor. Years, during which we saw nothing of one another, had passed since we lived in neighbourly intercourse, and I had heard nothing of his quick passage from narrow circumstances to prosperity, when I was stayed in a quick walk along the southern side of the Strand by the sound of my name, uttered in a high treble key by some one behind me. Turning quickly round I looked upon a small, fragile, little man, dancing about the pavement in high excitement, to the considerable inconvenience of wayfarers. There was no doubt he was the man who had called to me. Only in one respect was he different from the James Hinton of my Charterhouse Square days. Instead of wearing seedy clothes, he was dressed like a prosperous gentleman. Jumping up to me he shook my hand with convulsive tugs, as he ejaculated,

'I am so glad, so very glad, so inexpressibly glad to see you. I have so often wished to see you and tell you all that has happened.'

Having by this time shaken my hand with much more than sufficient cordiality, he went back a few paces from me, and in doing so blundered against a stout lady, and knocked a small boy down into the gutter. After viewing me in the right perspective, my emotional friend danced up to me again, and then danced before me, ejaculating in the highest notes of his shrill voice,

'I am so delighted to see you. There is so much for us to talk about. So many things have happened that I want to tell you about. Do you know, I am a successful man—a very successful man? I became a success all in a moment. Isn't it ludicrous? You never expected me to be a successful man. No one thought it in the least degree possible that I should be a success. No one,—no one,—no one. See, that's my carriage, those are my horses. Is it not absurd?—do, my dear fellow, say it is absurd that I should drive about London in my own carriage.'

He went on talking in this strain, laughing at himself and his success, and entreating me to come as soon as possible to his house, so that he might explain to me how the ridiculous change in his circumstances had come about. It mattered not to him that he and I were surrounded by a ring of greatly amused listeners,—that he was blocking the way. To escape from a slightly embarrassing position, I assured him I would soon call upon him, and at the same time spoke of an engagement that compelled me to say good-bye and be off. He was the most benevolent of men. As soon as he had grown accustomed to his success he ceased to talk about it, and henceforth strove in various ways to use his prosperity for the advantage of unfortunate people. There never lived a man with a whiter soul, a warmer heart, or a shriller voice.

Whilst I was James Hinton's neighbour in Charterhouse Square, I was a frequent visitor at a house in Finsbury Square, where I made the acquaintance of several of the leaders of the medical profession, together with other interesting and influential persons. It was the house of my cousin Henry Jeaffreson, M.D. Cantab, the honourably-remembered physician of St. Bartholomew's Hospital, who, besides being one of the most successful physicians of his period, was the best whist-player, the best billiard-player, the best shot, and the most popular member of the medical profession. Social changes have so greatly reduced the number and status of 'the city doctors' during the last thirty years, that it is well to remind the younger readers of this page how large a proportion of the foremost physicians and surgeons of London lived within a mile of the Mansion House in the opening decades of the present reign. From 1834, the year in which he began his professional career at No. 2, Finsbury Pavement, till December, 1866, the month in which he died at No. 8, Finsbury Square, Henry Jeaffreson had his London home in a quarter that was known as 'the Medical Quarter.' Eminent physicians and surgeons were scattered here and there about the western districts of the town: in Spring Gardens, in Savile Row, in Brook Street, in Grosvenor Street, in several of the thoroughfares near Cavendish Square; but the *one* Medical Quarter of the town comprised Finsbury Pavement, Finsbury Square, Finsbury Circus, Broad Street, and St. Helen's Place.

Of the medical celebrities, whose acquaintance I made at No. 2 Finsbury Square, perhaps the most amusing was Dr. William Withey Gull, on whose departure to the western side of the town, my cousin moved from No. 2 to No. 8, which latter house Gull had occupied for several years. At the time of his migration from the East to the West, Gull had a painful misgiving as to the consequences of so hazardous a step. Having enjoyed a lucrative practice and enviable position in medical society for many years, he may well have been doubtful whether he should enlarge his income and improve his position by moving to a more fashionable district. Even at the last moment, he would have relinquished his ambitious design, and remained in Finsbury Square, could he have withdrawn honourably from his engagement to assign the remainder of his lease of No. 8, Finsbury Square, to my cousin. The engagement was merely verbal; but whilst Henry Jeaffreson was a man to act on a friend's word, as though it were a deed duly signed and delivered, Gull was not a man to withdraw from his mere promise. In reliance on the verbal engagement, Henry Jeaffreson was quick in disposing of the remainder of his lease of No. 2, and he had scarcely done so, when Dr. Gull told him that after all he had determined to relinquish or at least defer his design of moving westward. For a moment the position was slightly embarrassing to both physicians, but it caused neither of them any serious discomfort; for on learning the state of the case, and seeing that he was bound in honour to withdraw from his house, Dr. Gull found courage to take the step, on which he had in later time so much reason to congratulate himself. Had Dr. Gull deferred the important step, he would perhaps have never taken it, and remaining in Finsbury Square would have died without winning his baronetcy, and making the largest fortune ever made by an English physician.

Dr. Gull was neither a brilliant nor highly humorous *raconteur;* but he often chatted to me lightly, and with a communicativeness that was flattering to so young and insignificant a person as myself. Moreover, though he could not be highly commended for humour, he garnished his table talk with touches of drollery that were very amusing. On one occasion he told me in his best style a capital story of two elderly and bird-like maidens, who dwelt in a Georgian mansion near Croydon, and were regarded by their neighbours with the respect due to two mature gentlewomen, who kept a coach, a pair of horses, and three or four male servants. They were sisters of different ages, and closely resembled one another in their tenuity, their profiles, and their general air of severe and old-fashioned gentility, albeit the elder was something taller, thinner, more severe and more bird-like in face than the younger. Whenever the doctor made a remark in the presence of these two sisters, he was answered by both. The elder sister having replied in precisely accentuated words, that rarely exceeded the limits of an ordinary sentence, the younger sister gave utterance to the same words, but imparted something of individuality, if not of originality, to them, by reversing the order of the clauses of the one sentence.

On the occasion of a professional visit to these sisters, Dr. Gull prescribed tonic medicine for both of them, and advised each to take two or three glasses of port wine every day.

Elder Sister. 'That is most distasteful advice to me and my sister, dear Dr. Gull, as we dislike wine.'

Younger Sister. 'Dear Dr. Gull, as we dislike wine, that is most distasteful advice to me and my sister.'

Dr. Gull. 'My dear ladies, you *must* take the wine,

as medicine. If you like, you may take it in the way of hot negus.'

Elder Sister. 'I thank you, dear doctor, for that suggestion, negus being far less disagreeable than wine.'

Younger Sister. 'Negus being far less disagreeable than wine, I thank you, dear doctor, for that suggestion.'

A week later, Dr. Gull paid the ladies another visit, and found them sipping their negus at luncheon; and at their urgent invitation he took a glass of the pure port wine.

Though he adopted the fashionable prejudice against port, when he had been for some years a supremely fashionable physician, Dr. Gull in his earlier time amongst the citizens honoured the wine as it should be honoured, drank rather freely of it, and was a fine *connoisseur* of the generous drink. He was, therefore, greatly shocked to find that the sisters had used for the making of their negus some superlatively good 1820 port.

Dr. Gull. 'Dear ladies, this is superlatively fine '20 port,—'tis as fine as '20 port can be.'

Elder Sister. 'As my dear father had the very highest opinion of the wine, Dr. Gull, I am not surprised that you like it.'

Younger Sister. 'I am not surprised that you like it, Dr. Gull, as my dear father had the very highest opinion of the wine.'

Feeling how important it was, for the highest interests of society, that such super-excellent wine should be withdrawn from the hands of the two gentlewomen, who were making it into negus, Dr. Gull explained to them that they might sell their 1820 port for ten pounds, and even more, per dozen, and buy at forty shillings per dozen wine that was of equal medicinal virtue and quite as palatable in negus. The sisters (daughters of a British merchant) came readily into the notion of turning a nimble and honest penny, by selling their choice wine and replacing it with cheap wine that would be quite as effectual for medicinal ends. They came into the notion the more readily, because they lived so nearly up to the limits of a good and sure income that they sometimes wished for a larger balance in their favour at the bank. The suggestion being regarded with approval by the sisters, Dr. Gull went more fully into the matter, and ascertained how many dozens they had of the wine. The result of the conference was that the physician was authorized to speak about the wine to certain of his friends, and enquire what price they would give for it. That he might act the more decisively in the interest of the two sisters, the physician carried with him to town a bottle of wine, that should be submitted to his friends as a sample of the stock in the cellar.

A day or two later, three gentlemen—to wit, Henry Jeaffreson, his brother-in-law Burnett, and Dr. Gull—dined together in Finsbury Square, and agreed to take all the wine, and offer the ladies a price much higher than any price that either to their knowledge or the knowledge of living man had ever been given for '20 port. Their common and chivalrous sentiment was expressed by the trio in these words:

'We mayn't profit by the simplicity and ignorance of the two ladies. Our honour requires that we should pay them more than anyone else would give them. Let us offer to take the whole lot at a guinea a bottle.'

Acting on this resolve, Gull at his next visit to the sisters announced to them that he and two of his friends wished to take all the wine at twelve guineas a-dozen. Instead of looking as he expected them to look at this liberal and even prodigal offer, the elder sister's thin face assumed a hard, cold, disdainful look. The same expression came over the younger sister's countenance.

Elder Sister, with contemptuous severity. 'Dr. Gull, though I and my sister live in the country, we do read the *Times*.'

Younger Sister, in the same tone of severe contempt. 'I and my sister *do* read the *Times*, Dr. Gull, although we live in the country.'

Elder Sister, with scornful ridicule in her voice. 'It is clear to me, Dr. Gull, that you haven't read to-day's *Times* with much care.'

Younger Sister. 'That you haven't read to-day's *Times* with much care is quite clear to me, Dr. Gull.'

Dr. Gull. 'What on earth is it, my dear ladies, that I ought to have seen in this morning's *Times*?'

Elder Sister, putting the paper in the doctor's hands, and pointing to a particular part of a particular column. ''Tis only that, Dr. Gull; do read it for yourself.'

Younger Sister. 'Do read it for yourself, Dr. Gull; 'tis only that.'

From the particular part of the particular column

to which his attention was directed, Dr. Gull learnt that on the previous day some choice '20 port had been knocked down to a bidder of the sensational price of sixteen guineas a-dozen at the public sale of a famous cellar. 'After this,' said the writer of the note in the *Times*, 'it will not astonish us to hear in a few months that twenty guineas a-dozen have been paid for this favourite wine.' As they were manifestly under the impression that he and his two London friends had attempted to get possession of their wine at a price much beneath its real value, Dr. Gull took his leave of the sisters without saying anything more on the affair of business. The negotiation for the sale and purchase of the wine 'dropt through;' and a few years later, when '20 port had 'taken the turn,' and was steadily falling in price, the sisters had reason to regret their refusal of the offered twelve guineas *per* dozen. The moral of the story is obvious:—When ladies have a lot of choice wine and are desirous of selling it, they should confide in the honour of the friend who offers them a high price for it, and should be careful to sell it before it begins to deteriorate.

Dr. Gull told me another good story, whilst I sat next him at my cousin's dinner-table, after the withdrawal of the ladies.

'The last patient I visited this afternoon,' he said, 'is an old lady who lives at Highbury, and is just now much troubled by a question, touching the greater part of the third edition of William Lawrence's *Lectures on Physiology, Zoology, and the Natural History of Man*,—the lectures, whose free thought and free speech raised such a storm in the religious world on the occasion of their publication in 1819. My old friend, Mrs. .... the widow of .... has the large remainder of the third edition of those so-called scandalous lectures stowed away in her house.'

'How on earth,' I inquired, 'did that remainder come into the hands of an old lady living at Highbury?'

Dr. Gull answered my question with a circumstantial statement, which I introduced into an obituary notice of Sir William Lawrence, Bart., that appeared in the *Athenæum* of 13th July, 1867:

'The commotion caused by the Lectures,' I wrote in the *Athenæum*, holding as closely as possible to Dr. Gull's words, 'did not soon pass away; but, although they were liberally aided by denunciation, the published addresses met with no quick sale. The second edition appeared in 1822; and in the following year was issued a third edition, which disappeared from the trade under circumstances that gave rise to the generally believed, but not strictly accurate, story that the author had suppressed it. The fate of this edition deserves a place amongst the comic *ana* of literature. Only a few of its copies had been sold when Lawrence was implored to suppress it by an intimate friend, who believed the book to be no less hurtful to its writer's professional interests than injurious to young students. Lawrence, after long contention with his importunate friend, promised that when the third edition should be exhausted he would not publish a fourth until a considerable period of time had elapsed, but said he would not do so imprudent a thing as to expose himself to hostile criticism by actually suppressing the edition. On receiving this promise, the anxious friend bought the entire remainder of the edition, and packed it away in the cellar of an official residence which he then occupied. Years passed on, when the owner of these several hundreds of cellared copies of a pernicious work was much troubled in the last days of his life by his inability to decide what ought to be done with the mass of pestiferous literature. The worthy man did not like to destroy what it had cost a large sum of money to acquire; his conscience would not permit him to sell the hurtful stuff. Eventually he died without having taken any further steps in the matter. Succeeding to her husband's possessions, his widow also succeeded to his responsibility with regard to the bought-up edition, which was carried from the official residence, in which its purchaser died, to a house in a London suburb, whither the widow removed. There this third edition still remains in the house of its unfortunate owner, who is continually worrying her aged brain with questions as to what she, as a Christian lady, ought to do with those awful books. In all probability this fat remainder, about nine-tenths of a heavy edition of Lawrence's *Lectures*, will eventually float into the hands of book-dealers, who, if they are clever tradesmen, will put a high price on the volumes, in consideration of their remarkable history.'

My cousin, Henry Jeaffreson, M.D., at whose house in Finsbury Square I used to meet Dr. Gull, in the opening years of my manhood, was a younger son of John Jeaffreson, surgeon and apothecary of Upper Street, (or High Street, as it is called now-a-days,) Islington, and the maker of the practice, in which he was succeeded by his eldest son, John. In all, there have been three family doctors in Islington—father, son, and grandson—each of whom bore the name of John Jeaffreson. I will say a few words of the earliest of of these three John Jeaffresons, of Islington.

A son of the earlier of the two Christopher Jeaffresons, who were successively rectors of Tunstall-cum-Dunningworth, co. Suffolk, John Jeaffreson I., of Islington, was the younger brother of the clergyman who was honourably famous in pugilistic circles, whilst he officiated as domestic chaplain of the Marquis of Hertford. In his youth he was apprenticed to the famous surgeon, John Abernethy, of Bedford Row and St. Bartholomew's Hospital, who conceived a warm affection for him in his boyhood, and lived in cordial friendship with him, till death divided them. Bearing a strong personal resemblance to his father and brother, this John Jeaffreson was a tall and remarkably handsome man, and by his mental endowments and moral excellence became a social power in Islington and its neighbourhood. Enjoying a lucrative practice at Islington, when it was still a small village, he became more and more prosperous in his vocation as the village extended its bounds and became a populous suburb. Beloved by people of all sorts and conditions for his benevolence, he was commended by severe moralists as a bright example of goodness.

In several respects he differed notably from those of his neighbours who may be styled the principal gentlefolk of Islington. Whilst they held aloof from the prosperous Jews, who were numerous in Islington and the neighbouring village of Stoke Newington, he showed his superiority to a cruel prejudice by living socially with those of his Jewish neighbours who were persons of education and refinement. The surgeon was well aware that his friendly way of treating the educated Jews was displeasing to some of his Christian patients, that it would probably cause some of the most powerful of them to employ another doctor, that it might even incite whole sets and connections of his Christian patients to turn away from him. But he was not a man to be deterred by considerations of self-interest from doing what he thought right. Animated by the spirit of neighbourliness, that was so powerful in the county from which he had sprung, he thought the Jews had a moral title to the good-will of their Christian fellow-countrymen, and were debarred from the enjoyment of one of their chief social rights by the Christians, who refused to have intercourse with them, simply because they were Jews. This being his opinion, the strong and kindly man persisted in holding out the hand of good fellowship to the Jews, and being, in his suburban village, a protector of and advocate for them.

Now that Jews are received at Court, occupy some of the highest offices of the State, are admitted to the House of Lords, and intermarry with noble houses, it seems ridiculous to speak of a suburban doctor as having favoured and protected the members of so powerful a class some two or three generations since. It is, however, certain that, so late as a hundred, ninety, eighty years since, the Jews needed the social countenance of their Christian neighbours, and were grateful to the few Christians who gave it.

Whilst John Jeaffreson was making his fine practice at Islington. Dr. Aikin was ministering to his few patients at Stoke Newington, though he made the larger part of his income by literary labour. In her *Memories of Seventy Years*, Mrs. Le Breton, the grand-daughter of Dr. Aikin and the grand-niece of Mrs. Barbauld, wrote these words:

'My relations,' (to wit, Dr. Aikin and Mrs. Barbauld,) 'had not many congenial friends in the dull village of Stoke

Newington, when they first went there. There were a good many Quaker families—nice, kind, respectable people, but not inclined to visiting beyond their own set. There were also many Jewish families. One, old Mr. Israel, Dr. Aikin was called in to attend on his death-bed; he was the grandfather of the late Lord Beaconsfield.* Jews were then in a very different position from that they now enjoy. They were treated with the greatest coldness and dislike by the other inhabitants of the place, and not visited by anyone.—Mrs. Barbauld's benevolent liberality was shocked at this ungenerous treatment; and, being the secretary of a Book Society she had lately established, she with difficulty prevailed on the other members to admit one or two Jewish ladies into the society. They received the invitation with surprise and gratitude, one of them saying, with tears in her eyes, " I never thought to live to see the day when one of *us* would be allowed to join such a thing."'

The picture of that poor lady, shedding tears of gratitude for so faint a show of neighbourliness, disposes the sensitive reader to weep also. What a cold kindness to stir a human heart! Permission to subscribe to a book-club!

Living sociably with the Jews of Islington and Highbury, John Jeaffreson numbered amongst his friends Isaac D'Israeli, author of *Curiosities of Literature*, only son of the old Mr. Israel, of Stoke Newington, and father of the famous statesman, Benjamin Disraeli, who passed a considerable proportion of his childhood at Islington.

Though I have been told by sincere witnesses that

---

* From a passage in Lord Beaconsfield's memoir of his father, it would appear that 'old Mr. Israel,' as Mrs. Le Breton styles him, had at one time lived further away from London than Stoke Newington. The lady is, however, accurate in saying that Isaac D'Israeli's father lived in his closing years, and died, at Stoke Newington.

Isaac D'Israeli was a householder of Islington, and, during several of the earlier years of his married life, was tenant of a small house in the open country, north of the ground now occupied by Canonbury Square, I have failed to obtain conclusive evidence of the accuracy of the statement; and I am more inclined to think that he occupied furnished lodgings or a furnished house, held for a term of months, than that he was a regular and rated householder of Islington, during his terms of residence in the parish, which had enjoyed a high reputation for salubrity from an early date of the seventeenth century, and even within my own personal observation was visited and used by Londoners of the middle classes as a convenient 'health-resort.'

That Isaac D'Israeli often stayed at Islington after his marriage with Maria Bassevi, and that their children used to be taken to Islington in their infancy for country air, are matters of certainty. It is also an affair of sure evidence that, in his childhood, the future statesman was a frequent visitor at John Jeaffreson's house in Upper Street, and was the familiar playmate of the surgeon's children, and so great a favourite in their home that he was allowed, and indeed encouraged, to take extravagant liberties with his good-tempered host, who delighted in the little fellow's singular beauty, extraordinary intelligence, and audacious 'pranks.' One of these pranks will suffice to show that the marvellous child was not chiefly remarkable for reverence for his elders. Though he was no fop, (indeed, the badness of his coats and the general carelessness of his attire live to this day in the recollection of Islington gossips) John Jeaffreson was particular about the dressing of his superabundant curly tresses, which were drawn together in accordance with a rather antiquated fashion, and tied with ribbon into a short loop-queue at the back of his neck. It struck little Ben, *œtat.* six or seven, that the doctor would look better without this appendage to his hair.

As he was a very early riser, it was John Jeaffreson's daily practice to retire to his consulting-room after his mid-day meal, and sitting in a chair to refresh himself with half-an-hour of sound slumber, before he started on his afternoon's 'round' to his numerous patients. On awaking from one of these sound naps, the surgeon saw on the table what he recognized as his loop-queue, with its silken fillet. Little Ben, the pet of the whole house, had stolen noiselessly upon the surgeon, and with a pair of sharp scissors had removed the tail without rousing the sleeper. Springing from his chair, the tall doctor went in pursuit of the urchin who had offered him so strange an indignity, and, after chasing the 'little Pickle' upstairs and downstairs, captured him in the hall, to the extreme delight of a party of small children, whose laughter made the whole house ring from basement to garret. After tickling the lovely 'little rip' for a punishment till he almost cried from laughter, the big man took the small boy in his arms, and carried him into the garden for another game of romps. Instead of destroying it, John Jeaffreson and his wife preserved the queue as a memorial of the angelic devilry of the lovely child, whose astonishing cleverness had already moved them to predict that he would not live to old age, without winning a place amongst the celebrities of his period. The hair of the queue still exists in the form of a bracelet which one of John Jeaffreson's still surviving daughters guards as an interesting relic.

John Jeaffreson's oldest daughter, Amelia, was born in the same year as Benjamin Disraeli, and in their tender childhood they exchanged vows of perpetual devotion to one another. Of course, it was settled by the precocious and romantic infants that they would marry one another as soon as they should attain to a fit age. Instead of being broken in a few months, after the wont of such compacts by nurslings, this engagement endured for years, before it perished from separation and the birth of new interests. Throughout successive years, a separation of a few months only intensified the mutual affection of the two little spouses. Absence made the heart of each grow fonder to the other, and the arrangement, which caused their elders not a little laughter, was regarded with equal tenderness and seriousness by the two young people. On coming to the fit age, of which she spoke with suitable gravity to her mother, on asking for the maternal consent to her arrangement with that 'dear boy Ben,' Miss Amelia Jeaffreson married one of her first cousins, the Reverend Christopher Jeaffreson, a chaplain in the East India Company's service, and lived to see another clergyman, her only son, take to his heart for better or worse one of the daughters of William Makepeace Thackeray's old schoolmate and Cambridge friend, James Reynold Young. Living as happily with the Oriental chaplain as Benjamin Disraeli lived with the lady to whom he made so admirable a husband, Mrs. Jeaffreson never shed tears for having missed wedlock with her 'first choice;' but in her declining age she sometimes spoke to her children with mingled tenderness and drollery of the sincerity and fervour of her infantile attachment to the little boy who had lived to be Lord Beaconsfield.

Since Lord Beaconsfield's departure from this life, it has been the use of certain journals at each anniversary of his death-day to publish letters of enquiry for the place of his birth. The statesman's birth has been assigned to several different places. With his own hand he represented that he was born at St. Mary Axe, and also that he was born in the chambers of the Adelphi, which Isaac Disraeli ceased to inhabit at some time shortly before his marriage. It is certain that the celebrated man was not born at the Adelphi chambers, and the statement that he drew his first breath at St. Mary Axe was a mere jest, which he did not conceive anyone would take seriously. A large house at the south-west corner of Bloomsbury Square is sometimes pointed to as the mansion in which he was born, and there is some weak evidence that the famous Tory statesman, who liked to obscure the details of the early chapters of his personal story, gave some countenance to the erroneous notion that he was born there. Because Isaac Disraeli paid rates in the opening years of his married life as the occupier of a house in King's Street, Holborn, it has been assumed too confidently that Disraeli the Younger came to life in that street. There is no need to produce evidence that a lady's first-born child is not invariably born at her usual place of abode. As Islington was a favourite health-resort of prosperous Londoners in the earlier decades of the present century, and as Isaac Disraeli and his wife were in the habit of staying in the healthy suburban village in the opening years of their wedded life, there would be nothing strange in the statement that the young husband and wife were resting in the Upper Street of the bright and pleasant village, whilst they were the legal occupiers of a house in foggy Holborn.

The story respecting the place and circumstances of the Younger Disraeli's birth, which John Jeaffreson I., of Islington, used to tell in his vigorous old age, and also in time before he had crossed the line that divides middle age from old age, was to this effect. In December, 1805, Isaac Disraeli was dwelling, together with his wife, in a house adjoining the surgeon's house in Upper Street, Islington, when Mrs. Disraeli was seized with the pains of labour, sooner than she had expected. Promptly answering a summons from his next-door neighbours, the surgeon entered their house none too soon. Provided neither with a nurse nor with clothing suitable to the little stranger who was on the point of entering the world, the sick lady would have been in an especially miserable plight, had not Mrs. Jeaffreson (the surgeon's wife) bestirred herself to send a competent female attendant to the sufferer, and also to supply from her own stores the needful linen and raiment for the infant.

As he was a man of clear and vigorous mind when he first told this story, as he was not a man to 'romance' and weave idle tales, as he was a man of good fame and condition, and had no conceivable motive for saying he attended Mrs. Disraeli on the occasion of her famous son's birth, if he were doubtful about the matter, the surgeon's testimony must at least be rated as the testimony of a credible witness. If he erred, his error was guiltless of bad faith. It is difficult to think he was mistaken in aught he said so positively of Isaac Disraeli and his wife, whom he numbered amongst his familiar friends, and of their eldest son who in his childhood was the favourite playmate of the surgeon's children. So sober and sensible a man cannot have been the mere fool of his own disordered fancy in thinking he attended at the accouchement of a lady who was his intimate friend. It is, however, just conceivable that, having attended Mrs. Disraeli at one of her several accouchements, he may, after a lapse of years, have misremembered some circumstances of the affair,—may, for instance, have thought it her *first*, when it was in fact her second or third confinement.

It being far more interesting to know the places in which celebrated men passed the happiest seasons of their childhood, than to know the particular houses in which they entered this life, I should not be pained to learn that, instead of being born in a particular house of the Upper Street, Islington, Benjamin Disraeli drew his first breath in some other parish in or near London. As the evidence that he was born in the Upper Street, Islington, is perhaps something less than conclusive, I am not wholly without doubt whether or no he came to life there. But it is a matter of certainty that the future statesman spent much of his childhood in Islington, that he passed some of the brightest hours of his childhood at my cousin's house in the Upper Street, and that in his youth he used to appear from time to time at the festivities of his old friends at Islington, even up to the time when he flashed upon the world as the author of *Vivian Grey.*

CHAPTER VIII.

MY FIRST AND SECOND NOVELS.

My first Novel, *Crewe Rise*—Messrs. Hurst and Blackett, Publishers—Mr. S. W. Fullom, Author of *The Marvels of Science*—Edward Whitty, Author of *Friends of Bohemia*—Young John Parker, Publisher and Editor of *Fraser's Magazine*—Holidays at Cheam and Boulogne, in the Channel Islands and the Suffolk Woodland—Changes in the Woodland—The New Agriculture—Steady Impoverishment of Suffolk Farmers—Weeks spent in Devon, at Exeter and Honiton—Months spent in Paris—M. Ricord, the famous Parisian Surgeon—Thomas Chambers Wakley, Coroner for Middlesex, and Proprietor and Editor of the *Lancet*—James Fernandez Clarke, M.R.C.S., Medical Journalist—I act as Hospital-Reporter for the *Lancet*.

AFTER settling into my quarters and duties at the boarding-house for Carthusian and Pauline schoolboys, I was quick to begin my first novel, which I composed for the most part as I walked to and fro between Charterhouse Square and the suburban home of the young man whom I was preparing for Oxford, and committed to paper at night, when my schoolboys had gone to bed. Begun when I was *ætat.* twenty-one, and finished within twelve months of its commencement, this boyish and artless performance was without loss of time submitted to the critical consideration of one of the literary tasters and advisers of Messrs. Hurst and Blackett, who had succeeded to the famous publishing business of the late Mr. Colburn of Great Marlborough Street. When I put my manuscript into the hands of the well-known publishers, I was told by a gentleman of their staff that the precious packet would receive due consideration, but I must not be impatient and think myself slighted, should several weeks elapse before I received another communication from 'the House.' The seasonable advice did not preserve me from impatience; but my lively fear that my tale would be declined by the publishers was extinguished by a letter from 13, Great Marlborough Street, that caused my heart to beat with joy. Messrs. Hurst and Blackett had been advised to publish my tale, and the writer of the welcome letter invited me to a conference.

On the following day I walked to 13, Great Marlborough Street, and was there received by Mr. S. W. Fullom, a tall, well-dressed, and rather stately gentleman. Literary eminence is so fleeting a possession that I question whether twenty readers of this page can remember aught of Mr. Fullom and his performances. But in 1853, the year in which I made his aquaintance, Mr. Fullom was a personage. Besides being the chief literary adviser of the Great Marlborough Street publishers, he was the author of *The Marvels of Science, and Their Testimony to Holy Writ*, a work that ran with speed to a seventh edition, and was soon followed by *The Great Highway*, which one of Mr. Punch's flippant writers re-christened *The Fulham*

Road. Decorated by the King of Hanover, to whom he had dedicated *The Marvels*, and extolled for his learning in the religious journals, Mr. Fullom was a celebrity, and now he is of no more account than any of the several authors of his period, whose works one and all fell still-born from the press.

As the offer which this gentleman had been instructed to make me was a fair proposal, I sold to Messrs. Hurst and Blackett the right of publishing a certain number of copies of my first distinct work, and in the season of 1854 the story was offered to readers under the title of *Crewe Rise.* Twelve months since I re-perused that story, and found it rather less feeble and contemptible than I thought it some five-and-thirty years agone, when I vowed never again to open one of its volumes. But though I think something less bitterly and disdainfully of my first book than I did when I made the vow, and at the same time put the offensive volumes out of sight, I am still of opinion that no weaker book ever won the approval of a considerable number of distinctly clever people. The book certainly was not a financial failure, for the edition (a rather large edition for a first novel by a young and quite unknown writer) was sold to the last copy, though not with the rapidity that would have disposed the publishers to issue a second edtion. It is remarkable that the artless and far from exciting narrative achieved the kind of success that is called a *succès d'estime.* Commended in journals whose judgment of literary aspirants seldom erred in the direction of mercy, the story hit the taste of a few critics who were regarded by their comrades of the ungentle craft as especially intolerant of the defects, that were conspicuous in every chapter of the tame and unskilful tale. Edward Whitty, whose tongue and pen were no less caustic than brilliant, came out of his way to make my acquaintance, because he had been stirred by the book, of which I soon became ashamed.

'You know nothing of the novelist's art, you don't know the rudiments of it,' he said, in his frank and hearty way, 'but you know human nature, and when you've learnt the rules and tricks of the business, you'll be a master of it. Your story is full of the bad faults of a raw apprentice, but it caught hold of me and made me blubber like a woman.'

Young John Parker, of the publishing-house of Parker and Son, West Strand, was neither a fool nor chiefly remarkable for sweetness of nature. On the contrary, he was an especially clever and strong-headed man. He was also a chronic invalid whose temper had been embittered by bodily suffering. Though people used to speak of him as 'young John Parker,' to distinguish him from his father and partner, he was a man of middle age at the commencement of our acquaintance. Youthful inexperience was therefore in no degree accountable for his judgment of literary aspirants. Yet this keen and hard-headed man of affairs and letters thought so well of my first puerile book that he invited me to contribute to *Fraser*, and after reading my second novel, and forming his own opinion of it, accepted it for the magazine, of which he was the sole editor. Written in 1854, and accepted for the magazine when I was only twenty-three years of age, *Hinchbrook*—a long novel of fifty-two chapters—appeared in *Fraser* in the following year.

'What a lucky fellow you are, Jeff,' said Tom Girtin, when I told him that, besides inviting me to contribute to the magazine, John Parker the Younger had accepted my novel for *Fraser*.

'My fear is that the luck won't last,' I replied, gloomily; for, even whilst I was elated by my good fortune, I was troubled by a strong opinion that it exceeded my desert. I was already out of conceit with my new story, though I had written it with a delightful and steadily growing opinion of its goodness. All my books have affected me in the same way. I never wrote a book without exulting in its goodness, or launched one upon the world without thinking it a miserable performance. And, when a book by my pen has fallen from my good opinion, I never again hold it in high esteem. No one can think more disdainfully of my earlier stories than I do; and the short-comings of my least faulty books have always been more apparent to me than to my severest critics.

During the two years and six or seven months of my first residence at 36, Charterhouse Square, I often left town for change of air and scene. I have pleasant memories of a trip that I made to Jersey, the first of several visits I paid the Channel Islands before my hair began to turn grey, and also of a short holiday I passed with Thornbury at Cheam, before his uncle Bouchier ceased to be curate of that parish, and settled for the remainder of his years in Wiltshire, as rector of Fonthill-Bishops. It must have been in the summer of 1854 that I crossed the Channel for first time, and in the company of Horace Gregory (a Doctors-Commons proctor, who just about a year since ceased to draw his pension from the Paymaster General), and spent from ten to fourteen days in and about Boulogne.

Thrice and again also I went to Brighton, where my incomparable eldest sister and my good sister Anne had become the mistresses of a girls'-school, that under their clever management became the most prosperous of the Brighton schools for young gentlewomen. And at least twice a-year I ran from town to my old home in the Suffolk Woodland, where my dear father and mother made as much of me as they could have done had I taken a first-class at Oxford, and gave cordial welcome to the friends I brought with me from the great town.

They were pleasant holidays in the old country; but it did not heighten my enjoyment of them, and of still later trips to the dear familiar haunts, to observe how steadily the neighbourhood was losing its old prosperity and picturesqueness. In those far-away days, I seldom went to Framlingham without hearing that yet another modest estate had passed from a small to a great landowner, or without seeing new signs of the social revolution which had for years occasioned my parents many a fit of dejection. Houses, that within my memory had been the picturesque homes of gentlefolk, were seen by their neglected gardens to have become the dwellings of mere tenant-farmers, too mean to care for flowers and ornamental shrubs, or too poor to cultivate them at an avoidable expense of a few pounds a-year. In places where several small farms had been made into one large holding, one saw that the houses, which were no longer required by farmers, had been divided into tenements for farm-labourers. It was about this time that one of the stateliest old halls near Framlingham—a grand old red-brick structure that had been for generations the Capital House of the Warners of Parham—was pulled down, so that no vestige but a workman's cottage was left of so interesting a residence.

Whatever good it may have done the country in other respects, the New Agriculture has done nothing to increase but much to diminish the picturesqueness of my native district. On discovering they were hurtful to the crops, by guarding them from breeze and sunshine, the New Agriculture lowered the height of the hedges, and had recourse to other measures for making the Woodland less woody. If the disfigurement of the country had resulted in the enrichment of the farmers, I would have pardoned the New Agriculture for making the parts about Framlingham so much less picturesque than they used to be. I do not say the New Agriculture did wrong in reducing the hedges. On the contrary, I believe it to have done right from the mere agriculturist's point of view. But, alas! ever since the New Agriculture cut down the fences, the tillers of the soil have steadily become poorer and yet poorer.

Whilst *Hinchbrook* was running through *Fraser*, I struck work in Charterhouse Square, and left London for several months, running in the first instance to Devonshire for a few weeks, that were divided between Exeter and Honiton, and then going to Paris for a stay of some months. Writing in this year of grace from mere recollection, I can state neither the month in which I left London, nor the exact time I spent in Devon, nor the route by which I journeyed from Devon to Paris. My memory of this period of my career is hazy and uncertain about several matters which I would fain recall precisely. On the contrary, some passages and incidents of my sojourn in the French capital live in my memory as though they were affairs of six months since. Through the kind offices of the eminent Parisian surgeon, Ricord, to whom I carried a letter of introduction from my fellow-townsman and staunch friend, Henry Thompson (in time's course to become a leader of the London surgeons), I gained admission to several of the Paris hospitals, and was allowed to visit their wards, as though I were one of their registered students. That I cared to watch the practice of the Parisian surgeons and physicians for no practical purpose, when I had made up my mind to enter one of the Inns of Court and study for the Bar, may be regarded as evidence of my taste and fitness for the profession, which I abandoned too lightly in my boyhood.

I rather think it was after my return from Paris to London, though it may have preceded my stay in the French capital, that I figured for awhile at the London hospitals as reporter for the *Lancet*. In justice to the leading journal of Surgery and Medicine, I should state how it came to pass that for a brief term (say some three months) I was permitted to occupy a place which would have been more suitably filled by a qualified surgeon. At a time when circumstances had deprived him of the services of the surgeon who had for several years acted as writer of the 'Mirror of Hospital Practice,' Mr. Thomas Chambers Wakley (coroner for Middlesex and editor-in-chief of the journal which he had originated) experienced some difficulty in finding an altogether suitable successor to the gentleman who had retired from the *Lancet*. At the beginning of this difficulty, Mr. James Fernandez Clarke, of 23, Gerard Street, Soho, M.R.C.S., a medical journalist, who for many years acted as Mr. Wakley's editorial assistant and right-hand man, enquired of Henry Thompson, F.R.C.S., whether he knew of a young surgeon, of sufficient journalistic address, who would like to fill the vacant place on the *Lancet*, or anyone who, without being a legally qualified surgeon, could and would act as *interim*-reporter at the hospitals, until an altogether fit person could be discovered for the post. As he could not point to a surgeon who would be likely to satisfy Mr. Wakley's requirements, Henry Thompson—ever thoughtful for my interest and welfare—suggested that Mr. Clarke should ask me to act as a 'stop-gap' reporter. Mr. Clarke, who knew a good deal of me, and in his student-days had been on friendly terms with my elder brother at University College Hospital, was quick to act on my friend's suggestion, and ere another week had passed Mr. Wakley accepted me as his reporter for the hospitals, after giving me clearly to understand that, however efficiently I might discharge the functions of the reportership, he should be looking out for a surgeon to hold the office, which no one but a legally qualified surgeon should occupy permanently. The event certainly justified Thompson's assertion that I was quite enough of a surgeon and physician for the place, whose functions were in no respect critical. Agreeable to me at the time, my brief connection with the *Lancet* was in several respects beneficial to me, after I had retired from the office to which I was admitted merely as a 'stop-gap' functionary. Enlarging my circle of acquaintance amongst the leaders of the profession, which several influences had trained me to regard with affectionate reverence, it gave me a few familiar associates whom in the course of years I had reason to number amongst my warmest and stoutest friends. Moreover, I am indebted to my brief connection with the *Lancet* for the pleasure I still take in startling my younger and newer friends of the faculty with a reference to the days when I was a worker on the 'medical press.'

CHAPTER IX.

JAMES HANNAY.

The *Idler* Magazine—My third Novel—Hannay 'at Home'—His charming Wife and lovely Children—His personal Appearance—Gabriel Rossetti's Portrait of Hannay—'Latinless Lubbers'—'Blood and Culture'—Examples of Hannay's Vocabulary—Hannay the Elder—Father and Son—Thackeray's strong Liking for Hannay—Thackeray's 'Thoroughbred little Fighting Cock—The Tumbler Club—The Tumblers—Quarrel and Reconciliation—Hannay stands for the Dumfries Burghs—Canonbury and Gunnersbury—Doran's Dinner-Party—Misdirected Complaisance—John Bruce, F.S.A.—His Modesty and Embarrassment—A dormant Baronetcy—Bruces of the Suffolk Woodland—A long Walk on a cold Night—Hannay's frequent Visits to Hatton House, Hatton Garden—John George Edgar—The 'Scot of a past Age'—His Opinion of the Queen's Lineage.

IN the year of our Lord, 1856, I passed quickly from slight acquaintanceship to close friendship with James Hannay, wrote a short story entitled *Gertrude's Guardian* for Edward Wilberforce's brilliant, but alas! short-lived, magazine, the *Idler*, associated with the Tumblers, ate dinners in Lincoln's Inn hall, and wrote my third novel, which was published in the autumn-season by Messrs. Hurst and Blackett under the title of *Isabel, The Young Wife and The Old Love*.

In his later time, when he had grown unhealthily fat and unwieldily corpulent, James Hannay retained little of the personality that fascinated me at the outset of our familiar intercourse. Descended from a gentle Scotch house, that entitled him to speak of himself as 'a cadet of the ancient Galloway family of Hannay of Sorbie,' Hannay was my senior by just four years, and very much my superior in literary experience and address, when he first delighted me with his brilliant talk, sunny humour, and eccentric views. Put into the Queen's navy in his fourteenth year, he quitted the service in his nineteenth year, and came to London at a time when domestic reverses required him to maintain himself. Some ten years later, he had established himself amongst the *littérateurs* of the metropolis, had married a young gentlewoman of uncommon beauty and goodness, and was living at Islington with his wife and two or three lovely babes, in a small house that overlooked the New River. Unless my memory is at fault, the little house stood within a stone's throw of the Lower Road, and was one of a lot of similar houses, that bore the pleasant name of Pleasant Row. A frequent visitor at this house, I was so fortunate as to win the favourable regard of Mrs. Hannay, who, according to her husband's serious and dramatic account of the affair, preserved my life from premature extinction by insisting that, instead of sending the essay to the press, he should commit to the flames a certain article, which he had written against me at the spur of generous indignation.

'By Jove, Jeff,' Hannay remarked to me, in the

most tragic tone of his agreeable voice, 'had it not been for her intervention, you would not be alive at this moment, to learn how she saved you from destruction. Had the lightning of that article struck you, you would have fallen dead. Upon the whole, I am well pleased that my arm was stayed as I was on the point of hurling the deadly bolt.'

The droll story points to one and more than one of Mrs. Hannay's womanly traits. Ever thoughtful for the interests of her husband, whom she idolized, she was ever on the alert to moderate the fiercer impulses of his fervid nature, and, as he was alive to the excellence of her judgment, he yielded to her will even in his most erratic moments. A sweeter or more conscientious woman than James Hannay's first wife never ruled a fond husband. Her voice was ever soft, gentle, and low. It was also sweetly musical and powerful for right on all questions offered to her wifely discretion. The dear lady, who preserved me from premature destruction, was an influence making for the peace and contentment of all who came under her gentle sway.

Slightly defective in height, something too short in the neck, and something too broad across the shoulders, Hannay's compact and active body was neither elegant nor stately. But his head was in every respect a head to be viewed with critical admiration. The high, broad, white forehead was surmounted by a fine show of dark curly hair. Nature's cunning hand had given his round face the most delicate contours, especially about the mouth, whose nervous lips (so straight and expressionless in later time) curled and curved as they were seen to curl and curve in the pencil-sketch which Gabriel Rossetti made of him, when they were both on manhood's threshold. But Hannay's striking face was chiefly remarkable for the splendour and beauty of its large violet-blue eyes,—so deep and dark a violet-blue that in certain lights they showed like black eyes. Strangely large and beautiful for colour, they were extraordinarily expressive eyes,—flashing grandly when he was stirred by anger, and overflowing with merriment when he was merry. Moreover, this striking and attractive head was pervaded by the air of distinction which is rarely seen in men who are incapable of achieving greatness.

In politics, Hannay was at heart a sincere and thorough conservative, unwavering in his devotion to his principles and party; but his conservatism was so tricked and bedecked with the conceits of Young England romanticism, that some people were more inclined to ridicule it than to believe in it. Some of his political views and social theories were in themselves very amusing, and he rendered them yet more diverting by the rhetorical extravagances with which he set them forth in his orations upon the pernicious temper and tendencies of the times. Holding that no one ought to take a leading part in politics unless he were a gentleman of ancient descent or a classical scholar, he overflowed with disdain for the many political leaders, who were neither scholars nor persons of gentle lineage. In the same spirit he spoke derisively of journalists, who were devoid of classic culture, as 'latinless lubbers.' And, in revenge, the 'latinless lubbers' spoke derisively of his views as 'blood and culture' views, and even nick-named the distasteful satirist Mr. Blood-and-Culture.

Teaching strange doctrine, Hannay took strange liberties with the English language for the more effectual diffusion of his sentiments,—sometimes using words of his own invention, and sometimes using a familiar word in an unfamiliar sense. At the outset of my friendship with him, I took occasion to ask him what he meant by 'blogg,' but he forbore to satisfy my reasonable curiosity. In the course of a few weeks, however, I discovered that 'Blogg' (with a large B) was the name of an imaginary individual, who was supposed to represent in the most offensive manner the temper and tone of the lower *bourgeoisie*, and that *blogg* (with a small *b*) was a symbol for all that was most disgusting in the prejudices and passions of the same unlovely class. 'Pleb' also was a word often heard on Hannay's lips; and I learnt, from vigilant attention to my friend's utterances, that he used the word as a contraction for 'plebeian,' and also in the sense of the latin word 'plebs.' When they speak of a man as 'a dog,' most persons wish to signify their lively contempt for the man of whom they are speaking. It was not so with the equally whimsical and brilliant Hannay, who often applied the word 'dog' to a gentleman he held habitually in high respect, but for the moment regarded with disfavour. At a time when he had recently failed to get a small appointment from a conservative minister. he remarked to me,

'By Jove, Jeff, if those *dogs* don't soon acknowledge my services in a proper manner, I'll take my flag over to the other camp!'

The reader may not imagine that Hannay was capable of ratting, or had the faintest thought of ratting, when he uttered these picturesque words. The speech was only my friend's light and airy way of saying that, if those dogs of ministers were wanting in proper gratitude to him, something terrible would happen. 'Tap' was another word he used in an unfamiliar sense. Blood, according to Hannay, was a peculiar property of our aristocratic houses, that passed from one house to another through a tap. He would speak of a man, who was well-descended in one and no more than one of his remote ancestral lines, as a person of a single tap. A man, whose gentle blood came to his veins from several sources, was the outcome of divers taps. In speaking of people whose ancestral story showed them to have proceeded from half-a-hundred noble or gentle stocks, the Professor of Blood and Culture would observe that they were drawn from countless taps.—If they were brought together and put in alphabetical order, the new words that Hannay coined for his oratorical convenience, and the old words which he endowed with new significance, would form a large vocabulary.

Delighting to expatiate on the grandeur and romantic vicissitudes of patrician houses, with which he had no ancestral connection, Hannay did not omit to speak much and handsomely of the Hannays of Sorbie, and all the other groups of Hannays who were genealogically related to his particular family. There were times, when he would have been better company had he said less of the virtues and alliances of his progenitors. I recall with amusement how his father (a charming old gentleman) on a certain occasion checked his brilliant son for being rather too eloquent about his ancestors. I was sitting one Sunday afternoon with the father and son in the dining-room of the Pleasant Row house, when Mr. Hannay the Elder, putting down his tumbler of whisky-toddy, checked my friend's loquacity on his favourite topic by remarking gently,

'There, there, Jamie, you have said more than enough about your pedigree. Don't you see you are just wearying your friend with o'er-much speech about people in whom he of course is not greatly interested? The Hannays were no such great people as you like to think them. One of your grandfathers, Jamie, was a highly respeckit Scotch shopkeeper, and I wish I could say as much for my ain son.'

For a moment my heart bled for my friend as these words came to him at one end of the table from the lips of his father, sitting directly opposite him. But Jamie was neither abashed nor rendered in any way uncomfortable by the parental rebuke, accompanied though it was by what I of course regarded as a domestic revelation, that could not fail to shock my friend and pain him acutely. On the contrary, the staggering speech brought a smile of amusement to Jamie's handsome face, and caused his magnificent eyes to overflow with silent laughter.

'Very good, wasn't it?' Hannay the Younger observed, in a low voice, as he covered me with his merry eyes. 'The dad has a happy vein of humour, and I never knew him in better trim.'

Half-an-hour later, when I rose to take leave of my friend, who had been entertaining me with a mid-day dinner, followed by whisky-toddy, James Hannay declared his purpose of attending me on my homeward way, at least as far as the *Angel* tavern, and on our way to that point, he was again at pains to impress on me that, in proclaiming him the grandson of 'a highly respeckit Scotch shop-keeper,' his sire had merely obeyed 'the happy vein of humour,' which sometimes moved him to utter the most astounding and groundless inventions with a seriousness that often caused the unwary to accept them as realistic statements. The father and son between them had so fairly puzzled me that I pursued my solitary course from the *Angel* corner to Charterhouse Square, in doubt whether I should believe the Elder Hannay to have spoken the simple truth, or should accept the gloss put upon his father's words by Hannay the Younger. And to this day I am uncertain which of the two views I should take.

Delighting in James Hannay's colloquial smartness and pleasantry, Thackeray thought highly of his literary address, and even admired the ferocity with which he fought his controversial battles.

'Hannay is a boy after my heart!' the white-headed novelist said to me more than once. 'He is a thoroughbred little fighting-cock! You can't find his match in the literary cock-pit for pluck and endurance. He is a perfect bird of his particular sort. Examine him as closely as you please, you won't find a white feather in him.'

Admiring Hannay greatly, Thackeray did more than a little for his advantage. Employing him to write the notes to the lectures on *The Humourists*, the great novelist induced his publishers to offer the author of *Singleton Fontenoy* four hundred pounds for another story, which for some reason or reasons Hannay never wrote. It was also to Thackeray that Hannay owed his introduction to the *Quarterly Review*. In his well-known obituary memoir of the author of *Vanity Fair*, Hannay spoke of himself as 'one whom Thackeray had loaded with benefits.'

I may be at fault in thinking Hannay was the originator of *The Tumbler*, the first of the several tavern-clubs to which I belonged before I became a member of *Our Club*, but it is an affair of sure recollection with me, that he was the controlling spirit of the brotherhood of authors, artists, journalists, and literary aspirants, who used to come together once a-week for social intercourse in the principal room of a public-house, standing in some street between Covent Garden and St. Martin's Lane, and that he closed the debate on the fittest name for the new society by saying, 'We are going to meet here not for dinner but for tumblers and talk. Let our club then be called *The Tumbler*, and let its members style themselves *The Tumblers*.' That there was need for this short-lived society appeared from the quickness with which it doubled and re-doubled its members. Alas! how few of the Tumblers remain! Kebbel is still writing in reviews and newspapers, Stigand still shows to the fore in the Consular Service, Edward Wilberforce is a placeman of the Law Courts, Sutherland Edwards still gives us delightful books, and this weary scribe continues to drive his far from ready pen; but gentle Sotheby, handsome Willshire Staunton Austin, brilliant Hannay, caustic and tender-hearted Whitty, honest Hodder, good Thornbury, clever William Jerrold, rollicking Mortimer Collins, manly and eccentric John George Edgar, and a score other clever fellows, whose faces come about me whenever I think of the earliest of my tavern-clubs, have all passed away.

I had not been on familiar terms with Hannay for many months, when our friendship was ruffled by a breeze. Without any purpose of annoying him, I wrote (in my third novel) about some of his Blood-and-Culture views with a levity that instead of moving him to laughter stirred him to wrath. Like many another professional satirist, Hannay had no liking for satire that tended to make him ridiculous; and on reading *Isabel, The Young Wife and The Old Love*, he so warmly resented my flippant way of dealing with his desire to restore the feudal relations of the higher and lower classes of society, that he took the earliest opportunity of showing his aversion for me.

The offensive book was in the first week of existence, when Hannay came upon me in Russell Square one Monday morning, and, instead of greeting me with his usual cordiality, gave me the 'cut direct.' Passing me in silence, he regarded me disdainfully as he went onwards to the British Museum. As both of us were just then assiduous and daily readers in the Museum library, he had frequent opportunities during the week for showing his hostility to me in the same impressive way, and he made the most of every opportunity. The article that would have slain me had it been published was written during that week; and if it accorded with the disdainful and scathing look which Hannay gave me whenever we met one another in or near the Museum reading-room, that review of my novel must have been a deadly composition. To this day I tremble at the thought of all that might have resulted from the delivery of the terrific bolt. But, for once, the gods were fighting for me. Gentle Mrs. Hannay was on my side. So was her father-in-law—'the dad,' as Hannay used to style him with much filial tenderness and no irreverence—who had so far taken me into his favour, as to declare me about the most agreeable of his son's literary friends. So were certain members of *The Tumbler*, to whom Hannay had spoken about the indignity I had offered him. Hence it came to pass that on Monday—the seventh day from the Monday on which Hannay had 'cut me' in Russell Square—I was surprised, as I sat over my work in the British Museum reading-room, by the sound of a familiar voice speaking to me these pleasant words:

'I am of opinion, Jeff, that we had better put an end to our little misunderstanding by shaking hands.'

Of course I sprang from my chair, and, seizing my friend's hand, shook it warmly. After shaking hands, we withdrew from the Museum for half-an-hour, and consecrated our reconciliation with suitable drinks.

The next year (1857) is memorable in the annals of the delightful author of *Singleton Fontenoy*, as the year in whose March he made at the general election a daring and unsuccessful attempt to wrest the seat for the Dumfries Burghs from Mr. William Ewart. From what source the young and far from affluent *littérateur* obtained the money for the immediate costs of this endeavour to get into parliament he did not inform me; but I remember the merry look his face wore, when, after repeating to me some of the happiest passages of his Address to the Electors, he remarked,

'I dated my address from Canonbury, instead of Islington. Everybody at Dumfries knows that Islington is a third-rate suburb of London; but in their ignorance of this over-grown capital the voters of my native borough will think that Canonbury is my country-seat. Canonbury rings upon the ear with historic significance. It sounds as well as Gunnersbury.'

Towards the close of this same year—to wit, on a certain Friday of November, 1857—I went to No. 4, Pembroke Terrace, Kensington, (the little house within a stone's-throw of Holland Park Gate, which Doran inhabited till he moved to 21, Royal Crescent, Notting Hill,) and there dined with Hannay at a very pleasant party, where he displayed several of his social peculiarities in a very entertaining manner. Mr. and Mrs. Hepworth Dixon and John Bruce, F.S.A., the honourably-remembered antiquary and archæological editor, were of the party; and, unless my memory is at fault, Dr. and Mrs. Doran had amongst their other guests Miss Geraldine Jewsbury. Without being too numerous for the small dining-room, the party would have been too large for the table, had another couple sought places at the merry board.

Hannay, sometimes a social force making more for

discord than harmony at a festal gathering, was in an exceptionally complaisant mood, and had clearly come to the party in a humour to make an agreeable impression on the lady who was entertaining him for the first time. It was not his wont to overflow with conversational blandishments, but on the present occasion he had civil speech for everyone. After complimenting Doran on the excellence of his Latinity, he staggered John Bruce by declaring him an unquestionable descendant of the royal stock whose name he bore, and to whose dignity he had given new lustre by his scholarly achievements. Blushing with confusion at a compliment that accorded so ill with his modesty and the truth of his ancestral story, poor Bruce faintly protested against Hannay's misconception.

'Indeed, Mr. Hannay,' gasped the sufferer from misdirected complaisance, 'you are quite at fault in regarding me as a descendant of kings. I can assure you I am in no way related to any one of the historic Bruces.'

But instead of accepting these disavowals of noble extraction, which he was pleased to regard as mere indications of the ingenuous modesty not uncommon in gentlemen of humble fortune and splendid ancestry, Hannay reiterated his assertion respecting the antiquary's lineage, and produced evidence in support of the statement. In his desire to convince Bruce of his royal worth, he brought his chair nearer and nearer to the seat of the greatly embarrassed 'chieftain' in spite of himself, or rather to the seat of the lady who sat between the persecutor and his victim;

and in order that she might not be thrown to the ground by the advancing professor of 'blood and culture,' the rather nervous and very much amused gentlewoman retreated on poor Bruce, who in like manner shifting his chair retreated towards the hostess, considerably to the disarrangement of the party on one side of the dinner-table. Bruce would have fared better had he possessed the colloquial readiness which enabled Mr. Russell, editor of the *Scotsman*, to bring Hannay to order, when the latter had set an Edinburgh dinner-table in a roar by declaring himself one of Mrs. Russell's cousins, and adding that there was a baronetcy dormant in the lady's family. In acknowledging this announcement, by which Hannay had designed to afford Mr. Russell lively gratification, the editor of the *Scotsman* remarked that, though he was pleased to hear of his relationship to the Hannays of Sorbie, he would rather have been told of a dormant bank-note than of the dormant baronetcy.

Unfortunately for his peace of mind, conversational smartness was not one of poor Bruce's social gifts, and he was the more troubled by the attempt to make him figure as a princely personage, because he was confronted by a young man from Suffolk, whom he had reason to regard as fully cognizant of his domestic story. Now that good John Bruce, his amiable wife, his 'rip of a brother,' and all the other members of his familiar connection have gone to the undiscovered country, I shall pain no living person by showing how wildly wrong Hannay was in styling my friend 'a Scottish gentleman of more than noble lineage.'

The gentle scholar and learned antiquary was the son of an eccentric and rather cranky Scotch tailor, who, after begetting two sons (whom in due course he educated for liberal professions), and making a moderate fortune in his humble vocation, bought a house and some two hundred acres of land at Rendham, within five miles of Framlingham, to which small estate he retired in his old age, when he ceased to measure his customers and make their clothes with artful care. The old tailor chose a place of retirement so far away from his native land and former city, because he thought that in a secluded district of the Suffolk Woodland he should have a better chance of escaping the social infamy of having been in his earlier time a tradesman and a needleman, than he would have in any corner of Scotland. For that matter, the old fellow might just as well have remained in his 'ain countree.' He had barely settled in my native Woodland, when, on the death of the fifth Earl of Rochford, the White House and appurtenant farms of Easton, near Framlingham, passed from the Nassaus to the Hamiltons,—a territorial incident that was soon followed by the arrival at Easton of divers Scottish folk in the service of His Grace the Duke of Hamilton and Brandon. Something later in the world's history, one of the great duke's Scottish retainers stumbled across the retired tailor in Framlingham, and recognized him as a former acquaintance, who had in time past made for his use certain mentionable and certain unmentionable articles of clothing. The ducal retainer should of course have held his tongue, and if he had not been a malicious loon would have said nothing to Mr. Bruce's disadvantage. But, as he was a vile loon and mere churl (the splendour of his livery notwithstanding), the varlet published his discovery on the very market-hill of Framlingham, the consequence being that, ere another week had passed, all the meaner folk of the neighbourhood were telling one another 'as how the new squire of Rendham was nobbut a fellow, who no long while since sate cross-legged on a tailor's board, and stitched away for his victuals and drink just like any other tailor-chap.'

As they were of the number of my father's patients, and as one of them—to wit, John Bruce's 'rip of a brother'—had practised as a solicitor in Framlingham in my boyhood, the Rendham Bruces had been known to me from my childhood. As he was related to me in no degree of blood or affinity, I could not rate John Bruce as a member of my family, but in London I always regarded him with a clannish sentiment. I was touched to the heart by the two or three glances of entreaty which the kindly gentleman threw at me, as he writhed, and gasped, and grew redder in the face, under Hannay's persistent endeavours to persuade him that he and Robert the Bruce were cousins. Bruce's imploring glances said, as plainly as words could have done, 'Can't you say something to get me out of this trouble? Can't you silence him or divert him to some other subject?' I could do nothing for the sufferer. As Hannay never looked at me, I could not inform him by a look that he was annoying the man whom he was set on pleasing. I should have done no good by assuring Hannay that he was arguing from erroneous data. I could not touch him with my hand, for we were on opposite sides of the table. Had I tried to hit him under the table with my foot, I might have kicked some one else.

Doran's other guests had all departed, and were in bed at their respective homes, when Hannay and I went forth from No. 4, Pembroke Terrace, and began to walk towards London in the small hours of the morning. As there were no empty cabs on the way till we neared Piccadilly Circus, it was fortunate for us that it did not rain. Though cold, the night was fine, and Hannay was a delightful companion as we moved along the main road. Twice or thrice he stopped in the brisk walk to give money and wholesome counsel to indigent pedestrians, whom he exhorted to withdraw their confidence from plebeian demagogues, and to compass an improvement in their worldly fortunes by consulting the wishes and winning the favour of the ancient gentry of 'these realms.' At a coffee and baked-potato stall he entertained so large a company of destitute wretches, that I insisted on contributing to the charges of the meal; and, whilst his guests were consuming their food and drink, he talked to them in a kindly way that pleased them not a little. As we continued our walk along the northern palisade of the Green Park, he told me how Mrs. Hannay had preserved me from the death that would have closed my career in the previous year, had she not entreated him to forbear from publishing a certain article. On coming to a quarter where night-cabs abounded, we found ourselves so refreshed by exercise in the frosty air that we decided to walk onwards for another mile. Life is worth living to young men, who can enjoy a march from Holland Park to Holborn Hill in the middle of a cold night.

My intimacy with James Hannay continued till he went to Edinburgh, in 1860, to edit the *Courant* newspaper. He was a frequent visitor at the rooms, which I and my brother Horace occupied for some twelve months in Hatton House, at the northern extremity of Hatton Garden, Holborn, and also came often to the chambers in Rolls Court, Chancery Lane, into which I moved from Hatton House, shortly before I was called to the Bar in 1859. During his residence at Edinburgh, he wrote me brief notes, sent me copies of his books, and reviewed *Live It Down* (1863), my best novel, at great length, and with cordial eulogy in the *Courant*; and after his return to London, to co-operate with Mr. Frederick Greenwood in establishing the *Pall Mall Gazette*, he visited me twice or thrice at No. 5. Heathcote Street, Mecklenburgh Square. But we never returned to the intimacy, in which we had lived from the beginning of 1856, up to the date of his migration from London to the Scotch capital.

He returned from Edinburgh to London, a very different man from the Hannay whose gaiety and comeliness and gallant manner had delighted me so greatly in the opening years of our acquaintance. Though they had not debilitated his intellect, anxiety and disappointment had shaken his self-confidence, robbed him of his early hopefulness, and darkened his soul. At the threshold of his fortieth year, he showed like a man of more than fifty years, and together with his bodily alertness he had lost the spiritual buoyancy, and the riant air that distinguished him in the time when his personality was so powerful in the literary coteries of London,—the time when Thackeray used to commend him for being 'a high-bred little fighting-cock.'

In the days when I saw much of Hannay, I of course saw more than a little of his special friend, John George Edgar, of whom he wrote so tenderly and strongly, in an article that may be found in *Characters and Criticisms*. 'Indeed,' Hannay remarks of his favourite comrade, in that elegant article, 'his appearance in the modern metropolitan world of wags and cynics and tale-writers had something about it that was not only picturesque but unique. He came in among those clever, amusing, and essentially modern men, like one of Scott's heroes. Profoundly attached to the feudal traditions,—a Tory of the purest Bolingbrokian School, as distinct from the Pittite Tory or modern Conservative, and supporting these doctrines with a fearless and eccentric eloquence, to which his fine person, and frank and gallant address gave at once an easy and a stately charm,—he represented in London the 'Scot of a past age.'

It lives in my memory how I observed this 'Scot of a past age,' on the several profane days of an entire week working in the British Museum reading-room, at an impressive collection of richly-bound books, touching the genealogy of England's sovereigns,—and how, at the close of his sixth day of severe and conscientious labour, he came to my seat in the great hall of study, and said to me in a deep and too sonorous undertone, that caused several students to look up from the desks, and regard him angrily,

'By Jove, Jeaffreson, I find that I have been for many a year under-rating the grandeur and dignity of the lineage of our Sovereign Lady the Queen. I have now spent an entire week in examining her genealogical evidences; and, by Jove, sir, now that I have gone through them carefully, I can assure you, *upon my honour*, that she is a devilish well-descended gentlewoman!'

CHAPTER X.

FRIENDSHIP, LOVE AND MARRIAGE.

Novels and Novelists, from Elizabeth to Victoria—My first Letter to Hepworth Dixon—His cordial Answer—His fine Nature—His Manliness—My Place on the *Athenæum* Staff—Applicants for ' a Friendly Lift '—An unscrupulous Enemy—Close Friends—Inns of Court Rifle-Corps—Serio-Comic Incidents—*Miriam Copley*, A Novel—*Sir Everard's Daughter*, A Novel—Life of Robert Stephenson, C.E., F.R.S.—Six Weeks in Northumbria—Stay at Darlington—George Stephenson and the Steam-Locomotive—Charles Manby's Home at Eastbourne—George Parkes Bidder, C.E., whilom ' the Calculating Boy '—His Talk about George Stephenson— Fallaciousness of Memory—Warning to Biographers—My Marriage—My Wife's Father—My admirable Mother-in-Law—Her brave and successful Fight with Adversity—Her noble Traits and beautiful Children—A Brighton School-Girl—Her Love-Match—Great Ormond Street, Bloomsbury—From Lodgings to ' our own House ' in Mesopotamia.

IN 1858 I published *Novels and Novelists, From Elizabeth to Victoria*, a work that was the result of much labour in the reading-room of the British Museum. Favourably treated by the critics, this book raised me in the esteem of literary workers, and increased the number of my readers.

In the same year, I began to write in the *Athenæum*, which had been for some five years under the editorial control of Hepworth Dixon, when I wrote him a letter, which he answered by word of mouth with a cordiality that delighted me. I had just ascended the steps in front of the British Museum, and was debating, far from hopefully, how he would be affected by my offer to write on his paper, when he came out of the Museum, saw me, and ran to me with outstretched hand.

'I intended to write to you this evening; this meeting relieves me of that trouble,' he said, in a hearty voice, as he shook my hand with energy. 'I got your letter this morning, and it put me in good spirits. I am delighted by your proposal, for I have a feeling that we shall work together harmoniously. I can't stop to talk now, for I am running to keep an engagement. But if you'll drop in upon me to-morrow at Wellington Street, in the forenoon, I shall be glad to have a chat with you. For the present, good-bye!'

As my personal intercourse with the editor of the *Athenæum* had hitherto been very slight, and strange stories had been told me of his overbearing temper and high-handed treatment of persons whom he regarded as his professional inferiors, Dixon's hearty manner on this occasion surprised, no less than it pleased me. Had I feared any humiliating rebuff, or any kind of direct incivility from him, I should not have written to him. My fear was that he would stand somewhat on his editorial dignity, and answer my letter with an official caution and coldness that would have nettled my pride. And now, in one brief utterance, he had declared his delight at my disposition to become his literary comrade. From the day of that meeting at the British Museum, his demeanour to me throughout the twenty-one years of our close association was invariably considerate, hearty, and sympathetic. I may also remark, that, in the long course of our intimacy, I never observed anything in his demeanour to other people that gave even a colour of justification to the strange stories of his overbearing temper and demeanour towards his professional inferiors.

It must be admitted that his manner was sometimes far from conciliatory. Towards comparative strangers and slight acquaintances he was sometimes wanting in deference. And towards those of his social equals or superiors, whom he suspected of a disposition to undervalue and suppress him, his bearing was at times aggressive and contemptuous. But at home, in the circle of his familiar friends, and in every society where he was at his ease, this disagreeable manner was never seen. And of the spirit which occasioned the rare exhibitions of this bad manner, nothing worse could be fairly said, than that it was a survival of the belligerent temper with which he had conquered the difficulties of his earlier time. At heart he was ever gentle, tender, and true.

In the *Athenæum* of January 3rd, 1880, when Hepworth Dixon had just been laid in his last bed in Highgate Cemetery, I wrote of him,

'If I had to express, in a word, the most distinguishing characteristics of this energetic worker, I should say " manliness." He had his failings, but he was always manly, in the brightest and bravest sense of the word. If he was deficient in tact, he was faultless in temper. He never failed to protest against the injustice of any remarks he might hear at a dinner-table or in the smoking-room, to the disparagement of an absent acquaintance. His view of a comrade's character and work often erred from excess of generosity, never from want of it. When his friends were in trouble, he always knew how to speak the right words of comfort, and, long after a trouble had passed, he could show with nicest delicacy his sympathetic mindfulness of the old grief. It was part of his manliness to be the keeper of his own troubles, and hold them bravely from the world's notice. He never talked melodramatically of his early struggles. On the morrow of a reverse, he went about as cheerfully as though it were the day after a victory. When his eldest daughter, the best beloved of all his children, died, his mere acquaintances suspected him of insensibility, because he disdained to wear his sorrow on his sleeve. Had he possessed a thousand a year from land, he could not have seemed more indifferent to the disaster that deprived him of the larger part of his careful savings, which he had invested in Turkish stock, with an unaccountable confidence in a hopelessly bankrupt and failing state. The explosion that shattered and almost destroyed his house near the Regent's Park canal did not ruffle his temper nor depress him for a single instant. He did his best to show the same fortitude under the blow that, falling upon him when he had for some time been getting out of health, was too much even for his marvellous pluck and endurance. On recovering from the first shock of surprise, that necessarily followed the sudden fall of the singularly vigorous and energetic actor, his friends were less moved by astonishment than by pain at the death, which was the natural consequence of his grief for the loss of his eldest son. From that stroke of calamity the man of vehement affections could not rally.— Just a month before his death, Dixon, ever so reluctant to admit that he was " hard hit," wrote to me in the postscript of a note, " Yesterday I was too ill to write. Excuse the scrawl. It is an awful thing to suffer from such a shock.' "

No writer ever worked under a more genial and considerate editor than Hepworth Dixon. Whenever complaints against my reviews came to him from angry authors, he displayed the nicest care for my feelings in his way of calling my attention to the wrathful letters; and, on the single occasion when I made a slip on an important matter of fact, he made light of the error, which the honourable practice of the *Athenæum* required him to acknowledge and correct in the next issue of the paper. It was seldom that he gave me a hint of the way he wished me to review a book. Indeed, I can recall only two occasions when he did so; and, on each of those occasions, the intimation was in the author's interest. On the earlier of those occasions, he remarked, as he pointed to a book by an equally benevolent and feeble writer, 'Of course, you must be thoughtful for the credit of the paper, but treat that kind lady's book as tenderly as you can. She is so bountiful to authors and artists in distress, that she is entitled to critical forbearance.' On the later occasion, he said, 'There is that fellow's book. Forget how badly he has treated me, while you are reading it and writing about it, for he has been very unfortunate of late. If the book is a good book, praise it heartily.' A staunch friend, Dixon was a most magnanimous enemy.

Having won a place on the regular *Athenæum* staff, I came into pleasant intercourse with several of the principal contributors to the journal. A less agreeable consequence of my connection with the leading literary journal was that literary aspirants (some of them being persons with whom I had only the slightest acquaintance, or no previous knowledge whatever) came to me with requests for favourable reviews of their books, and showed in various ways their displeasure with me for telling them frankly that I could not comply with their requirements. Because I declined, on the score of my duty to the paper and its proprietors, to give them what they were pleased to call 'a friendly lift,' some of the disappointed applicants charged me in the literary cliques with giving myself airs, and talking a lot of humbug about my obligations of honour to the proprietors of the *Fourpenny Annihilator*. One of these unhappy suitors took his revenge in a more reprehensible way. For years the malignant fellow went about telling persons, whose books had been roughly handled in the *Athenæum*, that I was the writer of the articles that had caused them annoyance; and, as he affected to have a secret and sure way of discovering the actual writers of the various articles in the *Athenæum*, this miserable fellow often succeeded in incensing people against me, by making them regard me as the writer of articles which I had not written, about books into whose covers I had not even looked. I forbear to publish the man's name, for though he long since went from the world, his widow and children are living.

After becoming friends, Hepworth Dixon and I quickly became very close friends. Going together to the same theatres and other places of amusement, we dined together at the same clubs, and, on the creation of the Volunteer Force in 1859, were prompt in joining the Inns of Court Corps, known to the flippant as *The Devil's Own*. For a few years, he and I marched together in the same company of that brilliant regiment, and should in all probability have continued to march side by side many more years, had not certain serio-comic incidents moved me to retire from the corps, before my captain had even thought of making me a non-commissioned officer. I have no wish to brag about my military style and prowess; for I can aver without fear of contradiction that, in the days when I wore the uniform of *The Devil's Own*, I was regarded by my comrades as the most incapable soldier of the whole regiment. Far from murmuring against this view of my military address, I cordially recognize its justice, albeit I still maintain that I was right on a question of taste, about which I and my captain were at friendly variance. I remain of opinion that I was right in declining to adopt the severe military *coiffure*, and that Dixon and I wore our hair none too long for citizen-soldiers.

A few words more about the serio-comic incidents, to which I have referred. The last time I went out with my corps was a certain field-day (at Richmond, if I remember rightly,) from which I returned with an agreeable sense of having distinguished myself by soldierly conduct, and more particularly by the rapidity with which I fired away all my blank cartridges in the concluding fusillade.

I returned to my peaceful home in this happy frame of mind without having heard of a rather ludicrous incident of the final shooting. In the excitement of the exercise a rifleman after reloading his weapon omitted to withdraw his ramrod, the consequence of the omission being that, at his next shot, he fired away the ramrod, which unfortunately struck a certain Mr. Briefless and wounded him. Some weeks later, during which weeks I had neither appeared at drill nor visited the Inns of Court, I received a letter from an officer of my company, informing me that I was generally regarded as the rifleman who had shot away his ramrod to the grievous injury of Mr. Briefless. The letter also informed me that my neglect to make enquiries respecting the state of Mr. Briefless, whilst he was undergoing surgical treatment for the wound inflicted upon him by my ramrod, had occasioned talk to my disadvantage in the coteries of the four Inns. This rather exciting epistle gave me my first intelligence of the accident that had caused Mr. Briefless and his friends to think ill of me. It was easy for me to vindicate my honour by producing my rifle and ramrod, but less easy to recover the equanimity of which I was deprived by the startling letter. As the citizen-soldier, who serves his country from pure patriotism, is above all things a creature of sentiment, it is not surprising that in my disgust at the series of serio-comic incidents, I retired from a service, in which I had been suspected of shooting away my ramrod, wounding a comrade, and then forbearing to express concern for his distress. It is needless for me to recall what I thought and said some five-and-thirty years since of the real culprit, who held his peace whilst I was being denounced for his misconduct.

The year that saw me don for the first time a soldier's uniform, also saw me assume the wig and robe of an English barrister. In the same year (1859), I published the earliest of the novels on which I reflect with a moderate degree of complacence. My earlier novels were puerile essays; but *Miriam Copley*, written in my twenty-eighth year, is a story of which I can speak as not altogether undeserving of the praise accorded to it by critics, or the favour with which it was regarded by novel-readers more than thirty years ago. After making good fun of the 'faults and glaring absurdities' of the book, Miss Geraldine Jewsbury, ever my severest as well as my most discerning and sympathetic critic, declared it a story that fairly took away the reader's breath, and pronounced its marvellous heroine an extremely amusing person. The critics, on papers with which I had no connection, spoke more strongly on my behalf. The *Press*, still in the fulness of its vigour and influence, and heretofore far from friendly to me, pronounced *Miriam Copley* my 'best book,' and predicted that it would 'attain great popularity.' The *Leader* declared it 'a very clever novel.' Of course the critics were not all on the right side. I recall an article in *Tait's Magazine*, in which I was handled severely for my audacity and recklessness in making my marvellous heroine commit murder with a gas too subtle and deadly for preservation. My censor called attention to the fact that my mal-odorous poison would necessarily be the death of any chemist who should produce it. I had therefore, according to my critic, been guilty of a bad and impudent blunder in arming Miriam with a minute and hermetically sealed flask, charged with a gas that could not be manufactured without fatal consequences to the manufacturer, and could not possibly be bottled in the alleged manner. I wonder what my censor thought of himself and did with his hair, on learning from a professor of chemistry that this particular gas, which no chemist could produce without losing his life, was often manufactured in laboratories and bottled without any fatal consequence to the manufacturer.

In 1860, I wrote *Sir Everard's Daughter*, a short novel that appeared in five successive numbers in the *Universal Magazine* (Allen and Co.), and was published three years later in a single volume. Whilst writing this tale, I was also working on *A Book about Doctors*, that was offered to readers in the ensuing autumn, when I was throwing off a hasty article on Dixon's *Life of Lord Bacon* for the *Temple Bar Magazine*.

In the same year (1860), Hepworth Dixon, ever thoughtful for the interests of his friends, did me a good turn. Robert Stephenson, the famous engineer, died in October, 1859, and in the following year Charles Manby, C.E. and F.R.S., acting in behalf of the representatives of the deceased engineer, asked Hepworth Dixon if he could tell him of a man of letters qualified to co-operate with Professor Pole, C.E. and F.R.S., in producing a fit biography of Robert Stephenson. Mr. Samuel Smiles's biography of the Elder Stephenson (George Stephenson) had appeared in 1857, and been so greatly successful that Dixon regarded the author of *The Life of George Stephenson* as the writer whom the Stephensons should invite to co-operate with Professor Pole, and told Mr. Manby so. On learning from Mr. Manby that, though they held Mr. Smiles's book in high esteem, Robert Stephenson's representatives were of opinion that Smiles should not be employed to write the Younger Stephenson's history, Dixon advised the negotiator to secure my services. The consequence of Dixon's words in my behalf was that in the summer of 1860 I was retained by the Stephenson family to work with Professor Pole. At the same time, Robert Stephenson's representatives decided that the new biography should be published by the Longmans. My legal agreement in the matter was an agreement with those eminent publishers; but I was chosen for the work by Robert Stephenson's representatives, and it was from them—to wit, Mr. George Robert Stephenson, Mr. George Parkes Bidder, their confidential agent, Mr. Charles Manby, and divers gentlemen to whom I was introduced by them—that I gained a considerable part of the documents and verbal information, which enabled me to tell the story of the Younger Stephenson's life.

It was arranged that, whilst I should act as the engineer's general and personal historian, Professor Pole should describe the engineer's works in separate chapters of the joint-biography, which chapters he should sign with his initials as portions of the book for which he was solely responsible; that Professor Pole should instruct and guide me on all engineering questions which I should deal with in my chapters of the 'Life;' and that I should write into the book nothing at discord with his instructions and guidance.

As the joint-biographers acted in accordance with these arrangements, and worked together in good faith and harmony from first to last, the authorized 'Life of Robert Stephenson, C.E. and F.R.S.,' is a work of the highest authority in respect to its matters of engineering; for no engineer of the present century knows more than Professor Pole of the science and history of his profession.

Though they were not exceedingly liberal, the terms on which I agreed to do my part of the joint-biography so greatly improved my pecuniary prospect for the next two years, that I determined to take a very important step in the following autumn. As soon as I had signed and sealed with the Messrs. Longmans and Co., I startled and delighted Dixon by saying to him,

'One consequence of this arrangement will be my marriage. I am now rich enough to marry, and in the course of the autumn I shall be in a position to introduce you to my wife. A certain young gentlewoman has had my heart in her keeping for full three years, and my influence over her is much less powerful than I conceive it to be, if I cannot persuade her to give herself wholly to me in September or October, when I shall have returned from Newcastle.'

In the August and September of the same year (1860), I spent some six weeks in Newcastle and the surrounding country, visiting Killingworth and Wylam and divers other Northumbrian places, where I gathered much new information about the Stephensons from their humbler kindred, ancient comrades, and former employers. Carrying with me from Newcastle several note-books filled with *data* and *ana* touching the two engineers, I broke my southward journey at Darlington, where I made the acquaintance of Mr. Pease, M.P., who gave me many particulars of his father's intercourse with the Elder Stephenson, and lent me a packet of letters, throwing additional light on certain passages of the Younger Stephenson's career. At Darlington I also had a long and very instructive interview with Mr. Hackworth, the maker of the locomotive *Sans Pareil*, that proved itself greatly superior to Messrs. Braithwaite and Erichson's *Novelty* and Mr. Brandreth's *Cyclops* at the Rainhill contest in 1829, although it was badly beaten in the same competition by Robert Stephenson's *Rocket*. Giving me some valuable intelligence respecting the merits of his own locomotive engine and the merits of the engine by which it was vanquished, Mr. Hackworth confirmed all that I had learned from competent instructors at Newcastle-on-Tyne about the early history of the locomotive.

I returned from Northumbria to London, in possession of conclusive evidence that, instead of being the original and independent inventor who had made Trevithic's 'iron horse' a thing of practical utility, as Mr. Smiles's memoir of the Elder Stephenson had caused the world to think, George Stephenson had in truth contributed nothing whatever of any importance to the great invention which had been so strangely misassigned to him by the popular biographer. I had discovered that George Stephenson did not discover the sufficiency of the adhesion of smooth wheels running on smooth rails; that, before he constructed the first of his Killingworth traction-engines, a locomotive with smooth wheels was running on smooth trams at Wylam; that he did not invent 'the blast'; that he did not invent the multi-tubular boiler; that, had the miscalled inventor of the locomotive never been born, we should have had our railroads and swift traction-engines just as soon.

In the last week of September, 1860, I went for a short visit to Mr. Charles Manby's country house, 'The Greys,' at Eastbourne, in order that I might receive from the lips of Mr. George Parkes Bidder whatever he should be pleased to tell me about the great engineer, with whom he had been closely associated in business and friendship. At that time, Mr. Bidder had lost something of the particular power that had made him famous in his youth as 'the calculating boy,' and during the earlier decades of his professional career had rendered him an effective witness before parliamentary committees on questions relating to 'quantities.' In his sixty-first year, Mr. Bidder told me that he should be happy to multiply four figures by four figures for my entertainment, as he could do so without distressing his brain, but that he had for some time refrained from performing any more difficult feat of mental calculation, because it pained him to multiply in his mind five figures by five figures. At the same time, to give me some notion of the process by which he dealt with figures in mental arithmetic, he told me that he worked the two sets of figures from left to right, *i.e.*, that in multiplying four figures by four figures, (say 9876 by

5432,) he multiplied the 9 thousands by the 5 thousands, and put the result in millions by itself, then multiplied the 8 hundreds by the 4 hundreds, putting the result by itself, and then dealt in like manner with the 70 and 30, and the 6 and 2. He said that after doing the four sums of multiplication, he saw the four results lying before his mind's eye, each of them lying in regular form like a pile of shot. He then added the results together, beginning with the two smallest sums, then adding their sum to the next pile, resulting from the first multiplication *i.e.*, 9000×5000.

'And before you add the four results together,' I said, ' you actually seem to see the four several piles?'

'Exactly so,' he answered quickly, as though he were weary of the subject, and wished to dismiss it, 'four several piles, like four piles of shot.'

In his youth and early manhood, Sir Wentworth Dilke, bart., (the father of the present Sir Charles Dilke,) was as remarkable in his private circle for his faculty of mental calculation, as Bidder 'the calculating boy' was remarkable under the world's observation for the same faculty. But I am unable to say whether the calculators worked their figures in the same way. For when Sir Wentworth Dilke told me of his former address in mental calculation, he forbore to tell me how he worked his sums.

When I had the good fortune to journey with him from London to Eastbourne in the same railway-carriage, and to pass at least an entire day (I think it was two whole days) in his society, Mr. Bidder was still a hale, vigorous, energetic, and strong-headed man; and, whilst he spoke to me with confidential freedom on matters relating to his intercourse with Robert Stephenson, he delighted me with his droll anecdotes, and his excellent manner of telling them. I have an object in impressing on my readers that, when I made the acquaintance of this remarkable man in his sixty-first year, he was in no respect whatever a shaken or failing man, and that he was so good as to give his best attention to all my numerous enquiries, and to answer them with equal thoughtfulness and lucidity. Yet more, he permitted me to take notes in writing of all that he told me, and to read my notes to him so that I might have an opportunity of correcting them under his observation, in whatever places they needed amendment.

Some time later, when I had thoroughly mastered a number of contemporary documents, relating to matters about which Mr. Bidder had instructed me from memory, I called upon him in George Street, Westminster, and drew his attention to several points, in respect to which his statements from recollection were in direct conflict with the evidence of the documents. As he was a man of unimpeachable honour, could have had no motive in misinstructing me, and was no less desirous than myself that his friend's biography should be accurate in every particular, I went to him in perfect confidence that the manifest errors of the information he had given me were wholly referable to defect of memory. After studying the documents to which I called his attention, he remarked,

'It is a very interesting and instructive demonstration of the fallaciousness of memory. Those writings put it beyond question that whilst I was instructing you so confidently, I was strangely misremembering the passages and incidents of my story, on which I have reflected most often and thoughtfully. In writing your book, use nothing I have told you from mere memory, unless you can corroborate it by documentary evidence.'

Biographers should take this story to heart. In preparing to write the 'Life' of a celebrated man whose course was run in the present century, it is usual for a biographer to hunt up the celebrity's early associates—his schoolmates, his college friends, the men who forty years since were his comrades in foreign travel, the servants who waited on him in childhood—and ask for their reminiscences of the notable individual's temper, character, tastes, and doings. Some of the persons, thus solicited for information, may be far gone in senility, and in their brightest time may have been poorly endowed with intelligence and discretion. I do not say that such persons are incapable of affording *data* of distinct biographical value; for I have more than once gathered from the feeble mind of a failing octogenarian particulars that showed me the way to surer and sounder informants. But as a veteran biographer, who knows much of the difficulty of getting good materials for personal history, I venture to assure my fellow-workers in a perilous department of literature, that in collecting materials for their books they should be suspicious of error even in the communications made to them by the most respectable informants. Above all things let them remember that a giver of information about a celebrated person may resemble Mr. Bidder in having a clear and vigorous mind, in being sincere as sunlight, and in having been the celebrity's nearest and dearest friend, and may still from defect of memory be extremely inaccurate and misleading in the details of his statements.

On the 2nd of October, 1860, I was married in St. Sepulchre's (St. Pulcheria's) church, hard by the Old Bailey, to Arabella Ellen, the only surviving daughter of the late William Eccles, F.R.C.S., whilom of 59, Old Broad Street, in the city of London. Like my own father, my father-in-law—or rather let me say the gentleman who would have been my father-in-law had he lived to witness his daughter's wedding—belonged to the highest grade of the medical profession. Surgeon of two London hospitals (the Devonshire Square Hospital and the Royal Free Hospital in Gray's Inn Road) and author of a treatise on a department of surgical practice, he had come to the front rank of 'the City surgeons,' when some of his City patients induced him to join them in railway speculations that resulted in his ruin. Prosperous in 1844, he imagined himself during several months of 1845 to be moving quickly to the possession of great wealth,—a delightful dream that was dissipated by the railway collapse of 1846, which impoverished so many sanguine speculators. Dying in the season of financial panic and disaster, the clever surgeon left five children and a widow (who was on the point of giving birth to a sixth child), with no provision apart from the thousand pounds for which he had insured his life at the time of his marriage.

A woman of great beauty, fortitude, and ability, my future mother-in-law was qualified to rise superior to a tempest of adversity that would have defeated her utterly, had she been an ordinary woman. Instead of yielding to despair, and requiring her several affluent relations to support her and her offspring, she determined to maintain herself and educate her children by her own exertions; and, in laying her plans for achieving her purpose, she decided to be more thoughtful for her *four* boys than for her *two* girls, in the earlier years of the long struggle on which she was entering. So that she might be in a position to send her sons to one or another of the great schools of the City Companies, she decided to open a boarding-house for boys attending those schools or the Charterhouse school as day-pupils; and her sixth child and fourth boy had not been for many weeks in possession of his cradle, when she acted on this resolve. Taking a large house in Charterhouse Square, she furnished it for the entertainment of a numerous party of schoolboys; and before the first anniversary of her husband's death, she was fairly and favourably launched in business as 'a Dame' for the City schools. At the same time she opened a morning class, for the instruction of small boys in the rudiments of English and Latin scholarship. The pupils of this preparatory class she taught herself with a success that attended all her enterprises.

I should vex my dear mother-in-law's shade, were I to speak of her good fortune in Charterhouse Square as resulting wholly from her excellences. Social sympathy with a woman, making a brave fight against adverse circumstances for herself and her six young children, was an influence to which she used in her latest years to declare herself largely indebted for the victory that rewarded her exertions. By the physicians and surgeons of 'the medical quarter' who had known and liked her husband, by their wives with whom she had lived in cordial neighbourliness during her married life in Old Broad Street, and by the family-doctors of the district around Charterhouse Square, she was strenuously and perseveringly supported. The Sollys, Adamses, Daldys, Langmores, Dempseys, Barringers, Masons sent their boys to her, and sounded her praises in the homes of their patients. Henry Jeaffreson rejoiced in doing his best for her and her children. And in the tranquil evening of her life, when the battle had been fought to a happy end, and she had lived to see two of her sons securely placed as assistant librarians in the British Museum, another of them flourishing as the principal secretary of a sound Insurance office in the City, and her fourth boy a stalwart settler in Canada, she used to think gratefully of Sir Risdon Bennett (whilom President of the College of Physicians) as one of those who had been on her side in the hard times, when she needed the help of every one of her many friends. Whilst 'the City doctors' aided her so effectually, she was fortunate in having the sympathy and encouragement of Dr. Saunders, head-master of the Charterhouse School, and Dr. Kynaston, the head-master of St. Paul's School.

A clever woman, who from her girlhood had been a thoughtful and critical reader of the higher literature, my future mother-in-law at the commencement of our acquaintance was well-informed on many subjects of which I knew little or nothing. She was also a mistress of the elegant accomplishments, in which highly-educated women usually excel their companions of the ruder sex. Sketching cleverly with pencil and brush, she was a proficient in music,—a good pianist, and a vocalist who still delighted critical auditors with her fine *contralto* voice, which had been trained in her earlier time by the best masters. A facile and charming letter-writer, she was the anonymous author of several articles in magazines and at least one delightful story for girls. She was also the anonymous author of a little educational primer, entitled *Harry Hawkins's H-Book*, that had an enormous sale, and is still used in primary schools for the advantage of infants who drop their h's.

Born in 1807, my future mother-in-law was in her forty-sixth year at the opening of our acquaintance; but though she was more than old enough to be my mother, and looked older than her years, she was remarkable for the buoyancy of her spirits and the animating gaiety of her conversation. A sweeter-natured woman never breathed. The beauty, which distinguished her in her hey-day, had passed from her to her children, who in 1852 were the loveliest lot of young persons I ever looked upon. But the one to please and interest me most strongly was the elder girl,—a tall slight slip of a child, still in her fourteenth year, with a long neck, small head, and a face of an unusual style of beauty.

In the summer of 1853, when she first set eyes on

this girl of an unusual style of beauty, my incomparable sister was 'so taken' by her, as to invite her to Brighton for an entire half-year, so that she might have the benefit of sea-air which the doctors were at that time prescribing for her, and might at the same time live the life of a Brighton school-girl. The invitation was accepted, and henceforth this girl of a singular beauty was educated, not for a single half-year but for four years, by my two dear sisters, of whose Brighton girls'-school I made mention in a former chapter.

As the young gentlewoman of a peculiar style of beauty returned every half year from the town upon the sea, taller in stature, more airily graceful in her carriage, brighter in her prattle, more winningly attractive in every element of her singular loveliness, it is not strange that my early interest developed into a state of feeling, which I did not venture to declare to her, so long as she was only a school-girl. Nor is it surprising that, when she had ceased to be 'a school-miss,' and had returned to her home in the quaint old square for good, I was quick to tell her of my love. I had ceased to live in Charterhouse Square before I made the prayer to which she consented; and I remember that, as I walked from her house to my rooms near Chancery Lane, with head erect, heart beating quick with elation, and steps that scarcely touched the pavements, my exultation at my good fortune was no greater than my amazement at it. More than a few times since that evening of violent delight, I have been visited with compunction for my selfishness in taking so young a girl at a disadvantage and binding her to my humble lot, when in her simplicity and ignorance of life she was unaware of her power to mate herself with wealth and dignity. I gave the love of a quite ordinary nature; she repaid me with a devotion that has glorified my obscure and ineffectual existence. In the secret chambers of her heart and brain, she must feel and know how much she has lost through giving herself to so ordinary a husband. Yet in her generosity she persists in speaking and acting, as though she were deeply indebted to me for doing her the great injury.

Our wedding-tour was a trip of ten days to Cambridge, where we had the college-gardens pretty much to ourselves. On one of those days we went to Dullingham to look at the tombs and memorials of *our* ancestors, and to visit the hall in which *our* people had lived for more than two hundred years.

On returning to London, too poor at the moment to take a house unless we ran into debt for furnishing it, we took furnished rooms in Great Ormond Street; and we lodged in that thoroughfare, so rich in Georgian associations, for just four months, with the exception of the three weeks of the Christmas holidays, which we spent at Framlingham, where dinners and dances were given in honour of the bride, who in her successive visits to the Suffolk Woodland had won the hearts of the town's-folk, from the members of the upper ten families down to the poor old bodies in the almshouses.

Seeing reasons, at the turn of the year, why we should find a home, in which we could have more quietude and privacy and security from disturbance than the lodging-house afforded us, we took a little house in Heathcote Street, Mecklenburgh Square, into which we moved on Tuesday, 12th February, 1861, after furnishing it with the economy which young people, who marry on a *very* modest income, do well to exercise in their domestic arrangements. We lived in that house for rather more than six years. I will not speak of those six years as the happiest years of my existence; for, thanks to my dear wife, till the sadness of declining age began to steal over me, all my years since my marriage were inexpressibly happy, notwithstanding death's frequent assaults on my felicity.

CHAPTER XI.

NO. 5, HEATHCOTE STREET.

Neighbourhood of Heathcote Street—*Littérateurs* of the District—Welcome Guests at No. 5—The Bensusans of Marylebone Road—Abraham Bensusan and Henri Quatre—Mrs. Bensusan's Last Will and Testament—*Olive Blake's Good Work*, a Novel—The Way in which it was Composed—Thackeray and his Characters—*Live It Down: A Story of the Light Lands*—The Story's Success—Mr. Petter's Praise—*Not Dead Yet*, a Novel—Coincidences of *Not Dead Yet* and the Tichborne Story—Vice-Chancellor Wood's Mention of those Coincidences—Athenæum Gossip—Rider Haggard's too hasty Critics.

FROM the front windows of our little house (No. 5, Heathcote Street, Mecklenburgh Square, W.C.) we looked to the south, along Mecklenburgh Street, and the eastern side of Mecklenburgh Square, down Doughty Street and St. John's Street, and onwards to the umbrageous trees of Gray's Inn Gardens. We could not complain of being 'built in' upon the south. From our back windows we overlooked the long and broad garden of one of our Gray's Inn Road neighbours, that separated us by a wide interval from the close-built and rather squalid district at the north-west of Gray's Inn Road. Near though it was to the main thoroughfare between Holborn and the King's Cross railway-station, our street had the commendable quality of quietude, for it was closed at its eastern end by 'a bar' that was in the keeping of an officer with much gold lace about his hat and blue coat.

Living in this pleasantly-placed house, we dwelt in a quarter favourably regarded by *littérateurs* and artists. Whilst we inhabited No. 5, Heathcote Street, Henry Dunphy (barrister, and literary editor of the *Morning Post*) lived in Heathcote Street, and Mrs. Newby the novelist was a householder of Mecklenburgh Street. Mrs. Maxwell (*née* Braddon, author of *Lady Audley's Secret*), James Hayllar the artist (my close and particular friend), and Serjeant Robinson (whose manuscript of *Bench and Bar*, I commended to the favourable consideration of my publishers, not long while before his recent death), all three lived in Mecklenburgh Square. Byron the novelist, in his later time the celebrated dramatic author, and Edmund Yates dwelt in Doughty Street. George Augustus Sala had his home in Guildford Street. In Gray's Inn, a favourite haunt of *littérateurs*, we had several friends. Though my friends in Westburnia and Kensington used to speak of it disdainfully as an out-of-the-way corner of Mesopotamia, Heathcote Street was very much in the way of writers and painters.

Though we lived quietly and on a curiously small income in our 'out-of-the-way corner of Mesopotamia,' our little house was visited by a goodly number of interesting people. The Thompsons (now-a-days Sir Henry and Lady Thompson), Miss Geraldine Jewsbury (no less dear and precious to my wife than to Mrs. Carlyle), the Hepworth-Dixons, the Dorans, the Diamonds (Dr. and Mrs. Diamond, of Twickenham House, Twickenham), the Lankesters (the coroner for Middlesex and Mrs. Lankester, brightest and kindliest of literary women), the Lockers (my old Oxford friend Arthur Locker, in those days spoken of as 'Locker of the *Times*,' and his sweetly gentle wife), the Bensusans whom everyone laughed at and delighted in, Charles Lamb Kenney (quaintest and most original of drollers), William Stigant or Stigand (barrister, poet, and Quarterly Reviewer), Frederick Lawrence (author of *The Life of Henry Fielding*), handsome Horace Mayhew (who never penned a cruel line nor ever uttered a savage *mot*, although he was a professional jester), scholarly, fastidious, chivalric Hans Sotheby (whose frigid manner belied his warm and generous heart), William Shedden Ralston of Lincoln's Inn and the British Museum (my friend for many a year before and after he took to writing and lecturing about Slavonic mythology and Russian folk-lore), good Walter Thornbury, delightfully loquacious Samuel Hatchard (a man of great promise and no achievement), James Hutton (the Anglo-Indian journalist), Ernest Hart (in the perfection of his youthful comeliness and cleverness), the Westland Marstons, were amongst the equally pleasant and interesting people, who came about my wife and her white slave in Heathcote Street, together with her cousins and my cousins from distant quarters of the town.

Of these amusing people, none were more striking as social curiosities than the Bensusans of No. 228, Marylebone Road, and of Beaudesert, Leighton-Buzzard, Bedfordshire. Israelites of Sephardim, they offered themselves to the world's respectful consideration as representatives of the style, culture, refinement, and dignity of their race. Well known in the city as a financial operator of unimpeachable integrity and stainless honour, Mr. Bensusan was chiefly valued in the western regions of the town for his similitude to Henri Quatre of France. Tall, stately, courteous, taciturn, he had a most agreeable smile, which never failed to brighten his royal features, when his striking resemblance to the handsomest of the Bourbons was referred to in his hearing. I once ventured to ask this interesting personage whether his family preserved any tradition that accounted for the marvellous resemblance; but, though he smiled upon me graciously, he forbore to satisfy my curiosity. It was, however, generally understood by the habitual visitors at No. 228, Marylebone Road, that Mr. Abraham Bensusan and Henri of France had a common ancestor in the far-away Princes of Sephardim.

Whilst her excellent husband had a silent tongue, Mrs. Bensusan was amusingly loquacious about the purity of her blood, the historic grandeur of the Bravos to whose lineage she was indebted for her descent from sacred princes, and the delight with which she, as a daughter of Israel, witnessed the mutual *rapprochement* of the English and Judaic peoples. According to her own statement of her case, this curious and rather charming gentlewoman was chiefly desirous that this mutual *rapprochement* should result in the perfect interfusion and commixture of the two noblest races of the whole human family. As the lady was an orthodox Jewess, and punctiliously observant of all the rules and precepts of her religion, I cannot conceive that she desired a perfect interfusion and commixture of judaism and christianity. I conceive that she looked forward to a happy time, when the English would be converted from their creed and adopt the faith of her people. But she was too considerate for the sensibilities of her christian friends to say so.

At Mrs. Bensusan's 'evenings' in the Marylebone Road one met celebrities of different sorts,—more especially the celebrities of the studios, the theatres, and the musical coteries, and a few personages of quality and fashion who liked to gossip with the 'indescribably queer people' whom she brought about her.

The way in which Mrs. Bensusan closed her financial accounts with the world was rather comical. To all persons, who knew anything of her pecuniary affairs, it was known that she had a power of disposing by will of certain moneys that had been settled upon her, for her own use and enjoyment during life. Of course, the amount of the moneys was exaggerated by rumour. By some persons the little bright-eyed, piquant woman was thought to have inherited great wealth, whereas I believe the fortune, held by trustees to her use, was something less than £20,000.

Whilst she was failing from an incurable malady, that would necessarily prove fatal in two or three years, the poor lady suffered also from 'the eternal want of pence.' A compassionate and free-handed woman, she had for years given to the poor more than she could afford to dispense in charity. She had even cumbered herself with a number of indigent pensioners. It was under these circumstances that she went to my friend A, and said to him,

'I want money to give to my pensioners and other poor wretches. I cannot bear to tell them I can help them no longer; I should provoke my too generous husband's anger by asking him to give me more money for my poor people; and I don't like to go to a money-lender for the loan, for it would pain me to tell a mere man of business the reasons why the transaction should be kept from Mr. Bensusan's knowledge. So I come to you as one of my old friends for a cheque of £100. If you will render me that service, I will leave you by my will a legacy of £1,000.* You will receive the legacy at no distant date, for my days are numbered.'

A. lent the money. He was not the only person to whom the lady applied for a loan of money in the same way. Several of my friends lent her money on the understanding that they should be repaid with handsome legacies under her will. Several persons, of whom I had no knowledge, did likewise. The doctors had not erred in their diagnosis of the childless lady's malady. In due course she died, leaving a will; but in it she had made no mention whatever of the

* Writing from memory so long after the incident, I may be at fault as to the exact sum she required of my friend, and as to the sum she promised to bequeath him. But I believe my memory is right as to both sums.

several persons who had accommodated her with the considerable sums of money. I never saw the lady's will; but I know from a sure informant that its most important clause appointed a comparatively young man (one of her near kindred, if I remember rightly,) the executor and residuary legatee.

Whilst the facts of this curious story were being whispered about, there was a lively stir amongst the people who used to figure at Mrs. Bensusan's receptions. One greatly excited lady came to me at No. 43, Springfield Road, St. John's Wood, to which house I had migrated from Heathcote Street, and implored me to tell her if I were one of the victims. Fortunately I could extinguish the lady's apprehension by assuring her that Mrs. Bensusan was too well aware of my poverty to think of asking me to lend her money. The next thing I heard of the strange business was that the disappointed lenders were combining to take legal action for the recovery of their money. But they had small cause for alarm, and no need whatever to take legal proceedings. For the lady's executor and residuary legatee was a gentleman of the nicest honour, and, on learning how strangely his eccentric kinswoman had acted, was quick to assure the so-called victims, that every farthing of the estate in his hands should be used for the satisfaction of their reasonable claims. In every particular this gentleman acted with admirable spirit, tact, and delicacy; and without any needless delay each of the lenders was repaid the sum he had lent.

If the poor lady designed to defraud the people who lent her money, her wrongful purpose should be regarded as resulting from bodily ailment and the medicines that were employed to mitigate the torture of her mortal malady; for it is certain that till her health failed she was a scrupulously conscientious woman. But I do not believe that her curious conduct proceeded from a fraudulent motive. My view of the invalid's case is, that she was actuated partly by need of the money for immediate and benevolent use, and partly by a humorous disposition to play upon the cupidity of her friends, and to demonstrate that christians were no less greedy of gain than people of her own race. Knowing that her residuary legatee would be sure to act honourably towards her creditors, she could with an easy conscience trifle with them in so droll a way.

Whilst I was working on the *Life of Robert Stephenson, C.E., F.R.S.* in 1861 and the three following years, I wrote three novels, (1) *Olive Blake's Good Work*, published in 1862 by Messrs. Chapman and Hall; (2) *Live It Down, A Story of The Light Lands*, published in March, 1863, by Messrs. Hurst and Blackett, and (3) *Not Dead Yet*, published in 1864 by the same last-named publishers.

In producing *Olive Blake's Good Work*, a complicated story, of nine books and eighty-one chapters, I worked on a new method. Before I blotted a single sheet, I designed the whole story even to some of its minutest details in my mind; and, in designing it, I perfected my scheme for the concluding portions of the tale before I filled in the outlines of the earlier parts of the narrative. After producing in this way a scheme of the whole story, and elaborating the final and initial portions, without committing a single thought to paper, I worked carefully and minutely within my own mind on those middle books of the story, that may be styled 'the body of the work.' In going forward with my design from the elaborated beginning to the elaborately finished concluding chapters, I worked at every point with thought for the positions and complications of subsequent sections of the composition, and especially for the *dénouement* towards which I was advancing. After thus designing the entire work, I wrote on a single sheet of foolscap the titles and descriptive headings of the nine books, and then in a space, left vacant for the purpose, I placed under the title and descriptive headings of each of the first eight books the titles of the chapters, which the book on being written and printed would contain. After perfecting this Table of Contents, I made lists of personal names, place-names, and dates,— to wit, the names of characters who would figure in the story,—the names of the more or less imaginary places in which the scenes of the story were laid,—and birth-dates, death-dates, age-dates, and other dates, to be borne in mind for the consistent development of the narrative. The story having been thus composed in my mind, even to most of its minutest particulars, I put it upon paper with a rapidity that astonished and delighted me. The whole novel was written from the first to the last line in six weeks and four days.

This way of producing a novel is the reverse of the way in which Thackeray wrote his comparatively plotless novels of character and humour. His plan was to create mentally two or three of his chief characters, and then to write away from time to time, with intervals of repose between the times of industry, and go onwards from chapter to chapter, with only a general notion of the course he would be taking a few chapters later. 'I don't control my characters,' he said to me. 'I am in their hands, and they take me where they please.' The great master's way of working was doubtless the best way for a supremely able novelist of his peculiar genius and style. But I have no doubt that the way in which I composed *Olive Blake's Good Work*, is the way in which second-rate and third-rate novelists—*i.e.*, mere tale-tellers—will work most easily and most effectually. *Olive Blake's Good Work* was in every respect successful beyond my not inordinate hopes.

Live It Down (1863) was even more successful. I lack the effrontery to repeat all the pleasant things that were said of this novel; but for their amusement I will venture to tell the readers of this page how highly Mr. Petter, late of the firm of Messrs. Cassell, Petter, and Galpin, thought of my story of the Light Lands. At the end of July or the beginning of August, 1863, I was in Suffolk, moving about sorrowfully in the haunts from which my dear mother had recently passed for ever, when the railway brought to Framlingham a clerical stranger, the Reverend Dr. Wright, who had journeyed from town, in order to invite me to write a serial story for the *Quiver*, one of Messrs. Cassell, Petter, and Galpin's serial publications. As the *Quiver* was produced by those eminent publishers for the religious edification as well as for the secular enlightenment of serious families, living for the most part within the lines of the non-conforming sects, I expressed a doubt of my fitness for the work I was asked to perform. But Dr. Wright made light of my reasons for hesitating to accept the proposal of the publishers, for whom he was acting.

'We don't want a theological story,' he remarked. 'All we require is an interesting story of wholesome morality, that shall contain nothing in direct conflict with the doctrines of Christianity. The readers of the *Quiver* do not object to stories about sinners, even flagrant sinners, provided their wickedness is not held up to admiration. Give them a story like *Live It Down*, and the proprietors of the *Quiver* will be more than satisfied. Mr. Petter, a most devout man, is most enthusiastic about *Live It Down*; he thinks it the finest work of fiction that has been produced in the present reign. Tears rise to Mr. Petter's eyes when he speaks of its most pathetic chapters. He said to me only yesterday, "Mr. Jeaffreson is a most remarkable man. He is the only living novelist who knows how to combine *sensation business* with *high religious tone!*"'

Before Dr. Wright started on his return-journey to London, I had agreed that *Not Dead Yet*, on which I was already working, should run through the *Quiver*, before its publication in three volumes. I regret to say that the story failed to please the readers of the *Quiver*. Either because its sensation business was excessive, or because its religious tone was inferior to the religious tone of the earlier story, *Not Dead Yet* proved distasteful to pious families in every part of the country. Horrifying the old ladies in countless villages, it wounded the nonconformist conscience to such a degree that the editor of the *Quiver* was severely handled by furious correspondents for allowing so flippant, worldly, and unedifying a tale to appear in his columns. Fortunately for me, the larger world differed from the subscribers for the *Quiver* respecting *Not Dead Yet*, which was in great demand at the circulating libraries, as soon as it appeared in three volumes. Successful in its particular season (1864) it came to be much talked about some years later during the successive Tichborne trials, on account of the strange coincidences in the story of its hero, the missing Edward Starling, and the story of the missing Roger Tichborne, and the even stranger coincidences in the career of the novel's imaginary impostor Rupert Smith and the career of the notorious claimant of the Tichborne drama.

How quick the public was to notice these two sets of coincidences in the tale of fancy and the drama of real life appears from the fact, that during the proceedings in the Court of Chancery, which preceded the great civil trial at Westminster, Vice-Chancellor Sir William Page Wood announced from his judicial seat that several correspondents had called his attention to the sets of coincidences. I do not know who wrote the letters to the Vice-Chancellor; but my pen produced the following note about the curious coincidences, which appeared in the *Weekly Gossip* of the *Athenæum* on 12th January, 1867,—

'The romantic story of the Tichborne baronetcy,—is it fact or fiction? Is it a daring reproduction of an imaginary tale, or a veritable drama, certain incidents of which are due to the influence of a fascinating novel, or an affair that, apart from several singular coincidences, has no connection with a popular work of romantic art? A singular concurrence of circumstances affords some countenance to a suspicion that the story about the Tichborne baronetcy, which has run the round of the journals, is nothing more than a bold adaptation of a well-known work of fiction. In 1864 Messrs. Hurst and Blackett published a novel, entitled *Not Dead Yet*, the hero of which is Edward Starling, at the story's outset the unacknowledged grandson, at its close the successor of Sir Frank Starling, Bart., of Gamlingay Court, Hampshire. Through a misunderstanding with his grandfather, this heir to a Hampshire baronetcy is severed from his family. Having received his education in France and the Channel Islands, he, on breaking with his grandfather, quits his native country, and after wandering in divers lands seeks his fortune in Australia, where he undergoes strange vicissitudes, and is struggling with adverse circumstances at the time of his father's death. On receiving intelligence of that occurrence, by which he becomes the premier baronet of Hampshire, he returns to England to claim his birthright; when, on reaching the old country, he finds an adroit pretender occupying his place. Thus runs the novel *Not Dead Yet;* and certainly the main points of the story bear a strong resemblance to the main points of the Tichborne romance. Like Sir Frank Starling of the novel, Sir Alfred Tichborne was a wealthy Hampshire baronet, his rank, like Sir Frank's, being of the first James's creation. Like Sir Frank Starling, he had a rupture with his heir, who, like Edward Starling in the romance, after receiving a foreign education, emigrated to Australia, and was residing there at the time of his succession to the dignity and estates of his family. Like Edward Starling, the heir to the Tichborne title and property was believed to have died in Australia, and like him he is said to have reappeared and proved himself—not dead yet. The situation and characteristics assigned to Gamlingay Court by the novelist accord, with those of Tichborne Park, near Alresford. At this point of the drama, or rather at this point in the series of their assertions, the journalists are asking whether the claimant of the Tichborne baronetcy is a pretender or true heir. If in the course of the next few months they should represent him to be a successful pretender, or, still better, an unsuccessful pretender, the narrative will bear a still more striking resemblance to the novel. Of course the writers in the daily papers will meet our suspicions by asserting that they deal with facts, whereas the novelist was merely a writer of fiction. But why should we believe them? Let them look at their own case thus. For argument's sake, let us suppose that, dates excepted, the facts of their story are unquestionable. Let us also suppose that those facts occurred four years since,—just two years before, instead of two years after, the publication of *Not Dead Yet*. In this case would they, on the appearance of the novel, have hesitated to charge the novelist with serving up old facts, instead of new fancies? And if he had replied, "On my honour I invented every incident of my tale," would they have believed him? Would they not have scornfully declined to give credence to his assertion? Why, then, should we have greater faith in the veracity of their statements of fact than they would have had in the imaginary character of his fictions? Anyhow, if the journalists have not been playing with the credulity of the public in this matter, the singular coincidences between the story of the circulating libraries and the statements of the newspapers should teach critics not to be over-hasty in charging novelists with borrowing their plots from the reports of the journals. *They should also incline critics to be slow in preferring an accusation of plagiarism against a novelist, simply because the plot or other principal features of his story bear some similitude to the inventions and devices of earlier writers.*'

The words printed in italics rose to my mind some years since, when certain critics were much too hasty in charging Mr. Rider Haggard with plagiarism, because some of his earlier stories bore in some of their devices and subordinate inventions a much slighter resemblance to certain old romances which he had never read, than the resemblance which my work of fiction, published in 1864, bore in its plot, chief characters, and leading incidents to the legal drama that opened more than two years after I had written my novel to the last line. I may add that, while I was writing *Not Dead Yet*, I had no thought of the Tichborne family, did not know the date of the creation of the Tichborne baronetcy, was not aware that the Tichborne estate lay in Hampshire, and had never heard anything of the missing Roger Tichborne's story.

CHAPTER XII.

RICHARD COBDEN AND QUEEN ELIZABETH.

Life of Robert Stephenson, C.E., F.R.S.—Mr. Smiles's *Lives of Boulton and Watt*—Popular Error touching the Elder Stephenson and the Steam Locomotive—David Roberts, R.A., on 'the Ignoromeousness' of Artists—James Hayllar's Picture, entitled *The Queen's Highway in the Sixteenth Century*—Richard Cobden's Part in the Production of that Picture—The Free Trader at Fault—His Inability to produce his Authority—An Essay in Literary Misdirection—Maud Ufford's Letter to Margery Pennington—D'Eyncourt's *Memoirs of Maids of Honour*—'Quaint old D'Eyncourt!'—Mr. Smiles's *Life of Thomas Telford, the Civil Engineer*—Explanation of Richard Cobden's Mistake—Light from *Murray's Handbook for Kent and Sussex*—'An ingenious Gentleman' of Queen Anne's Court—Prince George of Denmark—Charles VI. of Spain—Falsification of Personal History—Publication of *A Book About Lawyers*—Letters from learned Lawyers—Edward Foss, F.S.A., author of *The Judges of England*—Letter from the Lord Chief Baron—Sir Fitzroy Kelly's Confirmation of my Exposure of a spurious Anecdote—Sir William Follett's Health in 1844 and 1845—An Idle Tale touching Sir William Follett and George Stephenson—Migration from Mesopotamia to St. John's Wood—Joy and Sorrow—Holiday Trips.

Not Dead Yet having appeared in the spring of 1864, the *Life of Robert Stephenson, F.R.S.*—the joint-work of Professor William Pole, C.E. and F.R.S., and the present writer—was published by the Messrs. Longman and Co. in the autumn of the same year. Mr. Charles Manby was right in saying the biography would be none the more acceptable to the public, for proving that the Elder Stephenson neither invented the locomotive nor did anything of importance for its improvement. But the joint-authors of the Younger Stephenson's biography were less eager for popularity than desirous of telling the truth.

Twelve months later, when he had produced his *Lives of Boulton and Watt*, the last and concluding volumes of his *Lives of the Engineers* (1865), I observed with interest and approval that in his preface to the new book, Mr. Smiles forbore to speak of the Elder Stephenson, as though he were the inventor of the first steam locomotive to run with smooth wheels on smooth rails. But the popular biographer still spoke of his favourite engineer as 'the principal improver and introducer of the locomotive.' Consequently I opened my *Athenæum* review (2nd December, 1865,) of the *Lives of Boulton and Watt* with these words,—

'No longer specially claiming credit to George Stephenson for the discovery that locomotives with smooth wheels could work efficiently on smooth rails, by the adhesion of the two smooth surfaces; and no longer insisting that George Stephenson built the first locomotive that moved with smooth wheels upon smooth rails, Mr. Smiles in the preface to this last and concluding volume of his *Lives of the Engineers* clings to the statement that George Stephenson was "the principal improver and introducer of the locomotive engine." What do these words mean? It is now known to everyone interested in such matters that the Killingworth engineer was *not* the first to ascertain that the adhesion of smooth wheels on smooth rails was sufficient for purposes of locomotion; that in building his Killingworth locomotive he merely copied Mr.

Hedley of Wylam, so far as leading principles were concerned; that he did *not* invent the blast; that he did *not* even contrive an efficient blast sooner than Mr. Hackworth of Darlington; that he did *not* invent the multitubular boiler. Mr. Smiles does not venture to claim credit for his hero on any one of these points. Since none of these improvements on Trevithick's engine can be attributed to the keen-witted Northumbrian mechanic, how can he be justly spoken of as "*the* principal improver of the locomotive"? With no greater justice can he be designated "*the* principal introducer of the locomotive." If that title should be applied to anyone, it should be given to the late Mr. Hedley of Wylam, as the man who built the first travelling-engine that was a successful machine and actual substitute for animal power; but even to that ingenious contriver the term would be inapplicable, since he was only one of several persons, who combined to accomplish the work, the honour of which Mr. Smiles would fain ascribe to a person who was no more than a subordinate.'

That George Stephenson was neither the inventor nor an important improver nor the introducer of the steam-locomotive is a matter of historic certainty. The story that he invented the locomotive is a pure biographic fiction, which in some obscure and hitherto undiscovered way came into existence since his death. It is not to be supposed even for a moment that Mr. Smiles, no less honourable as a man than entertaining and powerful as a writer, had part in the original making of the untrue story. He merely came upon the curious fiction, and by the art of his delightful pen gave i a place in universal history. It is also only fair to honest old Geordie Stephenson to say that had any such story ever come to his ears, he would have been greatly pained by it, and would have used very strong language in repudiating it as a monstrous untruth.

In the same year (1864), which saw the publication

of the severely truthful and accurate *Life of Robert Stephenson*, I was guilty of a droll exploit in literary misdirection for which I can plead no better excuse than that I did it to help a friend in difficulty.

David Roberts, R.A., many years since made me laugh and gave me a good word, by telling me that he regarded artists as 'an ignoromeous class of persons.' I am far from thinking so lightly of artists; but in the spring of 1864, I observed a faint vein of ignoromeousness in the bright and well-informed mind of my old friend James Hayllar who occupied a big house in Mecklenburgh Square, whilst I was tenant of a tiny house in Heathcote Street. As we had been friends for years before I took possession of the tiny house, and as he had married a gentlewoman, who was one of my rather numerous somehow-or-other consins, it is not surprising that he and I became 'thicker than ever,' when our parlour windows winked at one another. I was continually dropping into his studio; his smiling face no less often brightened my little study. At night, when no article for to-morrow's paper held me to my desk, I used to run twice or thrice a-week into his billiard-room, for a game before going to bed. My little girl had no dearer friends than the little Hayllar girls, whom their father used in those days to paint into his pictures, and who now-a-days are applauded for pictures of their own painting.

Hayllar's picture for the Academy Exhibition of 1864 was *The Queen's Highway in the Sixteenth Century*, and it proved very attractive to picture-viewers at the Academy, though no policemen were put on special duty to guard the thing of art and beauty. There stood Queen Bess, with two ladies in attendance a few paces behind her, on the muddy and rutted road of a Sussex highway, keeping her eyes upon her coach, and at the same time watching the Sussex boors, who were labouring to get the ponderous vehicle out of the scrape, in which it was stuck fast. The Queen painted from a piquant Oxford Street *modiste*, the ladies-in-attendance, drawn from two Mesopotamian maid-servants, were examples of high-bred feminine delicacy and stateliness, and of the costume of the period. The big coach had been painted from a state-chamber on wheels, that was said to have been greatly admired in Dublin, when His Excellency the Lord Lieutenant of Queen Bess's Ireland used to ride in it through his rather squalid capital. The boors and the landscape were well painted. For the subject of this picture Hayllar (a Sussex man) was indebted to Richard Cobden (another Sussex man), who had pressed the artist to depict a scene, so eloquent of the difficulties and discomforts of travelling by carriage in an English county, towards the close of the Tudor period. Cobden averred that he had read an account of this incident of one of Queen Elizabeth's progresses in some old county-history, resting in his Sussex home. Liking the subject, from Cobden's simple and yet eloquent statement of the case, Hayllar had painted the picture without having studied the printed words of Cobden's authority. Cobden had watched the progress of the picture with interest, and on the occasion of his last visit to the painter's studio had been enjoined to copy from the old county-history the *ipsissima verba* of the passage, of which the picture was the artistic illustration. On the last sending-in day for outsiders, the post, instead of bringing the longed-for transcript from the text of an old book, only brought a letter, in which the great Free Trader told how he and Mrs. Cobden and their children had been overhauling and searching a dozen different folios, in a vain hunt for the needful description.

'Here's a fix, Jeff! What the deuce am I to do?' said Hayllar, when he had told me his trouble. 'Can't you give me an authority? Be a good fellow, and find up something at the British Museum.'

Said I, 'You ignoromeous fellow! Ignoromeous of the very matter that has been engaging your best thoughts for the last six months! I can give you sufficient authority, without going to the Museum. Here, I'll put it on that bit of paper.'

Sitting down at a writing-table, I wrote these words,—

'THE QUEEN'S HIGHWAY IN THE SIXTEENTH CENTURY.
J. HAYLLAR.

'" The journey was marvellous for ease and expedition, for such is the perfect evenness of the New Highway, Her Highness left the coach only once, whilst hinds and folk of a base sort lifted it on with their poles."—*Vide*, Maud Ufford's Letter to Margery Pennington in D'Eyncourt's *Memoirs of the Maids of Honour!*'

'Capital!' exclaimed Hayllar. ''Tis the very thing I wanted. What a marvellous memory you have, Jeff, to be able to bring that scrap out so pat and neat, at the very nick of time, from old D'Eyncourt's *Maids of Honour!*"

'Memory?' I answered, 'I go to imagination for my facts. There never was any old D'Eyncourt; or, if there was, he never wrote a book about Maids of Honour. There must have been a Maud Ufford,—the name sounds like truth; but, you may take my word for it, she never wrote a line to Margery Pennington. This child is a novelist. He invented this pleasant quotation.'

'But the selecting committee and the hangers will spot it,' Hayllar remarked, after coming out of his laughter.

'Not a bit of it!' I answered. 'It took you in,—and it will take them in. They are just as ignoromeous as you are.'

So the picture was sent off to the Academy, with the name I had given it, and the justificatory quotation I had invented. In due course, the little quotation figured very prettily in the Academy catalogue, and in most of the critical reviews of the exhibition. As Hayllar wished the fictitious quality of the historic *morceau* to be kept a secret during the exhibition, I forbore to talk of my successful imposture; and good fun it was to me to observe what airs the critics and the connoisseurs gave themselves, in affecting perfect familiarity with D'Eyncourt's delightful book. They usually spoke of him as 'old D'Eyncourt.' Sometimes they even went so far as to call him 'quaint old D'Eyncourt.' They were no less at home with the fair Maud and Margery. 'After all,' one of the humbugs said, 'it is from the frank letters by the high-bred dames and demoiselles of merry England, that we get much of our brightest and surest knowledge of our Tudor ancestors.'

The drollest and most instructive consequence of my successful essay in literary imposture was that Mr. Samuel Smiles, who was then meditating his well-known *Life of Thomas Telford, the Civil Engineer*, and was drawing together multifarious scraps of information about the roads of England in olden time, accepted my fiction of Maud Ufford's letter as a piece of sound documentary evidence, and popped it into his book. 'But,' says Mr. Smiles in his *Life of Telford*, p. 13, Standard Edition (1867), 'it was only a few of the main roads leading from the metropolis that were practicable for coaches; and on the occasion of a royal progress, or the visit of a lord-lieutenant, there was a general turn-out of labourers and masons to mend the ways and render the bridges at least temporarily secure. Of one of Queen Elizabeth's journeys it is said,—" It was marvellous for ease and expedition, for such is the perfect evenness of the new highway that Her Majesty left the coach only once, whilst the hinds and the folk of a base sort *lifted it on with their poles*."'

How came Cobden to imagine he had perused a record of this incident of Elizabethan travel, which he certainly never found in any book touching the high-handed Queen? No chronicler of Her Highness's doings tells any such story. A somewhat similar account is, however, given of the troubles that came from the badness of the Sussex roads in the eighteenth century to Prince George of Denmark, Queen Anne's husband, when he journeyed to Petworth, to welcome the Spanish King. In the preface to *Murray's Handbook for Kent and Sussex* (Edition, 1863) appears this passage,—'A letter " by an ingenious gentleman of the court" gives a curious account of the journey (in 1708) of Prince George of Denmark from Godalming to Petworth, where he met Charles VI. of Spain, who had landed at Portsmouth. "We set out," says the ingenious gentleman, " by torchlight, and did not get out of the coaches (save only when we were overturned or stuck fast in the mud) till we arrived at our journey's end. 'Twas hard for the Prince to sit 14 hours in the coach that day without eating anything, and passing through the worst ways I ever saw in my life. We were thrown but once indeed in going, but both our coach, which was the leading, and His Highness's body-coach, would have suffered often if the nimble boors of Sussex had not frequently poised it and supported it with their shoulders from Godalming almost to Petworth."' Much more is given in *Murray's Handbook* from the letter of 'the ingenious gentleman of the court.' Who was he? Was he a veritable personage, or as much a mere thing of romantic invention as my ingenious lady of an earlier court—Maud Ufford?

Few readers will doubt that Richard Cobden got the germinal notion of the subject of Hayllar's picture from this passage of *Murray's Handbook*; that in thinking over the narrative assigned to 'an ingenious gentleman of the court' he unintentionally substituted Queen Bess for Prince George; that, having so replaced the Prince with the Queen, the great Free Trader imagined the ladies in attendance, whom he spoke of, as having stood behind the Queen in a muddy Sussex road. It is thus that the facts of personal history are tossed about, and stories are mistold by honest narrators. By defect of memory and force of fancy, Richard Cobden, far from being the prosaic and unimaginative creature some persons conceive him to have been, gave so vivid an account of Queen Elizabeth's sufferings from the misadventures which are said in print to have befallen Queen Anne's husband, that the painter produced a picture of the mistold story. For Hayllar's advantage, I put a piece of false history on the false picture. My scrap of fictitious writing was reproduced as sound history by so grave a biographer as Mr. Smiles. 'Tis thus that personal history is sometimes falsified. How much fiction is there in Plutarch's *Lives*? 'There's nothing new and there's nothing true, and it don't much sinnify,' said Thackeray. It certainly matters little that James Hayllar's historical picture is wanting in historic truth. As a thing of beauty, the picture is all the better for the blunder. The queen of power and beauty and her daintily-attired maids-of-honour show more agreeably on the canvas, than the King of Spain, Prince George of Denmark, and two or three ingenious gentlemen of the Court would have done.

In 1865 and 1866 I was working upon my *Book about Lawyers*, which was published by Messrs. Hurst and Blackett in November of the latter year. In the concluding paragraph of a long review (nearly four columns in length), the *Times* said of this book,

'Mr. Jeaffreson modestly styles himself "a collector of anecdotes and gossip," but in spite of this self-depreciation, he has accomplished his work in a very creditable manner. *A Book about Lawyers* belongs, of course, to what is called the book-making department of literature—that is, it is made up for the most part of extracts from other books; but when we consider the number of the authorities which have been consulted and the careful use made of the information thus obtained, the epithet "bookmaker" need convey no sense of disparagement. But the compiler has taken pains to collect information from persons as well as books, and as every little scrap of old-world gossip about his legal brethren seems to interest him personally, he writes with a keen sense of enjoyment, which greatly enhances the reader's pleasures.' The only mistake my publishers made in respect to this book was that they liberated the type, after striking off a much larger edition than they hoped to sell, to the last copy. It was, therefore, necessary to re-set the type for the production of the 'Second Edition, Revised,' when the unusually heavy 'First Edition' had been exhausted within eight weeks of its publication. My time in Heathcote Street closed with this success.

The Lord Chief Baron Kelly and Mr. Edward Foss, F.S.A., of the Inner Temple, the laborious and accurate author of *The Judges of England*, were two of the numerous learned lawyers, from judges to solicitors, who wrote me agreeable letters about my volumes on *Lawyers*. Giving me some information for the amendment of the next edition of my book, Mr.

Edward Foss opened his interesting and characteristic letter with a courteous acknowledgment of my civil words about his chief literary performance.

'Sir,' said the historian of *The Judges*, dating from Trensham House, Croydon, January 30th, 1867, 'I have just had an opportunity of seeing your pleasant *Book about Lawyers*, and I thank you for the handsome manner in which you have spoken of me and my work.'

Eight months later, the Right Hon. Sir Fitzroy Kelly, dating from 8, Connaught Place, W., September 30th, 1867, wrote me a letter in confirmation of my reasons for saying that George Stephenson and Sir William Follett never came together at Sir Robert Peel's country house, and that consequently a familiar anecdote ('the gift of the gab' story) of their intercourse at Drayton Manor should be rated as an idle tale.

'The Lord Chief Baron,' my correspondent wrote, 'presents his compliments to Mr. Jeaffreson, and having lately, while on the Continent, read with much gratification Mr. Jeaffreson's *Book about Lawyers*, begs leave to offer a remark or two upon some passages which it contains, which Mr. Jeaffreson may think it worth while to bear in recollection, whenever another edition of the work shall be published. In confirmation of the statement (vol. ii, p. 139) denying the truth of an anecdote of Sir William Follett, concerning an occurrence reported to have taken place, to which Sir William Follett and George Stephenson were parties, the Chief Baron would observe that he met Sir William and Lady Follett at Bonn on the Rhine, on their way to Italy in August, 1844, and that Sir William passed the winter in Italy, and did not return to England until long after the period of George Stephenson's visit to Sir Robert Peel, and was then in a state of health which precluded the possibility of a visit by himself to meet a convivial party at a country house . . .'

Years have passed since I stept the stones of Heathcote Street; but for many years after my migration from that pleasant corner of Mesopotamia to No. 43, Springfield Road, St. John's Wood, N.W., I used to make pilgrimages to Mecklenburgh Square for the pleasure of looking at dear little No. 5,—the first tenement that I and my wife could call 'our home,' the only house in which I had the pleasure of entertaining my dear mother, the house in which I made the acquaintance of my only child, the house in which my brother Horace had his quarters during the interval between his return from Australia and his appointment to the place of Resident Physician of the Fever Hospital, in which he so nearly lost his life during the great epidemic. How much happiness we had in that little house, and also how much sorrow! Sad changes came to my life whilst I tenanted the tiny house. My dear mother died in the summer of 1863, my dear father followed her to the unseen land in November, 1865. To the brief obituary memoir, which I wrote for the *Lancet* immediately after my dear father's death, the editor of that journal added these words, 'Mr. Jeaffreson was one of the earliest contributors to the *Lancet*, and was a steady friend to progress at a time when its friends were few.'

Up to the time of my dear father's death, my visits to Framlingham were frequent and my sojourns there were long, for he liked to have me and my wife with him. But our trips to Suffolk were not our only trips from Heathcote Street. I bethink me of our merry run to Cambridge with the Hepworth Dixons, when the Devil's Own manœuvred with the University Volunteers,—of our North Welsh tour, which we enjoyed so immensely, though it rained in torrents nearly the whole time,—of the rapid run I and Dixon made to Bury, Lynn, Norwich, Thetford, Framlingham, and other places of East Anglia,—of the pleasant days we spent with the Dixons at Harwich and Felixstowe,—and my first Swiss trip, made with my good and ever hearty Dixon, when my dear wife was much too happy in the society of her newly-invented daughter, to care to accompany us. For *me*, Dixon was the best fellow-tourist imaginable. In some matters he was masterful, not to say despotic. He decided where we should go and what we should do, fixed the hours of starting, and chose the routes to be taken. On these points I neither had nor cared to have a voice. On the other hand, he rewarded my submissiveness to his will and energy, by relieving me of all the petty troubles of touring. He took the tickets, passed the baggage, selected the rooms, and at every turn provided for my comfort with characteristic cheeriness and considerateness. Had he been my paid courier, he could not have worked harder for my contentment. Ever alert and capable, he was a most unselfish and sympathetic fellow-traveller.

CHAPTER XIII.

' OUR CLUB.'

Augustus De Morgan on London Club-houses—Tavern Clubs—
The Tumbler Club—*The Sheridan* Club—*The Rambler* Club
—*Our Club*—Notable Members of the last-named Club—
Frederick William Hamstede, First Secretary of *Our Club*—
Thackeray's Affection for ' little Hamstede '—' I love little
Hamstede '—Messrs. Merivale and Marzials on Thackeray—
Cause of Thackeray's Tenderness for 'little Hamstede '—
Clunn's Hotel, Covent Garden—Dinners at ' Clunn's '—
Marrow-Bones and Marrow-Spoons—Drinking in 'the 'Fifties
and 'Sixties '—Table-Talk at *Our Club*—George Jessel on
Vulgar Prejudices—Songsters of *Our Club*—Robert Chambers on the Waverley Novels—Freedom of Action in Edinburgh—Robert Chambers on the Fictions of Biographers—
Insult offered to Frederick Lawrence—Garibaldi's Telegram
to Fred Lawrence—A Large Order on Modest Means—Mr,
Matthews of Sheffield—Théophile Gautier at *Our Club*—
' Who the Devil is *Dore* ?'—*Tête-à-tête* of an Englishman who
spoke no French and a Frenchman who knew no English—
'The Illustrious Goaty '—Théophile at the Salisbury Hotel
—Mr. Matthews entertaining ' the brightest Spirits of the
Age.'

WHEN John Doran (Dr. Doran) was pressed by
Shirley Brooks to become a member of the Garrick
Club, Augustus De Morgan (the famous mathematician, and for years one of the inner ring of the

Athenæum staff) advised him to resist Brooks's entreaty. 'To a man of your age, with a happy home and more friends than you need, a club is useless. London clubs are institutions kept up by a hundred men for the convenience of ten.' To Doran's remark that the members' roll of every good London club contained the names of men whom one would like to know, De Morgan answered, 'And they are just the members who never enter it, or at least never use it with a regularity and freedom that would give you opportunities for approaching them.' De Morgan had already advised me in similar terms to avoid the expense of becoming a member of a London club-house. To me he added, 'At the outset club-houses were instituted from considerations of economy, for the advantage of poor rather than of rich men. But they are managed so as to be the reverse of economical. What with the entrance-money, the yearly subscription, and the charges of eating and drinking at one of the joint-stock palaces, it costs more than a little to be a member of a London club-house, if you use it habitually. You will do better in every way for yourself by spending half the money in entertaining your friend's hospitably at your own house.'

Doran acted on De Morgan's advice, and to the last was remarkable amongst London men of his social quality for never joining a house-club. After acting for some time on the mathematician's counsel, I ceased to be controlled by it, and learnt from experience the soundness of the advice. During my life in London I have belonged to four different house-clubs,—two of them being clubs that *primâ facie* were peculiarly qualified to contribute to my contentment,—but I seldom entered any one of them. They neither afforded me diversion nor did aught else for my advantage. It was otherwise with the several tavern-clubs, to which I belonged in the earlier years of my London career—*The Tumbler* of which I have already spoken, the short-lived *Sheridan* (which numbered amongst its members George Augustus Sala, J. C. Parkinson, Burnand of happy thoughts, Fred Dickens, brother of the great novelist, George Hodder, author of *Memories of my Time*, James Hutton, Byron the novelist and dramatic author, Edmund Yates), *The Rambler*, from which I withdrew on the eve of my marriage, and *Our Club* into which I was elected towards the end of 1860, and of which I have been a member for thirty-two years.

Founded and raised to social celebrity by Douglas Jerrold, *Our Club* had enjoyed a bright reputation in literary London for a considerable number of years, when I dined at its table for the first time as Hepworth Dixon's guest. Honourably known in London, it was talked about and written about in Paris as a society, so remarkable for its convivial usages and so distinguished by the wit and achievements of its members, that no Parisian might plume himself on his familiarity with the literary and artistic coteries of the English capital, until he had feasted at its board. The importance of the club may have been slightly exaggerated by writers on either side the Seine, but to demonstrate that the society comprised a considerable number of clever and notable gentlemen, it is enough to mention a few of the persons who belonged to the brotherhood in its palmy days.

Forbearing to speak of individuals, who from death or voluntary retirement had ceased to be members of the society before I first dined at its table, I can mention as whilom members of *Our Club* within my own personal cognizance,—William Makepeace Thackeray, of whom I shall say a good deal in later chapters; Samuel Lucas[a] of the *Times*, successor to Samuel Phillips, as chief literary critic of that journal; Davison,[a] the musical critic of the *Times*; Mark Lemon,[a] original editor of *Punch*; John Leech,[a] *Punch*-draughtsman; Horace Mayhew,[a] *Punch*-writer, and one of the original staff of the famous comic paper; Shirley Brooks,[a] editor of *Punch*, next in succession to Mark Lemon; Hepworth Dixon;[a] James Hannay;[a] David Masson,[a] biographer of John Milton, and Professor of English Literature in the University of Edinburgh; Edwin Lawrence,[a] F.S.A., of the Stock Exchange, antiquary and artistic *connoisseur*; John Doran,[a] LL.D.; Henry Holl,[a] novelist, dramatic author, and theatrical mimic; Rear-Admiral Sir Edward Belcher, C.B., the Arctic navigator; Charles Knight,[a] historian, publisher, and popular educator; Robert Chambers,[a] LL.D., social historian and publisher; Robert Cooke,[a] publisher, nephew and coadjutor of John Murray; .... Evans,[a] publisher, of the firm of Bradbury and Evans; Alexander MacMillan, publisher; William Blanchard Jerrold,[a] editor of *Lloyd's Weekly Newspaper*, in succession to his father Douglas Jerrold; Norman Lockyer, F.R.S., the Astronomer; William Hazlitt,[a] Shakespearian scholar and Registrar of the Court of Bankruptcy, only son of the famous critic; Nicolas Trübner, Oriental scholar and publisher; Joseph Octave Delepierre,[a] the Belgian scholar and antiquary, and Secretary of Legation and Consul-General for Belgium in London; Lieutenant-Colonel Chesterton; Thomas Wright,[a] M.A., archæological explorer and antiquarian editor; Peter Cunningham,[a] antiquary, antiquarian editor, art-critic, and general journalist, son of Allan Cunningham; Colonel Francis Cunningham, *Saturday* Reviewer, brother of the aforementioned Peter Cunningham; E. M. Ward,[a] R.A., painter; Solomon Hart,[a] R.A., painter; Charles Landseer,[a] R.A., painter; Marcus Stone, R.A., painter; Joseph Durham,[a] A.R.A., sculptor; Thomas Woolner, R.A., sculptor and poet; W. H. B. Davis, R.A., painter; George Jessel,[a] barrister-at-law, in his later time Sir George Jessel, Master of the Rolls; John Humffreys Parry,[a] barrister, in his later time Serjeant-at-Law; Frederick Lawrence,[a] barrister-at-law, author of *The Life of Henry Fielding*; Douglas Straight, M.P., barrister-at-law, and in later time a judge in India; J. S. Ramskill,[a] M.D. Lond., of St. Helen's Place; Francis Sibson,[a] M.D. Lond., of Lower Brook Street, Grosvenor Square; Henry G. Wright,[a] M.D. Lond., of 23, Somerset Street, Portman Square, *Saturday* Reviewer; Hugh Welsh Diamond,[a] M.D., famous for his colloquial humour and his collection of British Pottery; Dr. Duplex,[a] L.C.P. Edin.; John Percy,[a] M.D. Edin., F.R.S., distinguished in scientific literature by his several works on *Metallurgy*, and an able contributor to the *Times*, *Athenæum*, and *Saturday Review*; Benjamin Ward Richardson, M.D., St. Andrews, and F.R.S., scientist and man of letters; Spencer Smith,

F.R.C.S., Lecturer on Surgery at St. Mary's Hospital; Ernest Hart, F.R.C.S., assistant-editor of the *Lancet* and in later time editor of the *British Medical Journal*; William Torrens McCullagh Torrens, M.P., biographer of Sir James Graham and William second Viscount Melbourne; Morgan John O'Connell,[a] the Liberator's handsome and humorous nephew; Charles Lamb Kenney,[a] dramatic critic and general journalist; Thomas Hamber, M.A., Oxon., editor of the *Standard*; Burton Blyth, journalist, editor of the *Morning Herald*, and in later time article-writer on the *Standard*; Lieutenant-Colonel William Haywood, C.E., architect of the Holborn Viaduct; William Stigand, poet and essayist; Sir Jules Benedict, musical composer; Frederick William Hamstede,[a] of 3, Adam Street, Adelphi, and the Garrick Club, for many years Honorary Secretary of *Our Club*; Charles Dickens the Younger, who succeeded Hamstede in the same honorary secretaryship; Walter White, Honorary Secretary of O. C. in succession to the same Charles Dickens; James Macmillan of the Common-Law bar; Sir Henry Anderson of the Indian Civil Service; William Ashurst, solicitor of the Post Office; F. Napier Broome, in later time Sir Napier Broome, a Colonial Governor; F. W. Cosens, Spanish scholar and art-connoisseur; E. B. Eastwick, M.P.; G. A. Henty, journalist and novelist; Major Moncrieff ('gun-carriage' Moncrieff); E. A. Moriarty, Irish humourist, and best translator of Charles Dickens's works into German; Benjamin Webster, actor and theatrical manager; Roger Fenton,[a] photographer; Andrew Maclure, photographer and songster.

These names I have written down as they came to my mind, putting the letter *a* over the names of those who were members of *Our Club*, when Thackeray was of the brotherhood. As I put the names on paper from recollection, unassisted by contemporary lists, I may have erred in respect to the spelling of one or two names, and from fault of memory omitted several names, that would shine forth brightly in a perfect record of the members of the society.

Special notice should be taken of the first secretary of O. C., because he was dear to both Douglas Jerrold and Thackeray; and fortunately one can speak frankly about him, without fear of paining his survivors, for many years have passed over his grave, and at his death he left neither widow, nor sister, nor brother, nor child. Originally a city-clerk, in some way associated with the Mr. Powles who induced the youthful Benjamin Disraeli to join him in mining speculations, Frederick William Hamstede was a kindly, honest, simple little man; but he was wholly wanting in the mental attainments and graces that qualify an obscure person to associate on equal terms with scholars and wits. His learning in no degree or direction exceeded the knowledge which a man requires for the performance of the duties of a subordinate clerk in a broker's office. He could cast accounts, knew something about the technicalities of the money-market, and could write a sufficient letter on familiar matters of business. In education, manner, tone, he was an old-fashioned city-clerk; but he differed from the majority of clerks, in his superstitious reverence for professional authors, his delight in associating with them, and his daily practice of covering sheets of letter-paper with the weakest doggerel that ever proceeded from the pen of an amateur poetaster. Year after year this odd little man poured letters upon me through the post, but he seldom wrote to me in prose. If I was absent from a meeting of *Our Club*, he seldom failed to write me a metrical account of what had taken place at Clunn's in my absence. When his humour was finely and greatly tickled under my immediate observation by an incident at O. C., I knew he would send me during the week a poem on the amusing occurrence. Pouring doggerel thus lavishly on the present annalist, he was no less liberal of his verse to other members of the club. He spent several shillings a year in sending poems of his own composition to Thackeray.

When Thackeray's 'dear little Hamstede' produced doggerel at an average rate of fifty lines a-day, he had ceased to be a clerk, and was living in lodgings at 3, Adam Street, Adelphi, upon the interest of a few hundred pounds, which he invested in the St. John del Rey gold-mine, before it became famous or indeed of any good repute. Whilst he provided thus fortunately for his own declining years, the little man rendered several of his friends the good service of inducing them to put their money into the same lucky venture. To little Hamstede's secret and sound information about St. John del Rey's, Frederick Lawrence owed it that he lived so comfortably during his later time, when he was earning little at the Bar, and still less by literature.

I question whether Thackeray towards the close

of his too short career cared more for Edward Fitzgerald than he did for the obscure, illiterate, and weak-minded little man, who kept the accounts and ordered the dinners of O. C. with commendable exactness and discretion. Some of the lighter spirits about Thackeray used to banter him about his excessive complaisance to so curious a *protégé*, until he silenced them by exclaiming, with a droll combination of 'gush' and irritability, 'No one shall say a word against little Hamstede in my hearing. I love little Hamstede; I tell you, I love little Hamstede; and as for his verses over which you have been making merry, all I care to say is that I take more pleasure in reading his poetry than I do in reading your prose.' Why did the scholarly and fastidious Thackeray love the old-fashioned little clerk who was singularly deficient in lovable qualities? To answer the question effectively, I must add something to what I have already said of the first Secretary of *Our Club*. Besides being a small man, he was a hunchback, and so crippled in his limbs that he could not move across a room without the help of a stick. In his infancy he had fallen from his nurse's arms to the ground, and from the fall sustained an injury— the dislocation of a thigh-bone—that was not submitted to a surgeon, until it was too late to reduce the dislocation. Resulting in the malformation of little Hamstede's body, this accident also occasioned the sour expression of his countenance,—the expression that usually distinguishes sufferers from severe spinal deformity.

Though I cannot think with Mr. Herman Merivale

and Mr. Frank Marzials, that Thackeray was especially remarkable for religious sensibility and devotional earnestness, and that his character and career were powerfully controlled by religious influences, I concur with them in thinking that Disappointment—i.e., the deep and enduring sorrow which came to him from his various distresses—was beneficial to his generous nature and fruitful of some of his finest qualities. Instead of dwarfing and deadening his sympathies, sorrow quickened them. Like the Queen of Virgil's poem, the great novelist learnt from his own misfortunes to pity the wretched. Sometimes cynical in the conceits of his brain and the freaks of his humour, in the arrowy utterances of his tongue and pen, he was never cynical at heart. Cynicism was only the outward robe with which he veiled a nature of almost womanly softness, a heart of heavenly compassionateness: and in the little hunchback Secretary of *Our Club* he came upon a weakling, with several titles to his pitiful regard.

Himself a sufferer from an accident, that made his countenance an example of disfigurement, the tender-hearted Thackeray found in the old city-clerk a fellow-sufferer who had been far more cruelly dealt with by accidental violence. A giant in stature, Thackeray pitied little Hamstede for being so minute. Enjoying the free use of a pair of remarkably long legs, Thackeray commiserated the infirm cripple who found it difficult to ascend a high flight of stairs or walk the length of a long gallery. Shapely in his own figure, the tall and stately novelist compassionated the dwarf for being a hunchback. Himself possessing a countenance that, notwithstanding the great and conspicuous disfigurement, was pleasant to all beholders, Thackeray pitied poor little Hamstede for having the sharp, sour, querulous look of a sufferer from spinal deformity. Instead of despising the dwarf for his lack of wit and culture, his want of breeding and the gentle air, the great Thackeray, whose taste was no less fastidious than his humour was subtle, and the perfection of whose social style was recognized even by those who disliked him, regarded the several defects and disabilities as so many additional reasons, why he should be gentle and tender and studiously benignant to his 'poor little Hamstede'—the victim of so many afflictions. Had people only been silent about the little man's social demerits, Thackeray's regard for him would not have passed beyond the limits of compassion; but when the tattlers took to decrying the luckless little fellow for the silliness of his doggerel and his general mental imbecility, Thackeray discovered that he loved little Hamstede, and would not allow anything to be said in his disparagement. In this way it came to pass that the compassionate giant loved the dwarf, who apart from his afflictions had no title to the love which Thackeray lavished upon him to the last.

From the date of its institution to the year in which the 'old house' was pulled down, *Our Club* dined on an upper floor (the floor immediately under the garrets) of Clunn's Hotel, whilom Richardson's Hotel, in the north-west corner of Covent Garden, next door to Evans's Hotel, whose large supper-and-music room on the basement was one of Thackeray's favourite haunts to the end of his life. Dining in this upper room of Clunn's once a week (Saturday, six o'clock, p.m.) from the beginning of November to the end of May, *Our Club* dined under the presidency of a Chairman, appointed for the one evening and no longer by the Committee. The members of O. C. always numbered forty (the normal strength of the able-bodied members living in London), and at times exceeded that number, as it was the practice of the Committee to keep chronic invalids and absentees from town on the club-roll, so that any one of them, on recovering his health or returning to town, could reappear at 'the mahogany tree,' on paying his annual subscription of one guinea for the current season. The members and visitors to sit at table at any ordinary meeting were seldom much under forty, and sometimes greatly exceeded that number. At the annual Shakespeare Dinner, when the large room was specially arranged for the accommodation of an exceptionally large company, some seventy or more persons would squeeze together in the crowded chamber. The annual Country Dinner, that took place in June at Blackwall, Greenwich, Richmond, or Hampton Court, sometimes brought together an even greater number of individuals. On the other hand, even in the club's palmiest days, there were meetings of *Our Club* so ill-attended, that members and visitors were together fewer than the fingers of a single hand. These poor meetings usually occurred during the short holidays (Easter, Whitsuntide, and Christmas), when most of the clubbists were out of town or overborne by festive engagements. The 'first night' of a theatrical performance, in which the playgoers were greatly interested, would also reduce the meeting to a handful. On these exceptional occasions, the diners, if they were so few as four, were at liberty to order for their own drinking a magnum of wine at the expense of the club.

Though he was a sorry poet, little Hamstede was an admirable Secretary. Taking the annual subscriptions (a guinea a-year from each member) and the payments for dinners (four shillings for each ordinary repast, without charges for wine) into his keeping, he did a great deal with the narrow income, though the clubbists used to tell him that, if his accounts were severely audited, he would be found to have made a pretty penny for himself out of the funds, committed to him In Trust for the uses of the Society. How he contrived to give us so many 'gratuitous punches all round' on ordinary evenings, to give us 'gratuitous private omnibuses' for homeward journeys from the country dinners, to pay for the 'gratuitous magnums' of wine for the parties of less than five individuals, to pay bills for printing and stationery, to give gratuities to our especially serviceable 'head-waiter,' and to defray a score of other incidental charges of O. C. out of so small a revenue as forty guineas a-year, is more than I can tell,—more also, I believe, than anyone can tell. My suspicion is that the worthy little man's yearly disbursements for O. C. exceeded that yearly income by a few pounds, for which he forbore to demand a whip from the members. His heart and pride were concerned in his efforts for *Our Club;* and it is pleasant to me to feel that he was abundantly repaid for his zeal in O. C.'s service by the respect with which the Society treated him. He was 'dear Hamstede' on the lips of all of us; albeit Thackeray was the only one of us with a heart large and warm enough to love the simple little fellow.

Of the *menus* of the extraordinary dinners,—to wit, the fish-dinners in the country and the dinners in celebration of Shakespeare's birthday,—I will be silent, as they differed in no important respect from *menus* that are familiar to all persons who dine sumptuously thrice or four times a-week during the London season. But a few lines about the ordinary dinners of O. C. at Clunn's will not be out of place in this chapter. Soup was never served at these weekly repasts. The fare consisted of (1) Fish,—cod, turbot, or salmon, according to the season,—cooked and dressed in various ways, (2) A multifarious course of some eight or ten dishes of divers viands, such as small joints of mutton, lamb, pork, calves' heads, ox-palates, veal-pies, eel-pies, pigeon-pies, stewed eels, venison, venison-pasties, curries, (3) Beef-steaks hot and hot from the grill, plain or flavoured with shalot or fried onions, (4) Marrow-bones and toast, and Welsh rabbits (rare-bits), (5) Cheese, butter, pulled bread. It is beneath the dignity of this historian to speak of vegetables and condiments. Besides the bread, cheese, and butter, with the usual additaments, there was no dessert. Whatever else he sent up for us, Mr. Clunn always gave us the beef-steaks, marrow-bones, and Welsh rabbits. The marrow-bones were brought round on dishes, eight or ten bones on a dish, each bone dressed in a white napkin and standing erect, so as to resemble a headless priest in a spotless surplice. Together with the bone of his choice, each feaster received a marrow-spoon,—a long silver scoop with which to dig and raise the hot juicy marrow out of the bone. When Clunn's 'old house' had been pulled down, the only house in which I ever saw silver marrow-spoons was the house of my dear and familiar friend, Dr. Diamond, who of course had a dozen or more of the scoops in his chests of old plate. I did not care for the marrow-bones, though I did my best to think favourably of them, until Shirley Brooks assured me that Clunn's stock of white bones had been in his possession for more than a quarter of a century, and that the marrow his cooks put into them for table-consumption was made in Gray's Inn Road out of suet and vegetables by a manufacturer who was also a great maker of grease for the wheels of railway-carriages.

Even Shirley Brooks lacked the hardihood to speak disrespectfully of the wines provided by Mr. Clunn, who had as good a cellar as any other taverner of all London. His claret wines were of the best vintages; his port wines were super-excellent; and his sherries were so fine that even Cosens, the art-connoisseur and Spanish scholar, collector of costly paintings and the largest importer of the best sherry sold in England, bore witness on more than one occasion to O. C. (of which he was a member), that Clunn's best sherries were as good as any sent out of Spain. Our host's wines were *very* good, and the clubbists knew them to be so, and drank freely of them,—far too freely, in the present opinion of Dr. Benjamin Ward Richardson, who, by the way, had not discovered in the later ''fifties' and the earlier ''sixties' how much poison lurked in a bottle of wine.

That we drank no more than was good for us, I will not aver. Most of the clubbists, after drinking ale and sherry at dinner, drank a bottle of port or claret—some even drank a second bottle—before they touched the punch and grog, which usually went about in the later hours of an ordinary *séance*. In doing so they drank no deeper than gentlemen were wont to drink on festal occasions in the later ''fifties' and earlier ''sixties.' At the close of a long sitting everyone was mellow and jolly with the drinks, denounced by Dr. Richardson in this closing decade of the grandest age of England's story. But with the exception of a single gentleman, who should have been content with a single bottle, I never saw a member of O. C. in the condition which used to be styled 'the worse for drink.'

Over the wine (which, by the way, each clubbist ordered at his own pleasure for himself and any guest or guests he brought with him) the talk at O. C. was brisk, merry, sometimes riotous, and never restrained by the rules of conventional courtesy. In our social brotherhood it was understood, that in the way of humorous persiflage we were at liberty to use our tongues without any care for the canons of etiquette, and that no one should resent any freedom of speech used for mirthful effect at the festive meetings. Speech was free, frank, and pungent with personalities. Members and guests were alike on 'hail fellow well met' terms. It was permissible for anyone to interrupt an orator on his legs with inquiries and comments, likely to put him to confusion. No member was allowed to propose another member's health in civil terms, or say anything that was in any degree flattering to any clubbist in the room. If an orator wished to express his satisfaction at meeting yet again so eminent a man as Mr. Thackeray, he might do so if he spoke of the great novelist as 'the writer of stories, chiefly remarkable for ignorance of society and human nature,' but was silenced with derisive uproar, if he ventured to speak seriously of the author of *Vanity Fair* as 'the Fielding of the nineteenth century.'

As a fair example of the contemptuous personalities of the table-talk, I may mention a lesson in good manners which I received from the late Sir George Jessel, when he still wore a stuff-gown. At a small meeting of four clubbists, who ordered a magnum at the club's expense, I incurred Jessel's displeasure. The fish having been removed, a single dish was put before Jessel as a sufficient prelude to the beef-steaks that were being grilled for the small party. Removing the cover with a flourish, the waiter displayed a small leg of pork, elegantly garnished with parsnips, to the four feasters—Jessel and Ernest Hart (two Jews), Spencer Smith and myself (two Christians). I was conscious of having glanced significantly at Spencer Smith, a glance that was of course a breach of good breeding, when Jessel, with perfect equanimity, but in a tone of severe parental superiority, said,

'Jeaffreson, what are you laughing at?'

'You wrong me, Jessel. I did not laugh;—if I smiled, regard it as a smile of gratification at the sight of one of my favourite creatures.'

'In that, at least, you show good taste,' Jessel returned, with Johnsonian severity.

We all four partook of the interesting joint, eating it with the orderliness and silence befitting four people who felt themselves on ground scarcely less delicate than the meat. Having eaten a fair portion of the forbidden flesh, the future Master of the Rolls helped himself a second time. On laying down his knife and fork after consuming the second portion, he remarked, with a lofty air of tutorial condescension,

'Now, Jeaffreson, take this lesson to heart, and let it cure you of at least *one* of your vulgar prejudices.'

Not content to charge me with one vulgar prejudice, my censor suggested that I nursed in my mind a large number of equally vulgar prejudices. I thought the speech so much to Jessel's credit, that before going to bed I wrote (not in doggerel) to little Hamstede, suggesting that he should record the matter in his Register of good things uttered at O. C.

Readers may not imagine that it was the wont of Our Clubbists to pelt one another with personalities incessantly throughout the six or seven hours of a *séance*. Desisting from the arrowy sport, we ever and again talked sociably on questions of literature and art, the scandals of the town, and the political doings of the parties and their leaders. Sometimes the talk was extremely interesting,—giving the latest news that would appear in the morning papers on Monday, and also secret and true intelligence not at all likely to appear in the public journals. We had also our songsters, who sung famous or unusual songs with delightful address,—Horace Mayhew, who sang the 'Marseillaise' with a passion which made his hearers feel as though the hymn were being chanted by a thousand voices; Edwin Lawrence, the gentle and kind, who trolled forth Sir Walter's drollest lyrics and old English staves in notes of mellow richness; Durham, the sculptor, who sang pathetic strains and love-songs with rare sweetness and feeling; Morgan John O'Connell, who used to recite, rather than chant, Thackeray's verses in ridicule of the Irish; Andrew Maclure, who entertained us with the quaintest of Scotch ballads; Hazlitt, who rattled out the ditties of Wiltshire and Somerset peasants; Thackeray, who trolled forth *Little Billee* and *Father Martin Luther*; and, in a later term of O. C.'s history, Charles Dickens the Younger, whose uncommon songs would have diverted us by their eccentricity, even if he had been deficient in voice and lyrical ability.

I say nothing of 'the flashes of wit' that 'set the table on a roar,' because 'the flashes' which affect convivial tables tempestuously are poor fireworks, when they are offered to critical consideration in the black and white of a printed page. Moreover, I cared less for the thunder of the roaring table than the less riotous sociability of the meetings 'about the old tree.' A sedate and slightly confidential gossip with Robert Chambers was more congenial to me than the clamour of the table in its more riotous moods. Never overbearing, his simple talk was always quaint, piquant, and natural.

'What have you been doing since I saw you last?' I inquired of the canny and humorous Scotchman, as I took a chair next him on the first Saturday of a new session of O. C., whilst the clubbists were paying their guineas to the Secretary, and only a handful of them had taken their places at the long table.

'I have joost been spending the time in Scotland with my ain people, and for my diversion I have been reading yet again Scott's novels. I went deliberately through the whole lot o' them. What do you think of a mon of my years spending the greater part of the long holidays in sic a way?'

''Twas in that way I first made acquaintance with the Waverley novels in a broiling hot summer and autumn. I went through them one after another, when I was a boy. How you must have enjoyed yourself!' I remarked, with sincere enthusiasm.

'Weel, weel, I canna say,' returned the Scotch publisher and man of letters. Pausing for a few seconds after this prelude to a confidential communication, he looked warily and suspiciously up and down the table, to make sure that he would not be heard by anyone but myself. Seeing that the Scotchmen of the party were standing in a knot at the farther end of the room, and that no one was paying any attention to us, he continued, 'I canna say I enjoyed the buiks so much as I did in my younger time. I would not say it aloud in Adinbro, but weel you believe me when I say that Sir Walter isn't all that he used to be to me? To tale you the truth,' he added, lowering his voice almost to a whisper, 'to tale you the truth, I fund him raether prosy. Ay, but dinna be laughing, or the lads there will be asking what I said to you. It is the truth that I tale you,— I moost conface I fund him at times a lectle prosy.'

On another occasion Robert Chambers reproved me for saying the sabbatarian narrowness of the Edinburgh people would render life in Edinburgh intolerable to me.

'That's joost one of your sooth-country prejudices, and nothing more. There's no sic teerany and intolerance in Adinbro as y' imagine. If you will only have a prudent care for local sainsibeelity and forbear to fly in the face of your neighbours' opeenions, you may amuse yoursel' in Adinbro on the sabbath vara moch as you do in London on the Sunday. In Adinbro I dine and sup with my friends on the sabbath joost as I do in London. Of course, when I drive out to dine with a friend on the Sunday in Adinbro, I don't get into the carriage at my ain door, but round the corner near by, where I have ordered it to be waiting for me. And, of course, I seize the occasion for slipping into it when no folk are watching me. You're quite wrong in fancying the sabbatarian saintiment of Adinbro is so teerannical as to prevent you from enjoying yourself on the Laird's day.'

'Anyhow, by your own confession, it is so intolerant and tyrannical that you dare not get into a fly at your own door, or even in any street of the neighbourhood on a Sunday, when people are looking at you. If that isn't social tyranny, what the deuce *is* social tyranny?'

'Ay, that's a soothron's pugnacious way of looking at the question,' replied my friend, with a merry twinkle in his eye. 'If y' had been reared in Adinbro in the right way in your youth, you would not speak so bitterly of the wholesome moral eenfluence o' your neighbours.'

We were one evening gossipping about the inaccuracy and sheer falsehood of personal histories, when Robert Chambers observed merrily,

'Nae doot biographies are for the most part highly seasoned with romantic inventions; but the lees are sometimes vara amusing, especially when the lee o' the author's text is eelustrated by a capable draughtsman. A short time since I had a good laugh over a pretty account of the history and rise of the Brothers Chambers, publishers and booksellers, in an eelustrated publication. The author told the world how my brother William and I came first into Adinbro on our shoeless feet to seek our fortunes, walking together side by side, each of us bearing at his back a bundle o' clo's secured by the crook of a stick, which he held over his shoulder. The artistic eelustration of this pretty invention was a picture of a broad, straight highway leading to Adinbro in the deestance, and twa puir, bare-footed laddies marching onwards to the ceety, each with a bundle of clo's done up in a kercher at his back. Whereas the seemple truth of our first entrance into Adinbro is this: I and my brother entered the capital o' Scotland for the first time sitting together side by side in a yaller po'-chay.'

Frederick Lawrence, the author of *The Life of*

Henry Fielding, was another of the clubbists, next to whom I liked to place myself at table, for the sake of their pleasant gossip. A close friend of John Humffreys Parry (Serjeant Parry), by whose side he had worked in his earlier time as a transcriber of titles for the British Museum Catalogue, Fred Lawrence had a large circle of acquaintances, whose cordial regard he enjoyed up to the moment of his sudden death in his Middle Temple chambers, in the last week of October, 1867. A fluent and at times even a brilliant speaker, he was especially entertaining in a confidential *tête-à-tête* chat, not so much for the wit of his words as for the unusual views he took of commonplace matters. He was talking with me one day of an unfortunate man who, after sinking in a few years from a gentlemanly estate, came to be an importunate beggar for money from his acquaintances (even from the neediest of them), when I observed,

'You would not speak so hardly of the poor devil, had he not drawn a good deal of money out of you.'

'My dear Jeff,' was the answer, 'he never got any money out of me, but he did what was quite as insulting,—he tried to get money out of me. It is an insult for a man of his sort to pester one for money in the character of an author in distress, when he never wrote a book or paragraph of any merit. He insulted me by showing he thought me fool enough to be likely to give him ten pounds, and I resent the insult.'

But though he held his money sternly against this unworthy applicant, and spoke with such comical indignation of the insult, Lawrence was more than duly free-handed to persons who had any title to relief out of his modest means. Lawrence was chairman of the Garibaldi Committee; and I never saw his comical countenance more expressive of drollery than it was when he told me of a telegram he had received from the Italian patriot, begging him to despatch promptly to Italian waters three warsteamers, well furnished with men and munitions. Coming to a private gentleman, whose entire income from the Bar, his pen, and his St. John del Rey shares was under £400 a-year, the startling requisition was certainly rather 'a large order.' Dining with Lawrence some twelve or twenty times a-year at O. C. during eight successive years, I used to partake of the little dinners he gave in his Temple chambers. It was at one of those dinners I met for the first time that able scholar and high-hearted man, Charles Wycliffe Goodwin.

In those earlier days of the society, to which this chapter chiefly relates, *Our Club* comprised three or four provincial gentlemen, whom Douglas Jerrold had introduced to the circle from motives of personal friendliness, and from benignant regard for their idolatry of men of letters. One of them was Mr. Matthews of Sheffield, whose ignorance of literature was commensurate with his superstitious reverence for its producers. A manufacturer, who had repeatedly filled the office of Master Cutler of Sheffield, Mr. Matthews expressed his worshipful devotion to the club in a curious way. Recognizing his inability to quicken the life of *Our Club* with keen and flashing epigrams, he decided to furnish it with bright and cutting blades of his own manufacture. Acting on this resolve, he gave each member of O. C. an ivory-handled pocket-knife with three blades of super-excellent quality, and a metal plate, engraved with the words, 'Our Club,' inserted in the white handle. Subsequently he gave me a second knife of the same kind, to replace the former gift should I lose it. Yet more, in his especial kindness to the youngest member of the club, he gave me a pair of ivory-handled razors. It is also in my recollection that he entertained me at a dinner, which he gave one Sunday evening at his London hotel in Salisbury Court, Fleet Street, in honour of Théophile Gautier.

Théophile Gautier, who neither spoke nor understood English, made his first appearance at *Our Club* as the guest of Horace Mayhew; and Mr. Matthews of Sheffield, who neither spoke nor understood French, was standing at the west end of Mr. Clunn's upmost dining-room, so that he faced the door of the apartment, when the French poet came upon the scene, side by side with his introducer. After introducing the illustrious Théophile to Mr. Matthews with a neat little speech in English, which informed the Yorkshireman that M. Gautier was in France all that Tennyson was in England, Horace Mayhew, passing smoothly from his mother tongue to the French of the Parisians, delivered another little speech, which informed the Frenchman that Mr. Matthews was one of England's greatest manufacturers and wealthiest capitalists. Before O. C. sat down to dinner, most of the members present were specially introduced to the illustrious Théophile, who throughout the dinner and to the last minute of the *séance* was the recipient of flattering attentions from the company.

When Bill Jerrold—*to wit*, William Blanchard Jerrold (Douglas's eldest son)—brought Gustave Doré with him to a big dinner, given in behalf of one of the literary charities, he had some difficulty in arranging that the chairman (no less a chairman than H.R.H. the Duke of Cambridge) should speak handsomely of the famous French painter in proposing the toast of the visitors. The Secretary of the Society was of opinion that the celebrated foreigner should receive the compliment due to his importance.

'Just write the gentleman's name on that slip of paper,' said the amiable Secretary, 'and I'll put it under the Duke's eye.'

Whereupon Jerrold wrote on the paper in clear letters, ' Distinguished Visitor—Gustave Doré,' but unfortunately marked the accent over the surname's last letter so faintly that it was invisible to His Royal Highness. Five minutes later, the Secretary came to Jerrold in full speed and bright heat and uttered these words, ' The Duke says, " By all means, certainly—but who the devil is *Dore*?"' For the chairman's sufficient enlightenment, it was necessary for Jerrold to write on a second slip of paper, ' Gustave Doré is the celebrated French painter, whose pictures are the admiration of the whole civilized world.' As the surname on this second slip was accented with adequate blackness, the distinguished visitor was in due time mentioned by H.R.H. with suitable encomium.

The chairman of O. C. knew all about Théophile

Gautier, or at least enough about him for the polite requirements of the occasion. What he said in Théophile's honour was loudly applauded, and Théophile's acknowledgment (delivered in French) evoked yet noisier acclamations. As he sat directly opposite 'the illustrious Goaty,' the good Mr. Matthews enjoyed the evening vastly; and towards the close of the *séance*, in his delight at having made the acquaintance of so interesting a foreigner, he induced Horace Mayhew to arrange that 'the illustrious Goaty' should dine with him (Matthews of Sheffield) at his hotel in Salisbury Court on the following day. As he was at liberty to consent to the desire of one of England's greatest manufacturers and wealthiest capitalists, Théophile accepted the invitation; and before I left Clunn's that night I had promised to dine at seven p.m. on the morrow at the Salisbury Hotel with the French poet, and the persons who should be invited to meet him in the rooms of the Sheffield manufacturer. I had also promised Mr. Matthews to come to the hotel twenty minutes before the appointed hour, to aid the gentleman, who spoke no French, in receiving the foreigner who spoke no English.

On arriving at the Salisbury Hotel on the following day (Sunday) at 6.40 p.m., I was welcomed by the chief waiter with an effusion that astonished me.

'Lord, sir, I am glad to see you, and only wish you had come an hour and half sooner,' said the servant, when I had told him of my engagement to dine with Mr. Matthews, and had replied in the affirmative to his question, whether I spoke French. 'The illustrious Moosoo Goaty has been here for nigh upon two hours. He came at ten minutes to five, and he and Mr. Matthews have been in a pretty fix. Mr. Matthews speaks no French, the illustrious Moosoo Goaty don't speak English, and there isn't a soul in the hotel capable of acting as interpreter. I ran out for a Frenchman who does the interpreter in the hotel, when an interpreter is wanted in the house, but he had gone into the country for a Sunday's holiday. I have a lad under me who is half-French, and can parlez-vous fairly well, but this is his Sunday out. I have been longing for some one to come, and so have the two gents upstairs. The illustrious Moosoo must have thought the dinner was ordered for five.'

On coming into Mr. Matthews's chamber of reception, I found him with a countenance that was wet with perspiration and worn with distress, whilst M. Théophile Gautier looked more than slightly bored, albeit he soon brightened up on seeing that I had come to his rescue. The state of the table showed that the good-natured, portly, broad-chested, round-shouldered Mr. Matthews had done his best to mitigate his unfortunate guest's discomfort.

The presence of wine, fruit, glasses, a bottle of cognac, an open box of cigars, indicated that the Sheffield manufacturer had been pressing cordial restoratives and milder refreshments on his visitor.

'Talk to the illustrious Goaty,' ejaculated Mr. Matthews, mopping and fanning his face with a big silk pocket-handkerchief, ' don't pay any attention to me, I shall soon be better now that you have come. Please, have the goodness to explain to him that had I known it was the fashion of illustrious Frenchmen to arrive two hours before the dinner-hour, I would have asked you and Polly' (Horace Mayhew used to be styled 'Polly' and also 'the wicked Marquis' by his most familiar friends) 'and Jerrold and the others to be here at 4.40. Do, for Heaven's sake, go at him quick and sharp in the language of his country, and pitch it into him hot and smart in the way of compliments. Tell him that I admire his country and honour him, and that, though I shan't be able to read a line of them, I mean to buy all his works. That's the line I want you to take. And now I'll be mum. What a blessing it is, you have come at last.'

I did all I could with my faulty French to render the position less unpleasant to Théophile Gautier, who laughed merrily as he replied in the affirmative to my suggestion, that he had started for the hotel under a misconception respecting the dinner-hour. The affair was explained in few words. Horace Mayhew had given the poet a card, on which he had written our host's name and London address, together with a note of the dinner-hour; the Frenchman had mistaken Horace's 7 for 5, and had consequently driven up to 'the Salisbury' two full hours before the proper time. I was still laughing over M. Gautier's droll account of Mr. Matthews's dumb-show efforts to put him at his ease, when handsome Horace walked into the room, gallantly attired in a long frock-coat of blue cloth, a white waistcoat, and lavender-colour nether-garments. He was followed at brief intervals by Stigand, Bill Jerrold, and the rest of the party, which, if I remember rightly, included George Augustus Sala.

The next five hours passed pleasantly. The dinner was good, the wine was good, the talk was amusing even to Mr. Matthews, though he did not understand a word of it; for the kindly and courteous gentleman insisted that the conversation should be in French, for the greater contentment of 'the illustrious Goaty,' who knew nothing of English. When the white cloth had been removed from the bright mahogany table, I turned to Mr. Matthews, at whose right hand I was sitting, and begged him to let me talk to him in English,

'No, no, sir,' the simple gentleman answered, stoutly, 'not a word of English, as long as the illustrious Moosoo Goaty honours me with his company. I shall be silent, but I shan't be dull. 'Tisn't much that I understand of the talk at Clunn's, when it's all in English. Two-thirds of it goes clean over my head, but all the same I like the riot of it, and enjoy watching the faces of the lads. This is a fine glass of port, and as I drink my whack I shall like the wine all the better, for thinking how I have brought about me some of the brightest spirits of the age. Not a word of English, if you please.'

CHAPTER XIV.

WILLIAM MAKEPEACE THACKERAY.

My Introduction to the Author of *Vanity Fair*—Thackeray's Regard for my Brother George—*Life of W. M. Thackeray* by Herman Merivale and Frank T. Marzials—The Novelist's Ancestors, gentle and simple—Hannay's Perplexity—Thackeray's Dictum touching 'three gentle Descents'—His Pride in his 'no Family in particular'—His Birth at Calcutta—His Preparatory School—Thackeray at Charterhouse School—The Youngs of St. Helen's Place, Bishopsgate—John Young—James Young—Emily Young—Edith Young—Thackeray playing with Children on a sunny Lawn—Thackeray at Cambridge and 'The Temple'—His Patrimony and Poverty—His Marriage at Paris and Married Life in Great Coram Street—His greatest Misfortune—Its sad Consequences—Mr. Edmund Yates's Sketch of Thackeray in *Town Talk*—The Thackeray-Yates Quarrel—Motley's Sketch of Thackeray's Face—Part taken by Charles Dickens in the Thackeray-Yates Quarrel—Thackeray's Avowal touching the Quarrel—Mr. Marzials on the Quarrel—Strife between Thackeray and Dickens—Thackeray's Ambition to surpass Dickens—Abraham Hayward's 'Airs'—His long Neglect of Thackeray—His Quickness in aiding the Successful Novelist—'The Inner Circle'—Thackeray's Admiration of Dickens the Novelist.

IN the season of 1857, I made the acquaintance of Thackeray, when I was in my twenty-seventh, and he was still in his forty-seventh year. As I made no written memorandum of my first interview with the great novelist, I cannot give the exact date of the meeting. Nor can I recall the circumstances under which I was introduced to his notice.* It is most likely that I met him for the first time at No. 16, Wimpole Street, the house occupied by Sir Henry Thompson during the earlier years of his professional career, and that I was indebted to the young and rising surgeon for my first introduction to the author of *Vanity Fair*. Possibly I was introduced to the novelist by my brother George, who, when he was a medical student of University College Hospital, had the good fortune to win Thackeray's kindly regard by rendering him some professional service, whilst he lay ill at No. 16, Wimpole Street. The London season of 1857 was still running its course, when Thackeray said to me,

'I like your young brother. I have not often seen an uglier fellow, but his " hugly mug " is a pleasant face. I like his strong, honest eyes, his fresh colour, and the hearty way in which he smiles outwards from his big white teeth. He's a kindly fellow, who will never cause you a heart-ache.'

---

*The reader, who is astonished by this confession, should bethink if he can state the circumstances under which he made the acquaintance of the persons whom he is most glad to have known. William Bewick deemed himself fortunate in having won the friendship of Hazlitt, the famous critic, but he says, ' I have no distinct recollection of my first interview with Hazlitt. It was probably at Haydon's.'—Vide, *Life and Letters of William Bewick, edited by Thomas Landseer, A.R.A.*

In connection with Thackeray's remarks about my brother's 'hugly mug,' I may observe that notwithstanding its defects, my brother's countenance bore in some respects a strong resemblance to Thackeray's face. The novelist's black-and-white caricature-sketches of his own face, some good examples of which appear in the *Brookfield Letters*, might be mistaken for caricatures of my brother's visage.

In the *Life of W. M. Thackeray*, by Herman Merivale and Frank T. Marzials, the best of the several memoirs of the novelist, Mr. Marzials says (*vide* p. 216), 'that a full Life will be published sooner or later may be taken for granted; and it were to be wished that the task should be undertaken by his daughter, Mrs. Ritchie, who has inherited so much of his literary gift.' Should Mrs. Ritchie ever give the world a comprehensive memoir of her father, in spite of the injunction he laid upon her towards the close of his career, the record would proceed from a writer peculiarly qualified to exhibit the most beautiful side of the novelist's character and story. But, even though she knew the whole of his life, which is improbable, the affectionate daughter would not be the best person to produce a perfect biography of the great humourist, who was very much of a Bohemian to the last, and whose domestic infelicity was fruitful of consequences, that should be neither avoided nor glossed, but should on the contrary be displayed with equal frankness and delicacy by the final historian of a man, so supremely interesting that his foibles and errors are almost as deserving of consideration as his brightest virtues and finest faculties.

The only son of an East Indian civil servant, who was himself the son of a member of the same service, Thackeray had for his great-grandfather in the direct male line the Dr. Thomas Thackeray, whilom a Fellow of King's College, Cambridge, who in George the Second's reign was for fifteen years head-master of Harrow School, during which period the flourishing school never numbered more than one hundred and thirty pupils, and who also in his later time figured in the church as Archdeacon of Surrey. No person of gentle ancestry, Archdeacon Thackeray was the son of a small yeoman landowner of Hampsthwaite, on the border of Knaresborough Forest, co. York, whose ancestors had held and tilled the same modest estate from the close of the sixteenth century.

It does not appear that any of these Yorkshire yeomen married women of superior quality, or that the blood of any aristocratic family passed to the novelist through the veins of any woman from whom he was lineally descended. To James Hannay, who liked to argue that genius was a fruit of 'blood,' it was perplexing that he could discover no 'tap' in Thackeray's lineage that would account satisfactorily for the genius of so fine a humourist and novelist. When he admitted, in his well-known obituary memoir of the novelist, that Thackeray 'by birth belonged to the upper middle class,' Hannay was careful to observe that the higher division of that comprehensive order was 'a section of our curiously divided society, which contained many cadets of old families, and formed a link between the aristocracy and the general bulk of the liberal professions.' Had the author of

Singleton Fontenoy discovered that Thackeray's grandmother, Miss Webb, or his great-grandmother, Ann Woodward, had descended through several obscure families from a ducal house, he would have ceased to marvel at the intellectual pre-eminence of the man of letters, whose ancestors in the direct male line had been simple yeomen for so many generations.

The discovery would also have been pleasant to the most famous of Archdeacon Thackeray's descendants; for, though he smiled at the claims of high descent, and was quick to ridicule spurious assertions of familiar grandeur, the keenest satirist of Victorian society was not at all disposed to undervalue his own rather slender title to be rated with personages of ancestral dignity. Reflecting with complacence on his descent from Dr. Thackeray of Harrow through a grandsire and a sire, who had both figured creditably in the Civil Service of the East India Company, he was often heard to say that three gentle descents were needful for the production of a gentleman.

'Then you don't think much of the influences of gentle lineage?' he once said to me, by way of rejoinder to some words that had passed from my lips.

'On the contrary,' I replied, 'I believe them to be fruitful of worth and dignity in a vast number of individuals. But the fact remains that some of the paltriest people who have come under my observation are people of good descent. And I infer from much of your writing that in this respect your experience accords with mine.'

'No doubt,' Thackeray returned, 'a man may be an earl of eleven descents, and yet be a pitifully mean creature. All the same for that, I am of opinion that it takes three generations to make a gentleman.'

'You are a gentleman,' I remarked, speaking at a time when I knew so little of my companion's pedigree, that I knew nothing of the Hampsthwaite yeomen, 'your father was a gentleman, your grandfather was a gentleman, your great-grandfather was a gentleman; but your great-great-grandfather was *not* a gentleman.'

'How do you know that, young 'un?' the great novelist inquired quickly, with an air of surprise and amusement.

'One often hears a man say that it takes a certain number of gentle descents, or a particular measure of ancestral gentility, to produce a true gentleman; and I have come to the conclusion that each speaker regards his own number of gentle descents as the true standard of ancestral gentility. Just now, Hannay is under the impression that he is descended from a knightly personage of Edward the Second's time. He is therefore of opinion that no one can be a gentleman of the finest quality unless he can push his ancestral line back to a knight of the same period.'

'Pooh!' laughed Thackeray. 'Hannay is a madman as soon as he has thrown his leg over his pet hobby. But he is a good fellow, and a thorough little fighting-cock.—And you had no other ground for speaking so disrespectfully of my great-great-grandfather?'

'I had no other ground.'

A merry smile stole over the great man's face as he observed,

'You made your point fairly, young 'un; and honour requires me to admit that you have scored. But no better gentleman than my great-grandfather ever trod English ground.'

'Although he could not boast a single gentle descent? How can he have been so good and true a gentleman, if it takes three generations to make a gentleman?'

'You have scored again,' the big man cried, with undiminished good-humour. 'If you go on in this way, you'll grow conceited. Now let's talk of something else.' But, before I could bring another subject up for discussion, he observed, in a graver tone, 'I give you leave, youngster, to laugh at my inordinate pride in my no family in particular, for I am fully alive to its absurdity. I was laughing at myself when I wrote of General Braddock that he was "not of high birth, yet absurdly proud of his no-ancestry." I am not exempt from the foibles of my weaker brethren, whom I lash so smartly in my books. I spoke the truth when I declared myself a snob in clear type on the title-page of a book you wot of.'

The son of Richmond Thackeray of the Indian Civil Service, who lived just long enough to make a more than adequate provision for his only child, William Makepeace Thackeray was born at Calcutta on the 18th of July, 1811, and had scarcely entered his sixth year, when death deprived him of his sire. A year later the fatherless boy was sent to England by his mother, who remained in India, and in due course became by her second marriage the wife of Captain (in his later time, Major) Carmichael Smyth,—a gentleman who proved a kindly and sympathetic, though scarcely beneficial, step-father to his wife's only son. Committed at so tender an age to the care of his aunt Ritchie at Chiswick, the future novelist was under that lady's charge, when he was sent to the preparatory school (at Southampton, unless my memory fails me), where he for the only time in his life endured the torture of a birching. In 1822 he entered the Charterhouse School, where he conceived a strong and enduring affection for James Reynold Young,—the 'Young of Caius' who figured in Thackeray's set of friends at Cambridge,—the Young who, after taking orders, became the rector of Whitnash, near Leamington, co. Warwick,—the scholarly and gracious clergyman whose daughter Edith Young married my cousin Herbert Jeaffreson, at present one of the clergy of St. Augustine's, Kilburn, and whose niece Emily Young married another of my cousins, William Julius Jeaffreson.

When Thackeray was a Carthusian day-scholar, living at a boarding-house in Charterhouse Square, his peculiar schoolmate lived with his parents in St. Helen's Place, Bishopsgate, where they kept a hospitable house, after the wont of rich and gentle citizens in George the Fourth's time; and Thackeray was so frequent a visitor at his friend's home that he came to be regarded by the Youngs as a member of their family rather than as a guest. Only a few months have passed since James Young's elder brother John was in the enjoyment of a green and vigorous old age; and no long time has elapsed since he was recalling for my entertainment how welcome a guest the Carthusian Thackeray was at St. Helen's Place, and how popular with the children of the house. A tall, bright, and companionable, though rather quiet, lad, he seized every occasion for dropping in upon his friends in St. Helen's Place, and seldom went back to his boarding-house without having thrown off half-a-dozen comical pen-and-ink sketches for the amusement of the boys and girls of the party.

To the Youngs of a later generation I am also indebted for several equally characteristic and pleasant anecdotes of the white-headed novelist. For example, my kind cousin Edith Jeaffreson, *née* Young, the aforementioned daughter of the Whitnash rector, told me no long while since, in her peculiarly vivacious style, how in her early childhood she and divers other children rushed in a troop upon Thackeray, as he lay on a sunny lawn, and required him to roar like a lion and in other natural ways to play the part of the great lion he was in London; and how the enormous man humoured the frolicsome children by putting himself on his hands and feet, and running after them on 'all fours,' whilst he tossed his white mane about and roared at them in an inexpressibly terrifying fashion; and how she and the other nurslings at last came about the terrible lion, and settled upon his enormous body and huge limbs, when he had returned to a recumbent posture on the sunny Dorsetshire lawn, after he had roared and gambolled himself quite out of breath, and they had screamed and raced about him till they were in no humour to continue the riotous game.

Though he was far from singular amongst men of genius for being one of those 'late developments,' who come slowly to the fulness of their powers, it is interesting to notice what little cause the observers of Thackeray's childhood, youth, and early manhood had to predict that he would eventually figure amongst the brightest and strongest men of the nineteenth century. In childhood he displayed no remarkable taste for the pursuits in which he achieved celebrity. At Charterhouse he neither distinguished himself by scholarly address nor came to the fore in the sports of the playground. The schoolboy's career was in truth chiefly remarkable for the fight, in which he was badly beaten and disfigured for life. His career at Cambridge was even more inglorious. After idling away something less than two years, he retired from Trinity College in his eighth term, under the transient discredit that usually covers an undergraduate who withdraws from his university without a degree. However fruitful of enjoyment it may have been to him at the time, his subsequent residence at Weimar and his first sojourn at Paris were attended by no incidents that caused his friends to regard him as a youngster of unusual ability. After studying for a few months in a pleader's chambers, the young Templar ceased to read for the Bar. After dabbling in art for a longer term, the art-student relinquished his short-lived ambition to distinguish himself in the studios, either because he recognized his unfitness for the attractive vocation, or because he revolted from the toilsome discipline that could alone render him a capable draughtsman. After throwing away his pencil, and deciding to make himself famous by his pen, he wasted time and money on two luckless ventures in journalism (the *National Standard*, a weekly journal of literature and art, and the *Constitutional*, a daily newspaper), into both of which unfortunate speculations he appears to have been drawn by his step-father, who should have used his influence to dissuade the youthful and inexperienced literary aspirant from meddling with the perilous projects.

Writing to his mother from Cornwall on the 25th of June, 1832, Thackeray said,

'I have been lying awake this morning, meditating on the wise and proper manner I shall employ my fortune in when I come of age, which, if I live so long, will take place in six weeks. First, I do not intend to quit my little chambers in the Temple; then I will take a regular monthly income which I will never exceed.'

The fortune—to be rated at about ten thousand pounds, *i.e.*, just one half of his reputed patrimony—which Thackeray intended to use so prudently, soon passed from his hands, even to the last shilling. It would be useless to discover how much of this modest fortune was lost at play, how much of it was wasted in luxurious living, how much of it was lent or given to needy comrades, and how much was thrown away in rotten investments. It is enough to know that Richmond Thackeray's handsome provision for his only son melted and slipt through the young man's fingers in something less than four years, and that when he mated with Miss Isabella Shawe at the British Embassy in Paris, on the 20th of August,

1836, he married on no grander income than the four hundred pounds a-year 'paid,' as he wrote to Mr. Synge, 'by a newspaper that failed six months afterwards.'

Up to the moment of this imprudent marriage, Thackeray's best writing had afforded no clear and conclusive indications of the gradually enlarging powers, that twelve years later clothed him with honour, and placed him in the front rank of professional authors. The young man, *ætat.* 25, who had left Cambridge without a degree or any such store of knowledge as could aid him materially in the struggle for existence, who had lost every penny of his patrimonial fortune, and who belonged to no one of the regular professions, was wholly dependent for subsistence on the most precarious of the liberal vocations, when he settled in Great Coram Street with his girlish bride, who had brought him little more than the proverbial 'chaplet of roses,' even though account be taken of the insecure fifty pounds a-year, which Mrs. Shawe had promised to allow her for personal pin-money. Under the circumstances, people, who regarded them with sympathy, had reason to fear that the young couple would find themselves face to face with urgent financial trouble.

From that trouble Thackeray and his young wife appear to have suffered less acutely in Great Coram Street than their prosperous and prudent friends predicted. But when Mrs. Thackeray had given birth to three children (one of whom died in earliest infancy), worse sorrow came to her and her husband than any of the griefs that proceed from mere want of pence. The calamity that befel them was a calamity for which both were entitled to profound and unqualified compassion. Before he had completed his thirtieth year, Thackeray was deprived of his wife's society by her incurable mental illness, which placed him in the cruel position of a widower who might not contract a second marriage; and, as the poor lady survived him, he remained in that cruel position to the end of his life. The grief which came to the novelist from deprivation of his wife's society and from frequent broodings over her pitiful fate was probably less depressing to his spirits, and certainly less hurtful to his general health, than the indirect consequences of the domestic affliction, which broke up his home near the Foundling Hospital, and compelled him to pass the remainder of his earthly existence under the vexatious conditions of unnatural celibacy. In truth, everything that was gravely irregular and hurtful in Thackeray's way of living, from the close of 1840 to the year of his death, was mainly referable to his conjugal bereavement. Had his marriage afforded him for twenty-five years the same measure of felicity, which it yielded him before the first manifestations of his wife's nervous failure, Thackeray might and doubtless would still have been rather too fond of gaiety and good cheer, but his wife's influence would have preserved him from the habits of gustatory self-indulgence, which resulted in the physical disorders that eventually deprived the world of his splendid genius. The same influence would also have preserved him from the trouble which compelled him to go so often in his closing years to Sir Henry Thompson for surgical treatment. Soon after the great novelist's death, Lord Houghton wrote to his wife, 'So Thackeray too has gone. I was not surprised, knowing how full of disease he was, and thereby accounting for much of the inequality and occasional perversity in his conduct.' The disease and the occasional perversity were consequences of the calamity that extinguished Thackeray's domestic contentment, and drove him from Great Coram Street in his thirtieth year.

Although the consequences of that calamity were deplorable, I do not say the same of all that resulted from the loss of patrimony, which several thoughtful writers have regarded as one of the grave misfortunes that befel Thackeray in his early manhood. Having regard to three of the novelist's characteristics—his pride, his sensitiveness, and his constitutional indolence—I am more disposed to rejoice than to regret that he threw away his patrimony so soon after he came into it. Had he held his small fortune with a close hand, the proud and sensitive man would have borne less patiently and bravely the petty rebuffs and discouragements and mortifications which he endured in his upward fight to literary eminence. I question whether he would have condescended to shorten *The Great Hoggarty Diamond* at the command of the editor of *Fraser*, or would have acknowledged with a conciliatory and almost meek letter Mr. Macvey Napier's treatment of his first contribution to the *Edinburgh Review*, had he retained possession of his patrimonial five hundred pounds a-year. It can scarcely be questioned by anyone who knew the real Thackeray, that the sharp goad of poverty, to which he used to refer so often and so feelingly in his subsequent prosperity, pricked him to exertions which he would not have made, had he been in the enjoyment of easy circumstances. To me it appears more probable that Thackeray with five hundred pounds a-year of unearned income at his back would have ceased to be a candidate for literary employment, practised at the Bar with moderate success, and eventually figured as a Master in Chancery or a stipendiary magistrate, than that he would have lived to write *Vanity Fair* and *The Newcomes*; in which former case he would have missed the celebrity that afforded him so much gratification in his later years, and the world would have missed the pleasure it has gained from the perusal of his masterly books. Taking this view of his case, I am thankful that poverty compelled him to persist in the toil, which in the long run was so fruitful of glory to the author, and of delight to mankind.

It points to the charm of Thackeray's attractive and winning personality, that I did not know him for many months before I conceived a strong liking for him; for I came to his presence for the first time with a strong disposition to find him a disagreeable acquaintance. Six-and-thirty years since strange stories were still current in society to his discredit; and one of these stories had caused me to imagine that the author of *Vanity Fair* was peevish, captious, and even more bitter in his ordinary conversation than in the most cynical passages of his brilliant writings. As it ceased to affect my regard for the novelist, as soon as he was pleased to show me his true nature, I forbear to set forth the particulars of the anecdote which caused me to think unjustly of a courteous and exceptionally benevolent man, before I knew him personally.

I had known Thackeray for a little more than a year, and for about the same time he had been in the habit of addressing me as 'youngster' and 'young 'un' (his usual way of addressing quite young men whom he regarded with favour), when the great novelist, who had hitherto shown me only his most agreeable characteristics, gave me a momentary view of one of his unamiable traits. To show how this came about, I must say something of a matter that in 1858 caused much angry talk in the literary cliques.

In the June of that year (1858), when personal journalism was in its infancy even in America, and was regarded with passionate disfavour in this country, Mr. Edmund Yates (a tall, slight, and very well-looking young government-clerk, *ætat* 26) wrote with his own hand and published in *Town Talk*, a slight sketch of the author of *Vanity Fair*,—a sketch in three sections, that dealt respectively with the great novelist's Appearance, Career, and Success. Forming just one-half of the essay, Section No. 2 on the author's literary career contained nothing that offended, and several things that were calculated to gratify, the sensitive novelist. But Sections No. 1 and No. 3— the shorter sections of the brief article—annoyed Thackeray acutely, and stirred him to fierce anger.

These divisions of the faulty article ran in these words:

'HIS APPEARANCE.

'Mr. Thackeray is forty-six years old, though, from the silvery whiteness of his hair, he appears somewhat older. He is very tall, standing upwards of six feet two inches, and as he walks erect his height makes him conspicuous in every assembly. His face is bloodless, and not particularly expressive, but *remarkable for the fracture of the bridge of the nose, the result of an accident in youth.* He wears a small grey whisker, but otherwise is close-shaven. No one meeting him could fail to recognize in him a gentleman; *his bearing is cold and uninviting, his style of conversation either openly cynical or affectedly good-natured and benevolent;* his *bonhomie* is forced, his wit biting, his pride easily touched; but his appearance is invariably that of the cool, suave, wellbred gentleman, who, whatever may be rankling within, suffers no surface display of his emotion.

* * * * * * * *

'HIS SUCCESS,

commencing with *Vanity Fair*, culminated with his *Lectures on the English Humourists of the Eighteenth Century,* which were attended by all the court and fashion of London. The prices were extravagant, the lecturer's adulation of birth and position was extravagant, the success was extravagant. *No one succeeds better than Mr. Thackeray in cutting his coat according to his cloth. Here he flattered the aristocracy; but, when he crossed the Atlantic, George Washington became the idol of his worship, the Four Georges the objects of his bitterest attacks.* These last-named lectures have been dead failures in England, though as literary compositions they are most excellent. Our opinion is that his success is upon the wane. His writings were never understood or appreciated by the middle classes; the aristocracy have been alienated by his American onslaught on their body, and the educated and refined are not sufficiently numerous to constitute an audience. Moreover, there is a want of heart in all he writes, which is not to be balanced by a most brilliant sarcasm and the most perfect knowledge of the workings of the human heart.'

For the convenience of readers, I have here printed in italics the passages of the article that provoked Thackeray's excessive displeasure,—passages that of course were printed originally in the ordinary roman type of the short-lived weekly journal of London gossip.

In the part of his autobiography, *Recollections and Experiences*, where he expresses in manly terms his frank regret for the faults of a piece of writing which he threw off with insufficient consideration under the stress of an editorial emergency, Mr. Edmund Yates observes, 'No one can see more clearly than I do the silliness and bad taste of the original article.' In these words of 'peccavi,' Mr. Yates is in my opinion much too severe on himself. Certainly the article is not chiefly remarkable for the failings of which its author speaks so stoutly. No doubt it contains a few passages that should not have been given to the public, and would not have been given to the public, had not the writer unfortunately been his own editor. The reference to the facial disfigurement, in respect to which Thackeray was extremely sensitive, though he often jested about it, was a mistake. The journalist was more gravely at fault in suggesting that Thackeray was usually insincere when he spoke in a kindly and benevolent strain. But, upon the whole, the note on the great novelist's personal appearance and address is a fairly accurate piece of verbal portraiture. If it speaks with insufficient tenderness of the broken nose, it calls attention to the grandeur and picturesqueness and to the lofty air 'of the cool, suave, well-bred gentleman.' Displaying no disposition to underrate the great novelist's genius or to disparage his literary achievements, the note on 'his career,' the longest of the three divisions of the memoir, is wholly void of offence. The third sentence of the third note, beginning with 'His success,' was unquestionably a serious literary indiscretion; but when the most has been made of its unfairness and incivility, it was no such offence as would have justified Thackeray in doing his utmost to humiliate and crush the writer of the offensive words,—a young man, still in his twenty-seventh year, who was of no great moment in the literary world when he produced the faulty sketch.

Stung to the quick by the passages of the article to which he referred in the letter which he wrote to Mr. Yates on the 14th of June, 1858, from Onslow Square,—the overbearing and contemptuous letter that made it impossible for Mr. Yates to set matters right with an apology,—Thackeray was even more sharply stung by the words about the broken nose, to which he made no reference in the insulting epistle. From Thackeray's habit of referring jocosely to his broken nose, some writers have inferred that he was in no degree sensitive about his facial disfigurement, but was on the contrary rather pleased with the blemish, of which he could talk so gaily. The inference is quite erroneous. As the blemish is scarcely apparent or wholly put out of sight in the popular pictures of the novelist, I may assure those of my readers who never saw him, or who having seen him retain only a vague memory of his appearance, that the blemish was no trivial disfigurement. I will not speak of it as a hideous disfigurement, for in spite of it Thackeray's face was pleasant to look upon. But I do not hesitate in calling it a grievous blemish and a striking example of nasal deformity. Writing to his wife on the 28th of May, 1858, Motley (no man to exaggerate the novelist's defects) spoke of Thackeray's face as 'a roundish face, with a little dab of a nose, upon which it is a perpetual wonder how he keeps his spectacles.' The frequency with which Thackeray called attention to this ridiculous dab of a nose, affords conclusive evidence that he often thought of the blemish, though he was too prudent to whine and wail about it, as Byron whined and wailed over his misshapen foot. Besides being sensitive and highly nervous, Thackeray was a rather vain man. Readers may be left to decide for themselves whether it is probable that such a man was either well pleased with so great a blemish or indifferent to it. Because a man makes the best of his personal deformity and talks lightly of it, it does not follow that he could with patience hear another person talk about the matter.

Angry at the outset of the squabble with no one but the writer of the article, Thackeray became very angry with Dickens, as soon as the latter had shown his intention to stand by Edmund Yates, and to do his best to preserve his young friend from the excessive punishment which the author of *Vanity Fair* wished to inflict upon him. It is almost needless to observe that Dickens failed to shield his *protégé* from the excessive punishment, and that Mr. Yates's name was erased from the list of the members of the Garrick Club on the 20th of July, 1858, when he had declined to apologize to Thackeray in submission to the requirement made by the majority of the clubbists at a General Meeting.

Having conceived anger against Dickens for standing by his young friend in a controversy, that should not have engaged the attention of the club's committee, Thackeray soon came to regard Dickens as the principal with whom he was contending, and to look upon Mr. Yates as a quite subordinate actor in the curious conflict. That the Thackeray-Yates quarrel had developed into a trial of strength between the two greatest novelists of the age, and that Thackeray had become even more furious against Dickens than he was against the writer of the article which occasioned the pitiful disturbance, first came to my sure knowledge from Thackeray's own lips.

To me the affair was nothing more than 'Thackeray's squabble with Yates about the article in *Town Talk*,' when I happened to come upon the author of *Vanity Fair*, as he was sitting alone in the dining-room of No. 16, Wimpole Street, waiting to be admitted to Henry (now-a-days Sir Henry) Thompson's consulting-room.

'Ah, young 'un,' said the great man, greeting me with a beaming smile, as I entered the room, 'I am glad you have come to bear me company. The dreariest hours of a man's life are those that he passes in a doctor's ante-room, whether the doctor be his physician, his surgeon, or only his dentist. Take that chair, and do your best to amuse me.'

In the earlier part of our *tête-à-tête* conversation, the famous novelist talked to me about one of my books, into which he had lately looked, and was pleased to inquire whether I had been fairly well paid for it,—a question which I answered frankly, though it cost me an effort to confess how little I had received from my publishers for so fine a work of genius. And on his pressing me with a delicate air of interest in my welfare for more information of the same kind, I told him the various prices I had received for my various books, and how I had contrived to earn my living since I left Oxford.

'You have done fairly well,' he remarked, when I satisfied his curiosity; 'yes, more than fairly well. I see you can get along without help.'

'Good Lord!' I answered, quickly, 'I want no one to help me.'

'How self-sufficient we are!' he rejoined, in a bantering tone, before he observed, 'At your age, young 'un, I had barely begun to earn money, and was still playing ducks and drakes with the remains of my fortune,'—words which he would not have spoken had he not either thought me younger than my real age, or forgotten the exact year in which he brought his young wife to Great Coram Street.

'I wish a benignant star,' I rejoined, 'had given me a chance of playing the same game.'

'Would you have played it?'

'For twelve months, but no longer.'

'If you had played it for twelve months, you'd have gone on playing it till your pockets were empty.'

Passing abruptly to a very different subject, he startled me by saying,

'What do people say, youngster, about my row with Yates?' Possibly because he saw in my face an indisposition to speak frankly on the delicate matter, he followed up the question quickly. 'Come, tell me what you hear.'

On being thus pressed to play the part of a reporter, I replied,

'You do not need to be told what your enemies and detractors say. Nor can there be any need for me to tell you what is being said of you by your extravagant partisans, who, though they applaud whatever you do, are scarcely to be called your friends. Your judicious admirers—all the people whose opinion on the matter is worth a rush, the people whose view of the affair will be everybody's judgment five-and-twenty-years hence—unite in saying you have made a prodigious mistake, and are forgetful of your dignity in showing so much annoyance at a few saucy words, and in condescending to quarrel with so young and unimportant a person as Mr. Yates.'

The immediate consequence of these words was that Thackeray, flushing with surprise and irritation, exclaimed, 'Confound your impudence, youngster.'

Rising to my feet at this outbreak of petulance, I looked steadily into my companion's face, before I answered, slowly,

'Pardon me, Mr. Thackeray, for not flattering you with an untruth, when you pressed me to give you information.'

Doubtless these words were spoken with a slight show of combativeness; for the youngster did not like being 'confounded for his impudence.' But I am sure they were not spoken in an offensive tone.

'You were quite right,' returned Thackeray, 'and it is for me to beg your pardon. You were right to tell me the truth, and I thank you for telling it. Since *Vanity Fair* people have been less quick to tell me the truth than they were before the book made me successful. But—but——' As he said 'but—but,' he rose from his seat to his full height, and looked down upon me with a face coloured with emotion. 'But—but,' he continued, 'you may not think, young 'un, that I am quarrelling with Mr. Yates. *I am hitting the man behind him.*'

Fortunately, my *tête-à-tête* with the great man was ended at that moment by Henry Thompson's appearance in the room.

To realize how fully time has justified the discreet and dispassionate persons, who in 1858 were of opinion that Thackeray had made and was persisting in a prodigious mistake, and has also justified my statement that in course of time their 'view of the affair would be everybody's judgment,' readers have only to read the eleventh chapter of the *Life of W. M. Thackeray*, by two of the novelist's most cordial admirers, and to peruse thoughtfully the well-considered words (*vide* pp. 196, 7, 8), in which Mr. Frank T. Marzials reviews and passes judgment on Thackeray's conduct in the unfortunate business.

'But' [says Mr. Marzials], 'granting to the full that the article was a peccant article, I fear it must be owned, even by Thackeray's admirers, that the punishment inflicted on the writer was disproportionate, and, which is worse, not of an altogether right kind. Several courses were open to Thackeray when Mr. Yates's animadversions were brought to his notice. He might—and this, I take it, was the right course—have shrugged his shoulders, and let the matter go by, remembering that he also, in his younger days, had said sharp things and personal things of his contemporaries, and had done so in periodicals more important than *Town Talk*. He might have appealed to Mr. Yates's better feeling, and asked whether the terms were quite those in which a recruit ought to speak of a white-haired veteran. He might, if his combative feelings were irrepressible, have inflicted such literary castigation on the offender as he had, in the "Essay on Thunder and Small Beer," inflicted on the *Times* critic, who had foolishly fallen foul of the "Kickleburys on the Rhine." The last, if bent on battle, was, I venture to think, his right course. Unfortunately, he did not take it. He first, on the 14th of June, 1858, wrote a fierce letter to Mr. Yates, a letter so couched as certainly not to facilitate apology or retraction . . . Thackeray next took the unusual course of appealing to the committee of the Garrick Club, on the plea that he had only met Mr. Yates at the Club, and that it was for the Club to protect him against Mr. Yates's insults. This, with all admiration for Thackeray, was scarcely, I think, *de bonne guerre*. The case was hardly one on which the Club ought to have been called upon to adjudicate; nor, in truth, did Thackeray himself come into court with perfectly clean hands, for he had made some of the members figure in his books, and not to their advantage.'

In 1858, Thackeray's judicious admirers said everything that is contained in this remarkable admission by one of his most fervid admirers, that in his action to the young journalist, for having written unfairly about him in an obscure paper, the great novelist was harsh, passionate, vindictive, and strangely wanting in magnanimity. As the latest, most satisfactory, and most authoritative of the several memoirs of the author of *Vanity Fair* came to us from the inner circle of his most critical and affectionate worshippers, it is manifest that the opinion which I communicated to Thackeray in 1858 as the judgment of his judicious and dispassionate friends has become the opinion of everybody who takes a critical interest in the character and story of the novelist.

'Still, even so,' Mr. Marzials observes, in his excellent account of the quarrel which agitated literary London so fiercely in 1858, 'it is difficult to understand why Thackeray was so ruffled by an article in an obscure paper like *Town Talk*. The explanation given at the time, and very current since, is that the whole affair was an outburst of long-smouldering jealousy between Thackeray and Dickens. Such a surmise must, from its nature, be difficult of proof or disproof.'

Speaking on the same point, Mr. Yates says, in his *Recollections and Experiences*,

'There is no doubt it was pretty generally said at the time, and it has been said since, and is said now, that the whole affair was a struggle for supremacy, or an outburst of jealousy, between Thackeray and Dickens, and that my part was merely that of the scapegoat or shuttlecock.'

It is already easier than Mr. Marzials imagines, and as the years go by it will be much easier, to prove that in the later stages of the fierce quarrel Thackeray was actuated by animosity against Dickens. The author of *Vanity Fair* was not more communicative to me, a recent and youthful acquaintance, than he was to several of his close and old friends about his motive in pushing his quarrel with the young journalist. He told them no less precisely than he told me that in striking Yates he was *hitting the man behind him;* and hitherto unpublished memoranda will in due course strengthen the evidence that he so spoke to them.

Though I never had any personal intercourse with Charles Dickens (albeit he wrote me two or three letters in 1858, and was so good as to give me a general invitation to visit him at Gad's Hill), I am not without grounds for holding a strong opinion that his action in the Yates-Thackeray quarrel proceeded in no degree from jealousy of Thackeray, that he never was jealous of Thackeray, that he never regarded himself as a competitor with Thackeray for literary pre-eminence, and that, from the dawn of Thackeray's success to the hour of his death, the rivalry of the two novelists was a one-sided rivalry. It is certain that Thackeray was keenly emulous of Dickens's literary success, and passionately desirous of surpassing it. There were times when this desire affected him so vehemently that he may be said to have suffered from Dickens-on-the-brain. He was enduring an acute visitation of the malady, when he went into Chapman and Hall's place of business, and begged to be told what was the average monthly sale of Dickens's then current story. On being shown the account of the monthly sales, he exclaimed, in a tone of mingled surprise and mortification, 'What!—so far ahead of me as all that!'

As his green leaves had a far larger circulation than Thackeray's yellow covers,—as ten persons went to his 'readings' for every individual who paid to hear Thackeray lecture,—as his works were no less generally read than Thackeray's books by the very classes who are said to have preferred the author of *Vanity Fair* to the author of *David Copperfield*,—as his professional position was strengthened by his possession of a singularly successful weekly periodical, whilst Thackeray never possessed any important periodical,—as his average yearly earnings must have been three times as great as Thackeray's average yearly earnings,—as his financial prosperity was never diminished or checked by Thackeray's success,—as he was read and applauded by the whole nation, whilst Thackeray had no strong hold on the public outside the lines of 'Society,' and was not universally admired by that small proportion of the English people, one fails to see why Dickens should have been jealous of Thackeray, or have regarded him as a competitor who was running him close, and might possibly get before him. Certainly Dickens was not jealous of his literary address and peculiar ability; for, though he recognized the greatness of his genius and admired *Vanity Fair*, *Pendennis*, and *The Newcomes*, he rated them none too highly, and saw little to commend in Thackeray's subsequent writings. Mr. Yates, who knew Dickens intimately, and studied him shrewdly, tells us in his autobiography that 'Dickens read little and thought less of Thackeray's later work,'—an announcement that may cause readers to remark, 'So much the worse for Dickens!'

Jealousy does not appear to have been one of Dickens's failings. He had quite as much reason to be jealous of Sir Edward Bulwer-Lytton (Lord Lytton) and of Wilkie Collins, when they were in the fulness of their powers and popularity, as he had to be jealous of Thackeray; but he lived in friendliness with them, and invited them to write for him. That Thackeray and Dickens were antipathetic would not of itself warrant a suspicion, much less would it justify a statement, that they were jealous of one another. The common notion that Dickens regarded Thackeray as a powerful and dangerous rival, and was therefore disposed to quarrel with him before the *Town Talk* embroilment, is neither supported by evidence nor even countenanced by the known facts of their never cordial intercourse. Moreover, sure facts account so fully for the displeasure with which Dickens regarded Thackeray from the summer of 1858 to the winter of 1863, that to account for it by an improbable hypothesis is to violate a first canon of biographical art. Dickens's friendship for Mr. Yates, to whom he conceived himself indebted for 'a manly service,' afforded a sufficient motive for his action in his young friend's behalf at the outset of the quarrel, and for his resolve to do his best to bring him out of a serious difficulty. Five weeks later, when Mr. Yates's name had been erased from the list of Garrick clubbists, Dickens's strong opinion that Thackeray had treated Yates with vindictive harshness, naturally caused him to regard the author of *Vanity Fair* with warm dislike,—a state of feeling that was aggravated by Dickens's annoyance at his failure to preserve his friend from the injury done to him by Thackeray. When it is remembered that, besides these reasons for disliking the author of *Vanity Fair*, Dickens had reason to resent the tone of the letter which Thackeray addressed to him from Onslow Square, on the 26th of November, 1858, there is no need to look beyond the incidents of the embroilment for the considerations which determined the by far most popular of then living novelists to hold aloof from the author of *The Newcomes*.

On the other hand, whilst there is no sufficient reason to charge Dickens with having been jealous of Thackeray, it is certain that Thackeray, from the dawn of his celebrity to the last year of his life, was greatly desirous of surpassing Dickens in the world's favour, and at times was keenly annoyed by his inability to do so. I question whether Thackeray had a familiar friend who did not at some time or other hear the author of *Vanity Fair* speak of himself as Dickens's rival, and declare his chagrin at failing to out-rival him. His ambition to get the better of Dickens may have originated in his natural appetite for social distinction, but I am rather inclined to regard it as having sprung from a seed that was planted in his breast by Mr. Abraham Hayward, whilst *Vanity Fair* was appearing in yellow-covered numbers.

Whilst Thackeray was a man of divers moods, Mr. Hayward was a man of divers airs. Though statesmen of light and leading smiled at his presumption in advising them on affairs of state, Mr. Hayward by his political airs caused a considerable number of rather intelligent persons to regard him as a politician whose secret counsel had sometimes controlled the policy of cabinets, and whose disfavour had resulted in the death of more than one administration. Though our best authors thought little and spoke lightly of his learning and his flashy articles, and Disraeli the Younger had been heard to style him 'the louse of literature,' Mr. Hayward's literary airs made him so great a power in the literary coteries, that young writers feared his frown, and were at much pains to win his favour. By his social airs, Mr. Hayward imposed himself on the idlers of Mayfair and clubland as a personage of the greatest social importance. It was the opinion of this gentleman, who flourished upon his airs from early manhood to extreme old age, that the intellectual and moral life of England was controlled by the intellect of London, that the intellect and higher morality of London were swayed by the Athenæum Club, that the brain and conscience of the Athenæum Club were governed by Mr. A. Hayward of that club, of the *Times,* and of the two leading quarterly Reviews.

But, though he was not quite so clever nor anything like so important a personage as he conceived himself to be, this gentleman of curious airs was a clever fellow,—especially clever in conciliating people of great influence, in discerning which of the new books it was his interest to praise and which of them it was his interest to condemn, and in seizing the happy moment for recognizing and aiding men of genius, who were on the point of becoming successful by virtue of their own powers. Leaving authors of genius to fight through their early difficulties as they best could, he was quick in coming to their assistance at the turning-point of their fortunes, so as to gain credit for helping them to achieve celebrity. Having known Thackeray for more than twelve years, known him from the early time when he was copying pictures in the Louvre, in order to qualify himself to be a professional artist, and having coldly watched his long struggles, without condescending to notice any one of his excellent works, or caring to give him a helping hand, Mr. Abraham Hayward no sooner saw from the opening numbers of *Vanity Fair* that it would make a great stir, than he hastened to congratulate the author on the excellence of the work, and to take prompt measures, so as to participate in his *dear old friend's* coming triumph, and even make it appear that he had done much to bring it about by his authoritative utterances in the press and at fashionable dinner-tables. Thackeray, of course, formed a correct estimate of the value and significance of Mr. Hayward's—his dear old friend's—admiration of the introductory numbers of the new serial in yellow covers, and his resolve to review the first eleven numbers in the *Edinburgh Review* of January, 1848. Knowing that the story had 'caught on,' as the phrase goes, before Hayward came to him about it, the novelist regarded his dear old friend's desire to introduce the book to 'Society,' as significant of Hayward's knowledge that the story was already being talked about in society, and also of his opinion that he must act quickly, if he would have the credit of being the first public writer to commend the book authoritatively to the world.

The gentleman of magnificent airs was at work on

the review, which would make him figure as the prime discoverer of the excellences of *Vanity Fair*, when he sent Thackeray the following brief note in acknowledgment of a sketch which he begged the novelist to give him for a lady's album,—

'Temple, Nov. 8, [1847].

'MY DEAR THACKERAY,

'A thousand thanks. It will do admirably, and I will not tax you again in the same manner. Don't get nervous or think about criticism, or trouble yourself about the friends; you have completely beaten Dickens out of the inner circle already. I dine at Gore House to-day; look in if you can.

'Ever yours,

'A. H.'

After laughing over this characteristic note from the gentleman of airs, Thackeray sent it to Mrs. Brookfield, together with a brief epistle, in which he encouraged the lady to laugh, as he had done, at the billet and its writer.

'Although,' Thackeray wrote to his dear Mrs. Brookfield, 'I am certainly committing a breach of confidence, I venture to offer my friend up to you, because you have considerable humour, and I think will possibly laugh at him ... Ah! madame, how much richer truth is than fiction, and how great that phrase about "the inner circle" is!'

The 'inner circle' was, of course, the circle of Mr. Hayward's friends—for the most part, members of the Athenæum Club—who felt, thought, said what he told them to feel, think, say. But, though he laughed at the 'great phrase about the inner circle,' I cannot doubt it tickled Thackeray's vanity, as well as his sense of humour, and was not without effect on his ambition to outstrip Dickens, and make him nothing more than the second novelist of his period of English literature. If it was not the seed of that ambition, it became by frequent repetition a part of the artificial soil that quickened the growth of the plant which sprang from other seed within his breast. The phrase, which soon became current in the drawing-rooms of the western quarters of London, points also to the atmosphere of flattery that encouraged Thackeray from the first season of his celebrity to think of himself as the novelist who, having driven Dickens 'out of the inner circle,' might hope to excel him in the open field.

From what I have said of Thackeray's desire to surpass Dickens—a desire of which he spoke with engaging frankness to his mere acquaintances as well as his closest friends—readers may not infer that it was a passion either mean in itself or likely to degenerate into envy and hatred of the more popular novelist. An essentially and uniformly generous passion, it was attended with a cordial recognition of the genius of Charles Dickens, and with enthusiastic admiration of his finer artistic achievements. Though he often spoke to me of Dickens and his literary doings, I never heard him utter a word in disparagement of the writer whom he laboured to outshine. I do not mean to imply that he admired everything that came from Dickens's pen, or that he was never heard to express dissatisfaction with a work by Dickens. I only wish to imply that I cannot conceive him to have ever spoken a word in censure of anything written by

Dickens that could be fairly attributed to the malice of jealousy. In remarking to Mr. Yates that 'Little D. was Deed stupid,' Thackeray said no more in dispraise of *Little Dorrit* than he said in dispraise of his own *Virginians*, when he spoke of it to Motley as a 'devilish stupid' book. He repeatedly avowed to me his desire to be thought a greater novelist than Dickens, but in doing so he always displayed a passionate admiration of the writer whom he was striving to precede. On one occasion, after descanting on the excellences of the new number of Dickens's then current book, he brought his fist down upon the table with a thump as he exclaimed, 'What is the use of my trying to run before that man, or by his side? I can't touch him,—I can't get near him.'

My whilom friend George Hodder, in his *Memories of my Time*, gives a similar example of Thackeray's enthusiastic admiration of the novelist whom he desired to surpass.

'Putting No. 5 of *Dombey and Son* in his pocket,' Hodder says of Thackeray, 'he hastened down to Mr. Punch's printing-office, and entering the editor's room, where I chanced to be the only person present except Mr. Mark Lemon himself, he dashed it on the table with startling vehemence, and exclaimed, "There's no writing against such power as this—one has no chance. Read that chapter describing young Paul's death; it is unsurpassed—it is stupendous"!'

On another occasion he said to me, with mingled sadness and magnanimity, that seemed to me both noble and pathetic, 'I am played out. All I can do now is to bring out my old puppets, and put new bits of riband upon them. But, if he live to be ninety, Dickens will still be creating new characters. In his art that man is marvellous.'

I know him to have spoken to other persons in the same strain and almost in the same words about the novelist, whom he admired so greatly.

Though the author of *Vanity Fair* was so good as to afford me many opportunities for studying his whims and foibles, as well as his noble qualities, and talked to me about his feelings for the author of *The Tale of Two Cities* as freely as he appears to have spoken of them to any person of his acquaintance, I never discovered anything rancorous, or petty, or ignoble in his rivalry of Dickens. On the contrary, I saw much that was admirable and beautiful in it. Thackeray would have been a happier man had he done his appointed work without thinking so often and so emulously of Gushy's prodigious circulation and strong sway over the reading populace. But, as his superb power fully justified the favourite novelist of 'the classes' in pitting himself against the favourite novelist of the whole people, I honoured him for the emulation that was so generous, so magnanimous, and so pure of envious malignity.

CHAPTER XV.

MORE ABOUT THACKERAY.

My Intercourse with Thackeray—An *Habitué* of Evans's—Paddy Green—The Cyder Cellars—Thackeray the Tavern-Haunter—His solitary Dinners at the Gray's Inn Coffee-House—His Divers Moods—Douglas Jerrold on Thackeray—James Kenney the Dramatist—His Whims and Eccentricities—Charles Lamb Kenney—Portraits of him in *Pendennis*—His Intimacy with Thackeray—His famous Review of *The Kickleburys on the Rhine*—Why did you 'do it,' Charley?—*Essay on Thunder and Small Beer*—Thackeray's Care for a Friend's Feelings—Thackeray at 'The Derby'—Comrades in Misfortune on Epsom Downs—Thackeray the *Bon Vivant*—His Delight in Good Cheer—The twopenny Tartlet—Consequences of his gastronomic Indiscretions—Curious Anecdotes about George III.—Thackeray and *Live It Down*—Thackeray in the Chair at a Shakespeare Dinner of *Our Club*—Geraldine Jewsbury's Review of *The Story of Elizabeth*—Consequences of that Review—National Shakespeare Tercentenary Committee—Squabbles and Misunderstandings—Thackeray's Withdrawal from *Our Club*—Hamstede's vain Endeavours to recover him to the Club—Thackeray's Death—His few Foibles and noble Qualities—Andrew Arcedeckne and Mr. Foker.

As I walked from Wimpole Street back to my lodgings, after the interview with Thackeray, in which he told me that he was striking Yates in order to 'hit the man behind him,' I was fearful that he would regret having spoken to me so frankly, and that the incident would diminish the friendliness of our intercourse. The fear was dispelled by the heartiness with which the novelist on meeting me a few days later invited me to walk with him. From that time till April 25th, 1863, the day on which I spoke with Thackeray for the last time, I saw a good deal of the famous novelist, under circumstances that increased my liking for him, and made me feel that I was growing steadily in his favour. But our pleasant intercourse would not justify me in speaking of myself as one of his intimate friends, for he neither invited me to his house nor crossed my threshold during the whole course of our acquaintanceship. I was never anything more to him than an acquaintance, with whom he liked to chat, when we came upon one another in the house of a common friend, at clubs and taverns, at the British Museum, in the public ways, and at places of public amusement.

Encountering him repeatedly at No. 16, Wimpole Street, I often met him on the pavements of the town; and when we met in a public thoroughfare he usually stopped to chat with me, and sometimes asked me to walk with him. It was at *his* request that I used to look for him at Evans's, when I was passing through or near Covent Garden at night, on my way to or fro between my home in Heathcote Street and the offices of the journals to which I contributed. Had he not asked me to seek him there, I should seldom have visited the supper-room on the basement of Evans's Hotel, of which Thackeray was an *habitué*;

for to me the hot, noisy cellar, in which journalists and gentlemen about town used to assemble and drink grog and toddy, and consume unwholesome suppers, when they should have been going to bed, was far from being a Cave of Harmony and Delight. Thackeray, on the contrary, enjoyed the music, the noise, and the smoky atmosphere of the hot, crowded cellar, where Herr von Joel used to whistle and 'do the farm-yard' to the lively delight of young farmers from the country. Dropping into Evans's late for 'a finish' after 'the play,' or a grand dinner or a rout, the author of *Vanity Fair* used also to go there early, for the pleasure of hearing the musical boys sing glees, and madrigals, and quaint old ballads. He would listen to them, song after song, for the hour— ay, for hours together, never speaking a word during the performances. Several of the singing-boys were church-choristers; and, in reference to their ecclesiastical employment, Thackeray once said to me, 'It does me more good to listen to them in this cellar than in Westminster Abbey.'

During the later years of Paddy Green's management of the big supper and music-room, when his health was failing and a priest was preparing his soul for the ordeal after death, the songs sung at Evans's were for the most part of great artistic merit, and no objection could be made to any of them on the score of morality. So much cannot be said of the songs which were sung there before Mr. Green had been admonished to reform his establishment. Thackeray greatly preferred the reformed to the unreformed supper-room, but he had been a supporter of the place in its earlier time. He used to go to the Cyder Cellars, when they were a school of vice for young clerks and students.

'Last night,' Albert Smith wrote to my old friend George Hodder, in some year of the earlier fifties, 'I met Thackeray at the Cyder Cellars, and we stayed there until three in the morning. He is a very jolly fellow, and no "High Art" about him.'

Thackeray had a good deal of 'High Art about him,' though he was too discreet to display it in a haunt where it would have been strangely out of place.

The worthy Irishman, who kept Evans's Hotel in the time when Thackeray was an *habitué* of the large supper-room on the basement, was a droll character. A short, squab man, with a purple complexion and the shortest neck ever put upon the shoulders of a licensed victualler, Mr. Green allowed his modish visitors to call him Paddy Green, or Paddy (without the Green), and repaid their familiarity by addressing each of them in turn as his 'dear boy.' Whilst Andrew Arcedeckne revenged himself on Thackeray, for describing him in Foker, by seizing every opportunity for addressing the great novelist as 'Thack,' Paddy Green used to greet the author of *Vanity Fair* with 'Ah, my dear boy,' as he opened his big silver snuff-box, and invited the dear boy to take a pinch. I am proud to say that Mr. Green used to accost me in the same affectionate manner, and that I must, in the course of years, have put into my nose a quarter-of-a-pound of snuff, taken in countless pinches from his capacious box. On discovering how poor an appetite I had for chops and stout, or devilled kidneys and brandy-grog, and that Thackeray was my only attraction to the social cellar, the no less kindly than comical Mr. Green often greeted me at the door of his place of nocturnal entertainment with, 'Have a pinch, my dear boy, and come in, for the dear boy is here,' or 'Ah, my dear boy, the dear boy isn't here, but have a pinch before you go off.'

Clunn's Hotel, next door to Evans's at the north-west corner of Covent Garden, was another tavern at which I saw much of Thackeray, when he had joined 'Our Club,' the meetings of which society for the promotion of good fellowship were agreeable to him, albeit he disliked the 'speeches' so greatly that he would sometimes fume about them and declare them insufferable. And I cannot conceive him to have ever been seen to greater advantage, than when he was sitting with a party of his congenial comrades at O. C., gossipping tenderly about dead authors, artists, and actors, or cheerily and in the kindliest spirit about living notabilities. It was very pleasant to watch the white-headed veteran, and also to hear him (though at best he sung indifferently) whilst he trolled forth his favourite ballads, touching Little Billee and Father Martin Luther. Better still it was to regard the radiant gratification of his face, whilst Horace Mayhew sang 'The Mahogany Tree,' perhaps the finest and most stirring of Thackeray's social songs, or was throwing his soul into the passionate 'Marseillaise.' Thackeray was in the latest stage of his too brief career when he joined 'Our Club.' I cannot say precisely and positively the date of Thackeray's election into the club, but I think he joined it in November, 1861.

I am at the more pains to say that my intercourse with Thackeray was held chiefly at taverns, because his habit of going to inns for refreshment and society, when he was a member of three such good and very different house-clubs as the 'Athenæum,' the 'Reform,' and the 'Garrick,' is an interesting illustration of one side of his social history and character. Joining the literary cliques at a time when authors-by-profession spent much of their leisure in taverns, —when young Alfred Tennyson used to turn into 'The Cock' in Fleet Street at 5 p.m. for 'a pint of port,'—when, indeed, some of the most able and distinguished authors-by-profession would have vainly sought to be elected into a house-club of good repute,—Thackeray contracted, from the habits of his early manhood, so strong a liking for tavern life, that he was to the last a frequenter of such inns as those in which he had cultivated the friendship of Maginn and Mahoney. He was, perhaps, the last greatly eminent man of letters, who preferred the old-world tavern to the modern club-house, as a place in which to take his ease and enjoy the company of his friends, —the last great English man of letters, to be fairly described as a tavern-haunter, in the most agreeable and quite inoffensive sense of the term. His liking for taverns was strengthened by his familiarity with the usages, and his sympathy with the spirit and humours of Queen Anne's London.

Going to taverns for intercourse with his friends, Thackeray sometimes went to inns, where the wine was especially good, for the enjoyment of his own society. I once brought a smile to his face by telling him, that a Lincoln's Inn barrister, struck by seeing him on several occasions walking eastward in Holborn, when the barristers of the Inns were walking westward after work, from pure curiosity turned about on a certain afternoon, and tracking him to the Gray's Inn coffee-house, saw him dine there in the coffee-room without a companion.

'Ah!' said Thackeray, with enjoyment of the story, and of the good wine which it recalled to his memory, 'that was when I was drinking the last of that wonderful bin of port. It *was* rare wine. There were only two dozen bottles and a few bottles over, when I came upon the remains of that bin, and I forthwith bargained with mine host to keep them for me. I drank every bottle and every drop of that remainder by myself. I shared never a bottle with living man; and so long as the wine lasted, I slipped off to the Gray's Inn coffee-house with all possible secrecy short of disguise, whenever I thought a dinner and a bottle by myself would do me good.'

The Thackeray, with whom I used to gossip at Evans's and Clunn's, at No. 16, Wimpole Street, and during our walks about town, differed greatly from the Thackeray whose 'bearing' struck Mr. Yates as 'cold and uninviting,' and in whom Mr. Frith, R.A., and Serjeant Ballantyne discovered divers unamiable qualities. But though he charmed me by his genial manner, his conversational communicativeness, and social kindliness, and caused me to think highly of his benevolence and his habitual considerateness for the feelings of his companions, I do not question either the honesty or the discernment of the several persons, who in published words have accused him of failings which he never displayed to me during the six years of our intercourse. As Mr. Yates was in his early manhood what he is at this late date of his career, a shrewd observer of human nature and a man of honour, I have no doubt that he had cause to think Thackeray 'cold and uninviting' in manner. Though I never saw anything in Thackeray to justify the severe terms in which Serjeant Ballantyne declared his dislike of the novelist, I think it more probable that in some of his weak and perverse moods Thackeray displayed the alleged infirmities, than that the caustic barrister was absolutely without grounds for declaring him very egotistical, greedy of flattery, and sensitive of criticism to a ridiculous extent. As Douglas Jerrold observed on more than one occasion, 'I have known Thackeray eighteen years, and don't know him yet,' I am not so immodest as to imagine that I knew the great novelist thoroughly, after associating with him for barely a third of that time. But I have grounds for thinking that my account of the author of *Vanity Fair* displays him in his most usual as well as his most agreeable moods; and I hold this opinion the more strongly, because my view of his nature closely resembled the view that was taken of him by several of my friends, who had known him for a much longer period,—notably, by Horace Mayhew, who, as one of the original staff of *Punch*, had known him from 1842, and Charles Lamb

Kenney, whose curious association with Thackeray began at a still earlier date.

Before I speak of Charles Lamb Kenney, one of whose sisters married my cousin, Samuel Jeaffreson, M.D. (Cantab.), of Leamington, I will say a little of his father, James Kenney, the dramatist—the author of *Raising the Wind*, the creator of Jeremy Diddler, the friend of Tom Moore and the Godwins. A dapper little Irishman, with a face remarkable in his earlier time for the comeliness of its features and the brightness of its complexion, the elder Kenney was a notability of literary London from the opening of the present century up to 1st of August, 1849, when he died in his eightieth year on the very morning that had been fixed for a performance for his benefit at the Drury Lane Theatre. Amusing the world with the productions of his pen, he afforded infinite diversion to his troops of friends by the sallies with which he set festive tables in a roar, and by eccentricities of behaviour, which seemed to indicate that his great wits were divided from madness by the thinnest of partitions. Shortly before his death in August, 1861, Henry Holden Frankum, who subsisted at Kensington in his closing years on a pension, allowed to him by the proprietors of the *Times* in consideration of his former services on the paper, threw me and Doran into hearty laughter by telling us how he had seen the elder Kenney in a solitary walk pause before a big puddle at the east end of Holywell Street, and had watched the process by which the small and nervous pedestrian lifted himself over the wide water. On first seeing the width of the puddle, resulting from an April shower and the stoppage of a drain, the dramatist turned white in the face, as he backed a few paces from the kerbstone that bordered the little lake. Five seconds later, under the influence of a happy thought, which restored the colour to his face, he moved quickly to the puddle, and grasped each of his high shirt-collars with a trembling hand. Another instant, and he had crossed the turbid pool without wetting his feet. Having come to the stones on the east side of the water without a splash, Kenney looked about him with the air of a man who had conquered a gigantic difficulty with almost superhuman cleverness.

'Ah!' he exclaimed, nodding triumphantly at the water, and addressing it as though it were a sentient being, familiar with the language of the country, 'you thought to stop my course, did you? You see, my lad, I am one too many for you. Now, you'd better clean out that drain, and go through it as quickly as possible. For, if you don't, bedad! all the street-boys will be laughing at you!'

Turning about, after he had ordered the water to slip away, the dramatist saw himself confronted by Frankum.

'Ah!' remarked the dramatist, 'you saw how I got the better of him. Then I have given you a wrinkle.'

'Yes,' replied Frankum, 'I saw how you lifted yourself over the water.'

'Ay,' returned Kenney, with equal seriousness and self-complacence, 'and wasn't it a pretty trick?—so simple and yet so novel?'

'Good heavens!' exclaimed Doran, when his more violent delight at the story had passed away, 'it reminds me of the man who, on returning to his house dead-beat from a long walk, put himself down in a big linen-basket and grasped its two handles, under the impression that he could lift himself up to his bed-room, and spare his feet the trouble of walking upstairs.'

On another occasion, Frankum was putting away his hat and overcoat in the entrance-hall of a suburban villa, at which he was in the habit of taking pot-luck dinner on Sunday, when he heard a familiar voice in the dining-room, the door of which was open.

'Yes, sir, you've been up to your little tricks again,' the familiar voice was saying in a tone of unusual severity. 'You self-indulgent, guzzling, guttling, drunken, dissolute dog, I see how you have been passing the last ten days! You have spent them, sir, in eating and drinking—ay, drinking and eating. Instead of working for your family, you have been feasting and carousing. Don't answer me, sir, or say a word in excuse of your conduct. Nothing you can say will affect my opinion of you. Good lord, what black lines there are about your dull, fishy eyes!—and what a complexion you have, yellow as an orange and muddy as ditch-water! You debauched, jaundiced, fish-eyed old scamp! You depraved, dissolute sinner, I'll punish you before I am many hours older! This very night, sir, I'll give you a pill,—such a pill!—a regular bolus! And to-morrow morning I'll give you a black draught,—such a nauseous draught!'

On passing noiselessly through the open door, Frankum saw Kenney the Elder, standing on a chair in front of the dining-room fire-place, and examining his yellow face and dark-rimmed eyes in the mirror over the mantel-piece. The dramatist had been the sole occupant of the room whilst he spoke so severely to his own likeness.

Inheriting his father's comely face and delicate figure, Charles Lamb Kenney also derived from his sire the peculiar gaiety—the whimsical, subtle, freakish humour—that made him so delightful a companion and so welcome a guest at convivial tables. A barrister who never held a brief, Charley Kenney was a journalist of considerable ability, and was for some time employed in Printing-house Square, to read the French newspapers and gather from them noteworthy items of continental intelligence. At the same time it devolved on Kenney to review books under the control of the Thunderer's literary editor, and to ply his pen in divers subordinate ways for the production of the daily issues of the *Times*. Had he been punctual, methodical, and habitually industrious, Charley would have been the right man to render the leading journal the various services of a literary under-strapper and a manipulator of news, taken from foreign journals. But he was incapable of the business-like habits that were needful for the performance of his duties in Printing-house Square. A Bohemian by birth and nurture, Charley was so averse to official drudgery, that he failed to peruse the continental journals with adequate care and regularity, and consequently lost the fairly good berth, to which he would have clung tenaciously had he been as prudent as he was brilliant.

When Thackeray was working on his own illustrations of *The History of Pendennis*, he induced his friend, Charley Kenney, to stand as model for some, if not for all, of the artistic sketches of Arthur Pendennis; and some of the novelist's portraits of the young man, who was his own greatest enemy, are close and curiously-exact likenesses of the Charley Kenney whom I met for the first time in some year of 'the mid-fifties,' when he had a strangely youthful and even boyish countenance for a man on the threshold of middle age. For example, the youthful Arthur of the illustration of the third chapter, which exhibits the young gentleman standing arm-in-arm with Mr. Foker in the cathedral yard of Chatteris, whilst they speak with Dr. Portman, is a good likeness of the Charley Kenney of my earliest recollections of him. The same may be said of the Arthur Pendennis of the sketch of the scene on the Castle Walk, when Miss Fotheringay passed poor Pen 'without any nod of recognition.' The subsequent pictures of Arthur are less close likenesses of Charley; indeed, some of them are so unlike the Arthur of the earlier illustrations, that they seem to have been drawn from another model; but the Arthur Pendennis, who holds in his right hand a glass of 'frothing lukewarm beer,' whilst he stands near Sam Huxter's cab on the Epsom race-course, gives another clear view of Charles Kenney.

Having stood as model for several of the sketches of Arthur Pendennis, when the novelist and artist was working upon the second of his greatly successful stories, Charley Kenney did his friend a far greater service in December, 1850, by writing and placing in the *Times* the absurd review of *The Kickleburys on the Rhine*, which gave the author of that flimsy tale an opportunity for making the leading journal supremely ridiculous for something more than nine days. If Mr. Theodore Taylor was right in saying that the review ' was generally attributed to the late Mr. Samuel Phillips,' the generality of readers made a mistake from which Thackeray's *Essay on Thunder and Small Beer* should have saved them. At a time when, in respect to literary reviews, Samuel Phillips was regarded by ' the town ' as the Thunderer himself, Thackeray told the readers of the famous *Essay* to attribute the review to ' Jupiter Jeames, trying to dazzle and roar like his awful employer.' But I question whether the critique was ever attributed to Mr. Phillips by people of light and leading in the literary cliques. If Thackeray for a brief hour suspected Phillips of having written the critique, he had survived the suspicion and discovered the actual writer of the notice, before he dipped his pen in ink to write the smashing answer.

That Kenney wrote the review first came to my knowledge from his intimate friend, Henry Holden Frankum, who was working on the *Times* during Charley's connection with the leading journal; and, in later time, Kenney himself admitted to me that he wrote the article.

' How on earth came you to do it, Charley?' I inquired.

'The book was a poor thing,' he answered.

'A poor thing, no doubt, to come from the pen of so great a writer; but, though it was a weak thing, Thackeray was your friend.'

'Surely he was my friend,' returned Kenney, in a magnificent vein, that set me laughing, as Charley meant it to do, 'but surely you don't mean to suggest that friendship, or any other personal feeling, should influence a critic when he is discharging one of the highest functions of a journalist.'

'Something had occurred to put you out of temper with W. M. T.? You were friends, but just then friends at feud on some question of small beer?'

'You are wrong,' he answered, with curious cynical levity, 'my only motive for pitching into the book was to please my employers. Thackeray was not liked by them, and I wished them to like me. My friendly regard for the writer of the poor book was overborne by a strong sense of my duty to the public, and a still stronger care for my own interest.'

Of course I took these words with a grain of distrust, and with due regard for my friend's freakish humour. I do not think he was actuated in the affair of the article merely by a sense of duty and a desire to benefit himself. But, freakish creature though he was, he would not have admitted he wrote the discreditable article if he had not written it.

It is strange that Kenney dealt so saucily and peevishly with his friend's Christmas story, when nothing had occurred to put them at open war with one another. As each of them was fervid in temper and rather stubborn in his resentments, it is even more strange that the reviewer of *The Kickleburys* and the author of *Vanity Fair* were friends in time subsequent to the publication of the *Essay on Thunder and Small Beer*. Whether the exchange of shots occasioned a transient rupture between the combatants I cannot say; but it is within my knowledge that, in his closing years, Thackeray maintained friendly relations with Charles Lamb Kenney.

Of Thackeray's care for the feelings of his friends I may give the following example. On looking for him one night in his favourite cellar, I saw his greatcoat on a chair near the principal entrance of the supper-room, whilst the owner of the garment was sitting in a distant corner of Paddy Green's chamber of entertainment. The chair, on which the greatcoat rested, was near the table at which A. (as he shall be styled in this page) was taking a chop and a pint of stout before going off to write a critique of some opera or concert for one of the morrow's papers. A. was a worthy fellow, but remarkable amongst the journalists of his set for 'hardness of hearing' (a curious defect for a musical critic), a dismally-displeasing visage, and a voice that, disagreeable to all hearers but the owner of the unmelodious organ, was at times excruciating to the nervous Thackeray. On coming to Thackeray's side, I told him that he had left his great-coat at a place whence it might be carried off by one of Paddy Green's least scrupulous customers.

'It must take its chance,' replied the novelist. 'I left it there for a purpose. I am not well enough to-night to endure dear old A.'s voice without wincing.

So I came across the room to this seat, but left my coat behind me so that A. might think I intended to return to him in a minute, and might not suspect I had run away from him. I would not, for the world, hurt the dear man.'

On two several Derby Days I came upon Thackeray on the Epsom race-course. On the earlier of these days, the friend with whom I was walking on the downs shortly before the grand race, asked Andrew Arcedeckne if he had seen Thackeray on the ground so recently, as to be able to point to the part of the course where he would probably be still loitering.

'I saw him there,' returned Mr. Andrew Arcedeckne, pointing to a particular booth as he spoke, 'a short five minutes since, but as you ain't a swell, you had better steer clear of Thack for a little time, for when I saw him and gave him the "Hullo, Thack!" he was walking with a lord.'

A few minutes later, when I came upon him, the great novelist greeted me with his usual complaisance, although he had been so recently seen in the company of a personage whose quality was likely to make him insolent and dangerous to ordinary mortals. At the second of these meetings on Epsom downs, Thackeray informed me of a loss I had sustained, but had not discovered before he called my attention to it.

'So, youngster, we are in the same plight,' he observed, as he glanced at what remained to me of a watch-guard, which a pickpocket had clipt. 'I have just lost my gold-repeater, and some rogue has taken your watch.' Unfortunately for my despoiler, my watch was no gold repeater, but a thing in a silver case, that had cost me about as many shillings as the guineas Thackeray had given for his watch. 'As comrades in misfortune,' Thackeray added, 'it behoves us to drink a consoling cup together; and I see a carriage where we can procure the cup.' Whereupon, the gentle giant conducted me to a carriage, from whose store of good cheer we received glasses of champagne.

I have already spoken so fully of the habits which wrecked Thackeray's health, that I shall occasion the readers of the present page no astonishment by speaking of him as an invalid, whose constitution was irrecoverably broken before I made his acquaintance. Had his appetites—especially his appetite for the pleasures of the table—been under his control, I should not be justified in using so strong an expression, to describe his bodily condition in the earlier years of my intercourse with him. Could he have acted steadily in accordance with the advice of his doctors, he might have recovered his health in 1860, or in a still later year, and kept it even to old age. But he was powerless to do as they advised him. Speaking to my friend, George Hodder, of his inability to live as his physicians urged him to live, the novelist said, with characteristic candour and vehemence (vide, *Memories of my Time*, p. 306),

'What is the use of advice, if you don't follow it? They tell me not to drink, and I *do* drink. They tell me not to smoke, and I *do* smoke. They tell me not to eat, and I *do* eat. In short, I do everything I am desired *not* to do, and, therefore, what am I to expect?'

These words were spoken to Hodder in 1857—the year of my introduction to the novelist, who on more than one occasion made the same confession of infirmity to me, albeit in different words.

'At a big dinner,' he said to me, 'I behave like a child, like a schoolboy at a Christmas feast, eating everything that is offered to me, everything that comes in my way. The season plays the devil with me, because I dine out a great deal, and I am in no sense my own master at any dinner-table but my own, and even at my own table I can't control my wicked appetite, when I am entertaining a lot of people. I can be admirably prudent, so long as there is no need for prudence; but with the first glass of champagne, away goes my prudence, and I must have something of whatever is going.'

Just as he on one occasion taught me to look for revelations of himself in the subordinate touches given to the creations of his fancy, by saying he was laughing at one of his own foibles when he ridiculed General Braddock's 'absurd pride in his no-ancestry,' he on another occasion gave me a similar lesson by telling me that he was thinking of his own 'contemptible gulosity' when he derided Joe Sedley for stuffing himself with different kinds of food, and then eating a lot of ratafia cakes. When Mrs. Brookfield offered him one of the smaller sweetmeats from a dish that held larger cates of the same kind, saying, 'Will you have a tartlet, Mr. Thackeray?' the novelist answered, 'I will, but I'll have a two-penny one, if you please.'

The story was more characteristic than the teller (Mrs. Brookfield) seems to have been aware. Taking a penn'orth of everything that was offered him at a dinner-table, Thackeray was sure to take a two-penn'orth of every nice dish, that was certain to do him harm. If in August, 1848, he stopt eating at the twenty-fifth dish at the *table d'hôte* of the Hotel Des Pays Bas at Spa, and rested from *gourmandise* whilst the fair, blue-eyed Flemish lady pegged away at subsequent dishes (vide, *The Brookfield Letters*, pp. 16, 17), he did so because the twenty-sixth and following *plats* were at no time acceptable to his palate. But, though he was a large eater, the superabundance of his meals escaped the notice of most of his companions, for he ate quietly and with due observance of the rules of good breeding.

Eating thus largely, he drank more than was good for him.

'You have drunk a good deal in your time,' I once observed to him.

'Enough,' he answered, jollily, 'to float a 74 gunship. Since I came out of my poverty, a bottle has been my daily minimum, and on three out of every four days I have taken a second bottle. I may be called a two-bottle man; and that takes no account of the two or three glasses of wine at mid-day, nor of the punches and grogs in the hours about midnight.'

But, though I have repeatedly seen him take in a few hours four and even six times as much alcohol as any one of his doctors would have authorized him to take in an entire day, I never saw him under the influence of the glass that used to be styled 'a glass too much.' Drinking wine as men used to drink wine in the days of Maginn and Theodore Hook, he 'carried it' like a gentleman.

As he delighted and indulged in good cheer thus freely, it is not surprising that the nervous man's stomach rebelled against a master who showed so little consideration for its weakness, and punished him with cramp and spasms, and violent fits of sickness and retching, in the last of which fits he died from the rupture of a blood-vessel in the head. Moreover, to realize fully how much the great novelist suffered in his closing years from bodily ailments, readers must bear in mind that, whilst he endured successive visitations of the stomachic disorder, that eventually put an end to his life, he was troubled by another disorder, even more wearing to the nerves and more afflicting to the spirits.

My most pleasant, and also my most painful, recollections of Thackeray relate to incidents of 1863.

In the first month of that year, I wrote a long review of *The Life of General Sir Robert Wilson, from Autobiographical Memoirs, Journals, Narratives, Correspondence, &c. Edited by his Nephew and Son-in-law, the Reverend Herbert Randolph*,' which review appeared in the number of the *Athenæum* for the 31st of January, 1863; and I think it was on the evening of the same day that I mentioned the book at *Our Club* in a way which caused Thackeray to tell me a curious story about George the Third. Containing much piquant gossip, to which no objection could be made on the score of indelicacy, the book contained also an anecdote of the Farmer King, so grotesquely indecorous and out-of-place in a work offered to readers of polite literature, that I did not venture to reproduce the story in the columns of the *Athenæum*. As an anonymous critic, I merely stated the page of the book on which the curious reader might find an anecdote so strangely improper that I attributed its appearance in the biography to editorial inadvertence. At the table of O. C., where I could speak without consideration *virginibus puerisque*, I told the story to a rather large party of listeners, who, with the single exception of Thackeray, were thrown into violent laughter by my communication: but, though he was silent, his face beamed with smiles of amusement, that assured me he was as much tickled by my contribution to the hilarity of the evening as I wished him to be.

Half-an-hour later, on his return to the room after a brief retirement to an adjoining chamber, the author of *Vanity Fair* seated himself on a vacant chair by my side, and said to me, in an undertone,

'I have come to you, like an honourable man, to pay you in kind for that droll story anent poor old George III. with a companion-story,—an unpublished anecdote from a manuscript journal, which Lord .... lent me, when I was gathering particulars of the King's personal story. A gentleman of the Household, the writer of the journal, was on duty at Court, when the King in his mental illness delighted in writing offensive words on the walls of rooms, and also on the walls of the grounds, in which he took exercise on foot, under the surveillance of an attendant, who was instructed to follow his liege lord and obliterate with a cloth or brush whatever the poor demented sovereign wrote with chalk or pencil on wall or gate. As it is a story I should not care to tell at the top of my voice to the whole table, take it quietly, laugh in your sleeve, so that the fellows neither hear nor see your laughter.'

After this prelude, the whilom lecturer on *The Four Georges* told me a story to the following effect. The courtly diarist was in the grounds where the King took his daily exercise, when he saw the royal invalid and his attendant coming along a straight path that was skirted by laurels and other shrubs, which screened a high wall. As he moved along the walk with quick steps, the royal invalid was seen ever and again to leave the path, run behind the shrubs, and reappear in a few seconds at the point of his momentary departure from view. The attendant at the invalid's heels was seen in like manner to dodge quickly behind the shrubs, and, after an absence of a few seconds, return to the straight and open way. Familiar with the invalid's taste for defacing fair garden walls, and with the measures that were employed to relieve walls of the marks he put upon them, the gentleman of the Household knew well enough what was done behind the shrubs by the sovereign, who led the way, and by the servant who followed him. But he was surprised at the unusual quickness of the King's steps, and accounted for it by supposing that the mental invalid was endeavouring to defeat his pursuer's purpose by superior agility. The monarch was passing within a few paces of him without observing him, when the courtly observer and diarist heard His Majesty say once and again with volubility and earnestness, 'I don't care a.... I don't care a.... I am four words ahead of him!' After glancing over his shoulder, so as to get a momentary view of the attendant, the King, as he hurried onwards, ejaculated in a yet louder voice of vindictive exultation, 'I don't care a.... I don't care a.... I am four words ahead of him!' To fit it for a page that will be submitted to fastidious readers, I have slightly altered the record of the King's brief utterance. In two places I have omitted a profane expression; I have also withdrawn an offensive word and replaced it with an inoffensive word.

Soon after the publication of my *Live It Down, A Novel*, in March, 1863, Thackeray spoke to me of the story in encouraging terms, as he sat beside me at Clunn's. He also observed,

'If you had told me of the title before you used it, I would have offered you fifty guineas for it.'

'I wish I had told you,' I returned, 'in time to get the offer. I should certainly have accepted it.'

'And I wish the title were mine. It is a book in three words!' he rejoined, warmly. After a pause he added, in a sad and lower voice, 'It would be the very title for my story of my own life,'—words which seemed to imply that he had some thought of writing his own biography.

Matters went thus pleasantly between me and Thackeray up to the time when he withdrew his favour from me, under a gust of angry emotion, which I had done nothing to occasion. On Saturday,

April 25th, 1863, he presided at the Shakespeare Dinner of *Our Club*,—a day memorable in my life's story as the day on which I exchanged spoken words for the last time with the author of *Vanity Fair*. Years syne it was the practice of O. C. to put before each 'cover' at a Shakespeare Anniversary Dinner some literary or artistic toy, or some trifle that was both literary *and* artistic, which the occupant of the place might put into his pocket, and, carrying away with him, might preserve as a memorial of the festal celebration. On April 25th, 1863, the trifle laid before each diner's napkin was a small white cardboard diptych in a white paper wrapper. Containing on the one half of its interior a photograph of a familiar portrait of Shakespeare, and on the other half of the interior a photographic reproduction of Ben Jonson's no less familiar verses, beginning with 'This Figure that thou here seest put,' the diptych displayed on one of its outer surfaces nine musical and deftly-worded verses by Henry Wright, M.D. The paper-wrapper of the folded card displayed on the interior surface the following metrical note by Shirley Brooks:

> As it fell upon a night,
> Came a thought to H. G. Wright,
> Loyal member of a club
> That at Clunn's doth meet to grub.
> 'To its Shakespeare's feast,' quoth he,
> 'Something shall be sent by me,
> And the Vanity is Fair
> That could meet approval there,
> Though I soar *ceratis pennis*
> In the presence of Pendennis,

> From the Second Folio (mine)
> I will take the Portrait fine;
> Add the verses writ by Ben
> On the foremost man of men;
> Get some rhymes (which here you see)
> From the virtuous bard, S. B.,
> And present the whole to each
> Who shall hear our Thackeray's speech.'
>
> SHIRLEY BROOKS.

Readers unfamiliar with the writings of the 'virtuous bard, S. B.,' may not regard as a fair example of his poetical address these rather feeble verses, which are interesting only because they relate to one of the latest banquets—possibly the *last* grand dinner at which Thackeray took the chair.

There was, of course, a large gathering at Clunn's Hotel on April 25th, 1863,* although Thackeray was known to be a very poor after-dinner speaker. Wearing his usual morning-dress, the author of *Vanity Fair* appeared in one of his high-collared white waistcoats at the banquet. Knowing how much he disliked the duties that would devolve upon him as chairman for the evening, I was not surprised that he looked nervous and full of trouble, as he entered the room and passed to his seat. At table he was supported on his right hand by Shirley Brooks, who, with smiles in his face and mischief in his eye, glanced alternately at me and Thackeray, when I greeted the

---

* The Shakespeare Dinners of O. C. used to be held on the Saturday next following April 23rd, so that they should not clash with the Shakespeare Dinners of the Garrick Club, held on what is generally regarded as the actual anniversary of the poet's birth.

great novelist before dinner as chairman, and when I came to him once and again with a piece of gossip, after the removal of the white cloth. Thackeray's speech on William Shakespeare was on the whole no better than his speeches usually were; but it contained a few sentences which fast-coming incidents rendered very pathetic to those who remembered them. He spoke of the atmosphere of rivalry and contention which Shakespeare breathed, while he was doing his appointed work and making his imperishable fame,—of the tattlers who talked saucily about him from mere mental flimsiness, and of the malicious detractors who from spiteful jealousy magnified the defects, and disparaged the excellences of his writings and character. Observing how the tattlers and detractors were remembered only by the few persons who remembered them with contempt, and how all their ineffectual efforts to defame their great master had failed to influence the world's judgment, he remarked how tenderly time and fate had dealt with the poet, in causing him to be known to us only by his writings. Avowing himself unwell, and from indisposition more than ordinarily incompetent to make an adequate speech about Shakespeare, the orator said that he should resign his chair to a worthier occupant at an early hour. And he did so, after discharging with a half-hearted and long-suffering air the formal duties of a dinner-table president. As he passed on his way out of the room, with Shirley Brooks at his elbow, Thackeray bowed slightly and stiffly to me, whilst Shirley Brooks regarded me with a look of exultation, which I could not at the moment account for. All that was clear to me as I wended my way back to Heathcote Street, Mecklenburgh Square, thinking over the incidents of an unsatisfactory evening, was that I was out of favour with Thackeray, and that Shirley Brooks knew it and exulted in the fact. What was in the air?

On the morrow (Sunday), I cut the leaves of my copy of the *Athenæum* (No. 1852), and after looking at my own review of George Augustus Sala's *Strange Adventures of Captain Dangerous* and a few other contributions by my pen, I came upon a closely-worded and trenchant notice of *The Story of Elizabeth* —a tale that had appeared originally in the previous year in the *Cornhill Magazine*, without any announcement of the author's name, and was republished in volume-form (again without the author's name) some few weeks before the appearance of the *Athenæum* review, which quickly made a lively commotion in the literary coteries of London.

The writer of this notorious review, which may perhaps be regarded as one of the several indirect causes of Thackeray's death before the end of the year, acknowledged the literary power of the tale. Calling it an 'undeniably clever' story, the critic also spoke of its 'facility of style.' But these words of strong praise were accompanied with severe censure of the subject of the narrative, and also of the spirit in which the undeniably clever writer dealt with the painful subject. The critic's opinion of the story was adverse. Yet more, the article, apart from its main verdict, contained passages that were peculiarly qualified to pain the writer of the clever tale, and to incense her affectionate and sensitive father.

Knowing that *The Story of Elizabeth* was the work of Thackeray's elder daughter, I did not peruse this notice without regarding it as the cause of Thackeray's coldness to me on the previous evening. On thinking over the article, and the several circumstances that had perplexed and discomposed me at Clunn's, I saw that I was regarded as the writer of the critique, which could not fail to cause Thackeray acute annoyance. The unusual way in which some people had looked at me, and the even more significant way in which others had looked away from me at a table where I had for some years been in more than general good favour, were accounted for. I saw why no one had spoken to me of the article, which most of the Shakespearian diners had doubtless seen in the morning, and would naturally have alluded to in my hearing as the prime incident of the hour, had I not been thought its writer. From the style of the article, I knew it was written by Geraldine Jewsbury,—a woman very dear to both me and my wife. On this point I could not have been more sure had I seen her writing the incisive sentences, and read them in wet ink. Clearly there was trouble ahead of me. As the writers on the *Athenæum* were in those days under an obligation of honour to refrain from avowing their contributions to the journal, and also to refrain from saying anything that might be likely to sacrifice in any respect the anonymity of the paper's judgments, I saw that I could not honourably disabuse Thackeray's mind of its apparent misconception respecting the authorship of the review, until I had Sir Wentworth Dilke's permission to do so. Yet further, I saw that, even should Sir Wentworth Dilke release me from the bond of reticence in respect to that particular article, I could not exercise the liberty without putting the suspicion, from which I wished to escape, on a lady who was one of my especial friends.

In form, presence, air, charm of manner, music of voice, and conversational address, I have never seen Geraldine Jewsbury's equal. Light, lissom, *spirituelle*, her tall, slight figure was singularly graceful. Had it not been for her complexion, which was deficient in brightness and transparency, she would have been remembered for her beauty as well as her wit. A woman of letters, living chiefly if not altogether at the point of her pen, she had need to be mindful of the petty financial economies, but in one direction she was self-indulgent in her personal expenditure. She enjoyed the favour of a most fashionable milliner, whom she honoured as an artist whilst employing her as a dress-maker. I do not mean that Geraldine Jewsbury was extravagant or light-headed in this particular. She would have gone about her business in mean attire sooner than have worn finery she could not afford. But she had a wholesome feminine delight in clothing her graceful figure with elegant and rich attire. Well-dressed at all times, she was sumptuous in her raiment on occasions of state. A consummate mistress of colloquial raillery, she was both witty and humorous. In her raillery she was sometimes finely satirical; but, instead of wounding, the light shafts of her airy satire only tickled those on whom they fell—ever hitting the exact point she aimed at. But she was less delightful for these social endowments than admirable for her benevolence, the sweetness of her sympathetic nature, her richness in charity to her neighbours, and the pious beauty of her whole existence. It is impossible for a daughter of Eve to be a better woman than Geraldine Jewsbury. Her books are in evidence that she had a fine literary taste and a lofty nature.

To the world she is chiefly known at the present time as Mrs. Carlyle's especial friend. But the Carlyles were not the only people to have her for a fireside intimate. She was my wife's intimate friend; and, singular amongst fascinating women for being even more acceptable to her own than to the harder sex, she was the especial friend of several ladies of my acquaintance.

To show how quick women of the finest discernment and sensibility were to love the gentle and charming woman, I may quote a few words that brighten a page of Mrs. Sutherland Orr's *Life of Robert Browning*: 'And, do you know, I was much taken, in London,' Elizabeth Barrett Browning wrote from Paris in 1851, 'with a young authoress, Geraldine Jewsbury. You have read her books .... she herself is quiet and simple, and drew my heart out of me a good deal. I felt inclined to love her in our half-hour's interview.' Tender and true when Mrs. Browning first saw her, Geraldine Jewsbury was no less sincere and sweetly sympathetic in 1863.

Such was the woman who reviewed *The Story of*

Elizabeth in the *Athenæum*. Should my daughter ever disappoint my expectations by writing a book and giving it to the world, I only hope she may be judged by critics as discerning and honest and incapable of jealousy—as just and generous and conscientious—as Geraldine Jewsbury.

The consequences of the review justified the prediction to which I gave utterance when I had studied the article. Too much has been made of Thackeray's sensitiveness and resentment of adverse criticism. That he felt the hostile judgments of the press acutely appears from his readiness to reply to them, when they seemed to him unjustifiable. But his resentment was transient. After paying Charley Kenney off with the *Essay on Small Beer*, he lived in friendliness with him. Though the *Athenæum*, upon the whole, treated him scarcely so well as he deserved, he joined the dinner-club of which Hepworth Dixon was a principal member. In his first chagrin at being blackballed at the 'Athenæum Club'—a mistake for which the club soon made the *amende honorable*—he could speak with good temper of a misadventure which he attributed to critical dislike of his writings. But I knew the affectionate father too well to have any doubt that his resentment against all persons, whom he held in any degree accountable for the unfavourable review of his daughter's first considerable literary essay, would be bitter and lasting.

Before another fortnight had passed, I received numerous indications of the disfavour with which I was regarded by the powerful connection of *littéra-*

teurs who looked up to the author of *Vanity Fair* as their 'Chief.' A few persons, with whom I had been on friendly terms, were moved to give me the 'cut direct' for having written in so ruffianly a style about *The Story of Elizabeth*. A larger number of persons straightened their backs and barely nodded to me, when we met in public ways or private rooms. Affecting to be my well-wishers, who would fain help me with good counsel in respect to 'this unfortunate business,' some meddlesome wiseacres urged me to be quick in setting myself right with the world. Receiving insolent letters on the affair from strangers who had the courage to sign their epistles, I was assailed through the post by despicable creatures—with a taste for stinging, but no disposition to smart under a retaliatory sting—who forbore to sign their spiteful notes. Matters had gone on in this way for several weeks, when Sir Wentworth Dilke (kindliest and most sympathetic of men) took occasion to tell me he knew what ill was said of me, and begged that, in dealing with the evil speakers, I would have no regard for 'the anonymity' of his critical journal. Thanking him for his license to speak, I told him I could not use it to the possible injury of Miss Jewsbury. Of the several persons who spoke to me of the ugly business, none in doing so pained me more than the individuals who told me that, after leaving Clunn's Hotel on the evening of April 23rd, 1863, Thackeray had, in their hearing, spoken of me as 'a man who, in order to give him pain, had slapped his daughter's face.' It is not surprising that my silence to the charge was regarded as a tacit admission that I had written the article. This is my first public denial of the charge. Of course, in well-informed literary cliques it has long been known that Miss Jewsbury wrote the article on *The Story of Elizabeth*, that moved Thackeray to speak so harshly of me. But even to this day there are people who think of me as the critic whose malicious pen caused Thackeray acute pain in his life's last year.

The defenders of anonymous journalism are wont to urge that the anonymous curtain does not conceal the writers of reviews from their brethren of the 'ungentle craft,' and to allege that the authorship of every anonymous critique which occasions much talk is an 'open secret' in the literary cliques. I venture to differ from the holders of this opinion. To this day no one has discovered the writer of the *Edinburgh* attack on Byron's *Hours of Idleness*, or the writer of the *Blackwood* onslaughts on John Keats. Before the actual writer of the *Quarterly's* famous assault on Shelley's peace of mind was revealed to the world, the article was erroneously assigned to divers writers. It makes nothing against the evidence of these cases that everyone knew from the first whose pen produced Croker's critique of the first instalment of Macaulay's *History*, and whose pen produced Macaulay's destructive attack on Robert Montgomery's poetical fame; for, in those and countless similar cases, there was no attempt at concealment on the part of the reviewer. My experience has been that, in nine cases out of ten, the literary coteries are as powerless as the outsiders to discover the author of an article, who wishes to take the full benefit of its anonymity. In nine cases out of ten, the open secret is nothing better than the secret error of an uncertain number of gossip-mongers. And sometimes the secret error is greatly injurious to a meritorious or inoffensive *littérateur*. One of the grievous results of the anonymous system in literature is the frequency with which a reviewer is punished severely for another reviewer's offence. The false rumour, that attributed to my pen Miss Jewsbury's article on *The Story of Elizabeth*, occasioned me much pain in the year of the review's appearance in the *Athenæum*, and for a much longer time was most hurtful to my professional interests.

The wretched squabble about the novel and the review was in the first stage of its slanderous course, when, mainly through Hepworth Dixon's action, the National Shakespeare Tercentenary Celebration Committee was set going, for the purpose of glorifying the poet with some grand monument that should be beautiful and otherwise beneficial. Dixon hoped for great things from this movement, which, after giving birth to half-a-hundred ludicrous squabbles, resulted in nothing more important than a modest sum of funded money, which may be serviceable to Shakespearian celebrants in 1964, and the planting of a small oak on Primrose Hill, which has hitherto declined to grow much bigger, though it was planted in the most complimentary manner, with much music of drums and wind-instruments, and several orations to which few of the Shakespearian Commemorators, then and there present, paid any attention.

For awhile, however, the National Shakespeare

Committee grew and increased in a re-assuring manner from the 25th of July, 1863, on which day it was publicly offered to an insufficiently sympathetic world in a column and a half of the *Athenæum*, with a sufficient staff of Honorary Secretaries. How it had been formed out of three other Committees, I cannot say precisely. But it is a matter of sure history that for some weeks peers spiritual and peers temporal, and other persons more or less exalted or insignificant, showed a satisfactory readiness to join the association, and subscribe moneys, for Shakespeare's honour.

When the other notabilities of the land were invited by circular to join this admirable Committee, a circular-invitation was, of course, sent to Thackeray, who was not likely to give his countenance to the undertaking in which Hepworth Dixon, the editor of the *Athenæum*, figured as one of the two General Secretaries, and as the chief projector of the enterprise. Joining the Committee, Charles Dickens forthwith became a Vice-President of the association; but Thackeray took no notice of the invitation. In late summer or early autumn, when the Committee was growing more and more unmanageably large, Dixon went off to the Holy Land, leaving me to act as General Secretary for him, till he should return.

Hepworth Dixon having gone off to the East, the Committee determined to make another attempt to attach Thackeray to the movement. It was felt by some of the Committee (*why* they felt it, I failed to discover), that in Dixon's absence Thackeray would do at a second invitation what he had not cared to do, when the editor of the *Athenæum* was in the country. Though I could not take their view of the case, I was too desirous to see the great humourist in the Committee, to be capable of opposing their wish. Moreover, I was under an obligation of honour to do the bidding of the Committee in all reasonable ways. Consequently, in compliance with the Committee's resolution to that effect, I wrote a special letter of invitation to Thackeray. As I anticipated, Thackeray took no notice of my letter. This failure to lure the novelist into the Committee's ranks was followed by a proposal that yet a third invitation should be sent to him.

Before this proposal was laid before the Committee in the shape of a resolution, it had been submitted to my consideration by one of a small knot of gentlemen who affected to be in a peculiar sense Thackeray's 'friends,' though I could not ascertain, and even at this date have no reason to think, that they were acting under his authority. These gentlemen perplexed and even alarmed me. The question whether there should be a grand celebration of the three hundredth anniversary of Shakespeare's birthday seemed to be closely associated in their minds with the question, whether Miss Jewsbury's article on *The Story of Elizabeth* was a piece of fair criticism. One of them even told me outright, that the National Shakespeare Committee ought to be wrecked, in order to punish the editor of the *Athenæum* for inserting the article in the paper. Some, but not all, of the gentlemen were possessed by a notion that, as Charles Dickens after joining the Committee had been made one of its Vice-Presidents, Thackeray ought to be invited to join the Committee in the capacity of a Vice-President, so that he should not even for so short a time as ten minutes hold a lower place than Dickens on the Committee. Had Thackeray joined the Committee, he would of course have been immediately placed amongst the Vice-Presidents by the unanimous vote of the Committee.

As I was surely informed that Thackeray had determined to have nothing to do with the Shakespeare Committee, and was in no humour to have any further intercourse either with the editor of the *Athenæum* or myself, and that a third invitation would be as ineffectual with the author of *Vanity Fair* as the two previous invitations had been, I opposed the motion that the Committee should for a third time invite the great novelist to co-operate with them in celebrating the tercentenary of the poet's birth. I was actuated in this matter by several considerations of policy and delicacy, and in the way of duty I told the Committee in the fewest possible words my reasons for thinking it would be unwise for them to trouble Mr. Thackeray at that juncture with a third request, that he would join in a movement from which he thought right to hold aloof. In my brief speech to the Committee I remarked that, should they decide to send Thackeray a third invitation to join the association, the letter of invitation ought not to be written by me. I said that I could not, would not write the great novelist another letter, as I knew I should pain him by doing so. I was the more explicit on this point, because I was acutely sensible of the magnitude of the mistake I had made in writing to him on a former occasion.

When it had been considered and debated by a full Committee of nearly sixty persons, the motion for sending Mr. Thackeray a *third* invitation was rejected by a large majority. Only nine persons of so large a meeting were in favour of the motion. The majority were of opinion that courtesy to the great novelist, no less than care for the interests of the movement in Shakespeare's honour, forbade the Committee to trouble Mr. Thackeray with another letter on a subject that was distasteful to him. I do not believe that a single individual of the majority was actuated by ill feeling to Mr. Thackeray in deciding that it would be better for the Committee to forbear for a brief while from troubling him with a solicitation that, under the existing circumstances, was much more likely to pain and irritate than to please and conciliate him.

A few days after Thackeray's death, there appeared in one of the weekly newspapers of London an equally sensational and malicious paragraph, announcing that 'the name of William Makepeace Thackeray had been proposed for the vice-presidency of the National Shakespeare Committee, and been rejected by a large majority.' Calling attention to this startling statement, Hepworth Dixon observed in the Weekly Gossip of the *Athenæum* of the 2nd of January, 1864:

'As this story has found its way into other journals, it is only respectful to the dead to explain that no such fact has occurred. Mr. Thackeray's claims to a place amongst the Vice-Presidents of the National Shakespeare Committee have never been raised, and of course they have never been discussed. This is the simple truth. Some months ago, a circular-invitation was sent to the author of *Vanity Fair*, as to many other eminent persons. By some mischance, or oversight, no answer was returned. A few weeks later the Committee, as a mark of honour to Mr. Thackeray, passed a resolution that a special invitation should be forwarded to him; which invitation was duly written and sent by the secretary of the day, acting for the General Secretary, who was then absent from Europe. At the next meeting of the Committee, a member proposed that yet another special invitation should be sent. A gentleman, who had taken an active part in voting the previous invitation, rose to inquire whether the reply to it had been received; and, on its being said that the answer had not yet come to hand, the chairman explained to the member who proposed sending a third invitation pending the receipt of an answer to the second, that it would be better to wait for Mr. Thackeray's reply. This being the apparent sense of a meeting nearly sixty strong. the proposer of the third invitation seemed to acquiesce; and no one imagined by adopting a course so decent the great humourist's claims would be in any degree put in doubt. Subsequently, however, the member pressed his motion, which, on being put to the vote, was supported by no more than nine; the great majority considering it not improper but merely ill-timed. These are the whole of the actual facts. We venture to say that the gentlemen who voted against this injudicious motion were Mr. Thackeray's true friends—those who felt most strongly his claims to a high place on the Committee, and who counted most strongly on his co-operation.'

Though I was not wholly without hope that Thackeray might after all be induced to join the Committee, if he were personally entreated to join it by the Duke of Manchester, the President of the Association, I was far from hopeful that the great novelist would be brought over to us. I therefore was not one of those members of the Committee who 'counted strongly on his co-operation.' When he penned those words, Dixon was not thinking of me, but of more sanguine members of the majority. No member of the Committee, however, felt more strongly than I did that, *if* he joined the Committee, Thackeray should be placed amongst the Vice-Presidents without a moment's delay. At the time when I was generally regarded in the literary coteries as the writer of Miss Jewsbury's review of *The Story of Elizabeth*, the most extravagant and fanciful things were said of my animosity against Thackeray. The pain which came to me from the harsh words Thackeray spoke of the youngster, to whose pen he attributed that article, never affected either my admiration of the novelist or my regard for the man.

When the time was drawing near for the members of *Our Club* to re-assemble after the Long Vacation of 1863, little Hamstede pressed Thackeray to return to the club, from which he had retired in consequence of Miss Jewsbury's review of *The Story of Elizabeth*. It is needless to say that the author of *Vanity Fair* declined to comply with the secretary's entreaty. As the great novelist based his refusal to reappear at Clunn's on his firm resolve never again to have friendly intercourse with the editor of the *Athenæum*, little Hamstede informed Thackeray that, if he would come back to the club, steps should be taken for excluding Hepworth Dixon from the society. At the instance of the secretary, a majority of the members of O. C. would request Dixon to withdraw from the society; and, should he refuse to retire in submission to their request, the majority would dissolve the club and re-constitute it without Dixon. To this proposal Thackeray replied that he had already driven one man out of a club for a personal reason, and was not so satisfied with the consequences of the affair as to be in a humour to repeat the operation, for the discomfiture of Hepworth Dixon. That little Hamstede made this audacious proposal to Thackeray, and that the latter declined to entertain it, came to my knowledge from Hamstede himself.

A few weeks later, when he was still endeavouring to draw Thackeray back to O. C., little Hamstede, with my permission, told the great novelist that he had erred in speaking of me as the writer of the *Athenæum* review of *The Story of Elizabeth*, and at the same time reminded him of his omission to answer my letter, asking him to join the Shakespeare Committee. I cannot state the exact day on which Hamstede spoke to Thackeray on these two matters. But in a letter, dated from the Garrick Club on December 1st, 1863, Hamstede gave me at Thackeray's request the substance of their quite recent conversation on the two points, and a day or two later gave me by word of mouth a fuller account of the conversation.

In respect to the more important point, Thackeray averred to Hamstede that he had never spoken of me as the writer of the article, but had, on the contrary, declared he did not believe I wrote it, when some person told him I was the writer of the critique. On the second point, Thackeray said he had neglected to answer my letter touching the Shakespeare Committee, merely because he mistook it for an official request for a subscription to the funds of the Society, and consequently regarded it as belonging to a class of applications which he was not accustomed to answer. At the close of the conversation he asked Hamstede to tell me what had passed between them.

'He,' Hamstede wrote to me, 'said you had been misinformed, as he had not reported you as the author of the article in question. One man had, at the time, told him he had heard you were, but he had replied he did not believe it. This,' he added, 'my subsequent statement of what you said at Richmond had confirmed. I then alluded to your note on the Shakespeare matter. He had thought it a request to subscribe. Such applications were so numerous that he left them unanswered. He then begged me to give you the substance of our conversation.'

A day or two later, in giving me his oral and fuller account of the conversation, Hamstede told me Thackeray had known for some time that Miss Jewsbury wrote the annoying article. In the course of the conversation, Thackeray spoke of Miss Jewsbury's share in the *Athenæum* onslaught on *The Story of Elizabeth*, as an affair of his own sure knowledge.

Thackeray's averment that he had never spoken of me as the writer of the article did not affect my confidence in sure evidence that he had so spoken of me on the night of April 25th, immediately after the Shakespeare Dinner. Nor did it affect in any degree my high opinion of his veracity. When he made the averment on a day at the close of November, 1863, seven full months had passed since he had at a late hour of a festal night spoken of me, whilst he was under divers disturbing influences, as ' the young man who, in order to give him pain, had slapped his daughter's face;' and it is not unusual for emotional persons to forget quickly the wild words they have spoken in gusty anger. Knowing him to be incapable of telling a deliberate untruth, or of paltering with the truth, I accepted the averment as an honest exhibition of what he believed at the time of making it.

How long Thackeray remained under the impression that I wrote the article which caused him so much pain, I cannot say. Nor can I say either when or how he gained his true knowledge respecting the authorship of the critique. But I am not without grounds for thinking the information came to him from Geraldine Jewsbury herself. As she never spoke to me of the article, which did me so much harm, I never troubled her with speech about a performance that had caused her much distress. On hearing how I was being punished for her act, it would be natural for the generous and brave woman to inform Thackeray that she was the real disturber of his peace.

On learning that Thackeray had ceased to attribute Miss Jewsbury's article to my pen, had clean forgotten what he had said to my injury in his first annoyance at the severe notice of the 'undeniably clever' story, and had not been actuated by ill-feeling towards me in forbearing to answer a certain letter, I could hope that in a few months Thackeray and I would resume our former intercourse. But the hope was disappointed. Before the few months had passed, he was dead. Everyone knows how he was found dead in his bed on the 24th of December, 1863,—close upon thirty years since. The shock given to England by the announcement that Thackeray had died so suddenly, resembled the shock occasioned by the letter from Missolonghi, which told the country that Byron was no more. In neither case had the nation been prepared to hear that the man who had for years been a chief force in her intellectual life, would never again pen a line, caustic or pathetic. In each case it was known to the great writer's personal friends that his health had long been impaired, and that his manner of living foretold a premature end. But even to those who knew how great an invalid he had been for several years, Thackeray's death was scarcely less surprising than it was to those who had known nothing of his ill health. To his personal acquaintance, no less than to the nation at large, it was as though some superb column, at which it was their use to gaze admiringly, had fallen suddenly to the ground, even while they were regarding it.

The great man's foibles would have been less generally known, had he forborne to call attention to them in his books, his private letters, and his gossip with his friends. There were moments when he was too mindful of his dignity and fame. In respect to one person of the gentler sex, who had caused him suffering, he was wanting in magnanimity. In moods of irritability, resulting more from bodily disease than from moral unsoundness, he once and again carried his private grievances and personal vexations to the public. Though he was never so obsequious to rank as Mr. Andrew Arcedeckne used to declare him, he was at times more strongly affected, than a man of his natural gifts should have been, by the accidental grandeur of exalted persons. Though Charles Knight thought him 'no idolater of rank,' and Harriet Martineau has been reproved for speaking sorrowfully of him as yet another example of 'the aristocracy of nature making the Ko-too to the aristocracy of accident,' it must be admitted that Charles Knight was not wholly right, and that Miss Martineau was not wholly wrong. It is noteworthy that, in one of the *Brookfield Letters*—the piece of a letter written 'From the Grange' in 1851 to Mrs. Brookfield—Thackeray acknowledged himself something of a rank-worshipper, and in doing so used the very expression which Miss Martineau used in her censure of the novelist, to the annoyance and resentment of so many of his admirers.

'How is it,' he wrote to his correspondent, 'that I find myself humbling before her,' (to wit, Lady Ashburton,) 'and taking a certain parasitical air as all the rest do? There's something commanding in the woman (she was born in 1806, you'll understand), and I see we all of us bow down before her. Why don't we bow down before you, ma'am? Little Mrs. Taylor is the only one who does not seem to Ko-too.'

But, when the most is made of Thackeray's imperfections, they are few and small in comparison with his manly virtues and generous traits.

Is it said that from my tribute to Thackeray's usual care for the feelings of others some drawback must be made, in consideration of the pain he inflicted on divers people—notably on the first Lord Lytton and the late Andrew Arcedeckne—by his treatment of their peculiarities? My answer is that no such drawback has to be made from aught I say in commendation of the Thackeray of my acquaintance. I made Thackeray's acquaintance long after the publication of the novel (*Pendennis*) in which Mr. Foker plays a part, and a much longer time after the young Thackeray was guilty of the lampoons on Sir Edward Bulwer Lytton. Moreover, much may be urged in Thackeray's behalf with respect to his treatment of both these men.

Joining *Fraser* at a time when writers in the lighter Maga were encouraged and even required by the public to indulge in excesses of personality, that would revolt the more fastidious readers of the present time, Thackeray acquired the style and contracted the bad habits of the literary school, in which he may be said to have served his apprenticeship. As Thackeray relinquished this offensive style of writing when his taste had matured, I venture to say he should not be judged hardly for having, when he was little more than a literary aspirant, written after the fashion of the leading magazine-essayists of his period. In respect to the lampoons on Bulwer Lytton, of which he lived to be heartily ashamed, Thackeray wrote in riper time to James Hannay, ' I suppose we all begin by being too savage,—I know one who did.' Moreover, in 1861 Thackeray wrote a frank apology for these old offences to Lord Lytton himself, saying, ' I wonder at the recklessness of the young man who could fancy such satire was harmless jocularity, and never calculated it might give pain.' The early indiscretions, for which he cried

'Peccavi' thus frankly, cannot with fairness be produced as evidence of the writer's unkindliness in his riper age.

The persons who enjoyed the high privilege of associating with Thackeray, and had also the questionable distinction of Mr. Andrew Arcedeckne's acquaintance, will not find it difficult to believe that, whilst he was writing *Pendennis*, Thackeray never imagined Mr. Arcedeckne would be hurt on recognising himself in Foker. The grandson of a West Indian planter, Mr. Andrew Arcedeckne had for his great-grandfather in the male line a barrister, who became attorney-general of Jamaica. Buying a small manorial property in Suffolk, and building in the small but picturesque park a rather stately mansion (which he christened Glevering Hall), the Jamaican attorney-general's son established himself as a Suffolk squire, within a few miles of Framlingham. Living on this not important Suffolk estate, the Arcedecknes sustained their local dignity for two generations by their Jamaican revenue, before they dropt into comparative poverty. Two of their daughters married Vannecks, members of a London commercial family, that acquired a large estate in Suffolk and an Irish peerage in the middle of the last century. But aristocratic blood came neither from the Vannecks nor from any of his near ancestors to Mr. Arcedeckne of the Garrick Club, who was, however, inordinately proud of his 'no family in particular.' To pass himself off as an aristocrat, who was far too jolly a fellow to be proud of his patrician quality, was this gentleman's chief ambition.

On becoming the head of his 'no family in particular,' he came into a small and debt-encumbered estate in Suffolk, and a fast-sinking interest in the West Indies. A smart, slangy, ludicrous person—an extravagant caricature of Albert Smith's 'gent,' in respect to his manners and speech—he was assiduous in his attentions to those actors and actresses of whom he was a sort of patron. Hanging about the theatres, he aimed at distinguishing himself as an amateur actor in low comedy. In Suffolk—where he was the laughing-stock of his county neighbours, and at ordinary times too poor to live at Glevering Hall—this indescribably grotesque personage lived chiefly at inns within an easy drive of his ancestral place. At 'The White Horse' of Ipswich, or 'The Bull' of Woodbridge, where for a few pounds a week he was lord of the host, and enjoyed the idolatry of the boots and barmaid, Mr. Arcedeckne made himself at home for days and even weeks at a time, revelling in the homage rendered to him night after night by the tradesmen of the town and the commercial travellers, to whom he sung his comic songs or performed his comic parts. The gentleman's language, style, humour were inexpressibly absurd.

Of course, Thackeray made a mistake in putting this eccentric person into his story as a typical young Englishman. But the author of *Pendennis* neither caricatured nor maligned the Suffolk squire. Minimizing his vulgarity, he toned down his more offensive characteristics and emphasized his genial qualities, so that the Foker of the novel became a far more agreeable fellow than the Arcedeckne of real life. Cognizant of Mr. Arcedeckne's wish to be rated as an eccentric 'aristocrat,' Thackeray humoured it by making Foker's mother an earl's daughter. At the same time, instead of making him the son of an impoverished proprietor, the novelist gave Foker an affluent father, who was a much more important person than Mr. Arcedeckne's father. It follows that, instead of being a malicious caricature, Foker was a genial and flattering portrait of Mr. Arcedeckne of the Garrick Club. Though he affected to regard the too personal portrait as an impertinence, that justified him in speaking of the great novelist as a tuft-hunter and snob, and in addressing him saucily as 'Thack,' I cannot imagine he was at any time acutely pained by it.

I agree with Mr. Marzials in thinking that no flood of light is thrown on Thackeray's art by the evidence that the novelist reproduced in Foker some of the laughable peculiarities 'of a certain Mr. Arcedeckne who frequented the Garrick Club.' On the other hand, as Mr. Arcedeckne was one of Thackeray's friends, and the novelist has been harshly judged for exhibiting one of his friends to public ridicule in the pages of a novel, I conceive Mr. Marzials will agree with me in thinking some advantage may accrue to Thackeray's reputation for kindliness from evidence that the portrait was not the malicious performance which many people have thought it.

END OF THE FIRST VOLUME.

LONDON : PRINTED BY DUNCAN MACDONALD, BLENHEIM HOUSE.

www.ingramcontent.com/pod-product-compliance
Lightning Source LLC
Chambersburg PA
CBHW031854220426
43663CB00006B/622